牧马图（局部） 〔唐〕韩幹

历代帝王图（局部）　［唐］阎立本

挥扇仕女图（局部） [唐]周昉

春山行旅图 〔唐〕李昭道

松荫图（局部）　〔唐〕李昭道

梅图

［唐］张祐

诗之巅峰，传诵古今

只此唐诗

许渊冲英译唯美唐诗（上）

许渊冲

编译

读者出版社

图书在版编目（CIP）数据

只此唐诗 ：许渊冲英译唯美唐诗 ：上、下册 ：汉
英对照 / 许渊冲编译. -- 兰州 ：读者出版社，2024.3
ISBN 978-7-5527-0788-5

Ⅰ．①只… Ⅱ．①许… Ⅲ．①唐诗—汉、英 Ⅳ．
①I222.742

中国国家版本馆CIP数据核字（2024）第036262号

只此唐诗：许渊冲英译唯美唐诗

许渊冲　编译

责任编辑　张　远
封面设计　樊　瑶

出版发行　读者出版社
地　　址　兰州市城关区读者大道568号（730030）
邮　　箱　readerpress@163.com
电　　话　0931-2131529（编辑部）　0931-2131507（发行部）

印　　刷　天津鑫旭阳印刷有限公司
规　　格　开本 880 毫米×1230 毫米　1/32
　　　　　印张 27　插页 2　字数 560 千
版　　次　2024 年 3 月第 1 版
　　　　　2024 年 3 月第 1 次印刷
书　　号　ISBN 978-7-5527-0788-5
定　　价　158.00元（上、下册）

代序

  21世纪是全球化的世纪。新世纪的新人不但应该了解全球的文化，而且应该使本华文明走向世界，成为全球文化的一部分，使世界文化更加灿烂辉煌。如果说20世纪是美国世纪的话，那么，19世纪可以说是英国世纪，18世纪则是法国世纪。再推上去，自7世纪至13世纪，则可以说是中国世纪或唐宋世纪，因为中国在唐宋六百年间，政治制度先进，经济繁荣，文化发达，是全世界其他国家难以企及的。

  唐代的全盛时期可以说是"礼乐"治国的盛世。根据冯友兰先生的解释，"礼"模仿自然界外在的秩序，"乐"模仿自然界内在的和谐。"礼"可以养性，"乐"可以怡情；"礼"是"义"的外化，"乐"是"仁"的外化；做人要重"仁义"，治国要重"礼乐"。这是中华文明屹立于世界文明几千年不衰的重要原因。就以唐玄宗而论，他去泰山祭天，行封禅大礼之后，经由曲埠祭拜了孔子，写下了《经邹鲁祭孔子而叹之》的五言律诗，可见他对礼教的尊重，对士人的推崇。

因此，唐代文化昌盛，诗人辈出，唐诗成了中国文化的瑰宝。不仅在中国，唐诗在世界文化发展史上也占有重要地位，正如诺贝尔文学奖评奖委员会主席谢尔·埃斯普马克说的："世界上哪些作品能与中国的唐诗和《红楼梦》相比的呢？"（《诺贝尔文学奖内幕》306页）

早在19世纪末期，英国汉学家翟理斯（Giles）曾把唐诗译成韵文，得到评论家的好评，如英国作家斯特莱彻（Strachey）说："翟译唐诗是那个时代最好的诗，在世界文学史上占有独一无二的地位。"但20世纪初期英国汉学家韦利（Waley）认为译诗用韵不可能不因声损义，因此他把唐诗译成自由诗或散体，这就开始了唐诗翻译史上的诗体与散体之争。一般说来，散体译文重真，诗体译文重美，所以散体与诗体之争也可以升华为真与美的矛盾。

唐诗英译真与美之争一直延续到了今天。例如李白的《送友人》就有两种不同的译法，现将原诗和两种译文抄录于下：

青山横北郭，白水绕东城。

此地一为别，孤蓬万里征。

浮云游子意，落日故人情。

挥手自兹去，萧萧班马鸣。

（1）

Green hills range north of the walled city,

The White River curves along its east.

Once we part here you' ll travel far alone,

Like the tumbleweed swept by the autumn wind.

A floating cloud—a wayfarer' s feeling from home,

The setting sun—the affection of an old friend.

Waving adieu, as you now depart from me，

Our horses neigh, loath to part from each other.

（《外语教学与研究》1991年第3期）

（2）

Blue mountains bar the northern sky;

White water girds the eastern town.

Here is the place to say goodbye;

You' ll drift like lonely thistledown.

With floating cloud you' ll float away;

Like parting day I' ll part from you.

You wave your hand and go your way;

Your steed still neighs, "Adieu, adieu!"

（吕叔湘《中诗英诗比录》133页）

比较一下两种译文，可以说第一种更重真，第二种更重美；第一种更形似，第二种更神似。自然，真和美是相对而言的，往往可以仁者见仁，智者见智。如以第一句而论，"青山"二字，第一种说是绿色的小山，第二种说是蓝色的大山；"北郭"二字，第一种说是城郭的北面，第二种为了避免重复"城"字，把"小城"移到第二行去了，说是北边的天空。由此可见，第一种写的是近景，第二种写的是远景。到底哪种译文更真呢？如以"青山"而论，第二种更形似，如以"北郭"而论，却是第一种更形似。全句最重要的是动词"横"字，第一种译文用了range，是"排列"的意思，读起来像是地理教科书中的术语，重的是真；第二种译文用了bar，作为名词，是"横木"的意思，作为动词，却是像横木一样横在天边，这个词形象生动，气势雄伟，合乎李白的诗风；加上英国诗人济慈在《秋颂》中用过这个词形容云彩，用在这里，更使全句显得诗意盎然，甚至有画龙点睛之妙，可见第二种译文重的是美。

再看第二句，原诗两句对称，"青山"对"白水"，"北郭"对"东城"，具有平衡的形美。第一种译文要求真，"青山"的译文只有两个音节，"白水"却有四个，这就不如第二种译文对称；"北郭"和"东城"的第一种译文也不平衡，没有传达原诗的形美。更重要的还是动词"绕"字，第一种译成curve，作为名词，是"曲线"的意思，作为动词，则是呈曲线形，这又是一个几何教科书中的术语，读起来仿佛在测量地形，未免大煞风景。第二种译文求美，用了gird一词，使人如见一衣带水的形象，又比第一种译文更有诗情画意了。

原诗第一、二句写景是"起"，第三句"此地"二字是"承"，"为别"二字"转"入叙事，全句是时空状语从句，第四句才是主句，转为写情。第一种译文把三、四句合译，把"万里"浅化为far（远），"孤"字等化为alone（孤独）移到第三句去；第四句只把"蓬"字等化为tumbleweed，却把"征"字深化为swept by the autumn wind（秋风横扫），这是求真呢？还是求美呢？可以商榷。据第一位译者研究，这首诗是李白送崔宗之写的。"崔家在嵩山之南，邀李同往，李因急于回家未从。李送走崔……"这样看来，友人并不是被迫离乡背井的，用秋风扫落叶的形象来描写，是译者自己的创造，恐怕不能算真了。能不能说比第二种译文更美呢？第二种译文的第四句借景抒情，把友人比作要"万里征"的"孤蓬"，惜别之心已经形象化了，可以说意美胜过第一种译文。至于音美，第一种译文没有押韵，各行音节数目不等，有长有短；第二种译文却隔行押韵，每行八个音节，都是抑扬格音步，没有"因声损义"，而第一种反倒不押韵而损义了！

第五、六句是全诗的高潮，是抒写离情别恨的妙句。李白善于借景写情，如"请君试问东流水，别意与之谁短长？""桃花潭水深千尺，不及汪伦送我情"，都是借流水、深潭来抒写离别的深情厚谊的。在《送友人》中又把惜别之心形象化为浮云和落日，更加显得依依不舍。第一种译文把"意"字译成feeling，把"情"字译成affection，译文形似，似乎忠实于原文。但"情""意"在中文是单音节，在诗词中常用，所以具有一种情韵美或意美。译成英文的对等词，因为在英诗中不如在中国诗词中常用，不能引起情韵的美感。例如"别意与之谁短长？""不及汪伦送我情"等句的英译文是：

（1）

O ask the river flowing to the east, I pray,

Whether its parting grief or mine will longer stay!

（2）

However deep the Lake of Peach Blossoms may be,

It' s not so deep, O Wang Lun! As your love for me.

如把grief（"意"）换成feeling，把love（"情"）换成affection，那散文味就太重，诗意却消失了。

第二种译文没有译"情""意"二字，却重复了float和part两个词，说成你和浮云一同飘然而去，我像落日一样离开了你。译文虽不形似，却说出了诗人的离情别意，可以说是一种创造性的翻译，"落日"也换成"正在消逝的白日"了。有人也许会说："孤蓬万里征"中的"征"解释为"秋风横扫"不也是创造性的翻译吗？朱光潜《诗论》中说"'从心所欲，不逾矩'是一切艺术的成熟境界"，我看也是翻译艺术的成熟境界。创造性的翻译"从心所欲"，但是不能超越作者的原意。"浮云"和"落日"的第二种译文只是超越了原文的形式，却没有违反原诗的内容，并没有"逾矩"；"秋风横扫"却超越了原文的内容和形式，"逾矩"了，所以我看不能算创造性的翻译。

最后一句"萧萧班马鸣"，第一种译文说是两匹马，第二种说是一匹，到底是几匹马呢？我看这不是"真"，而是"美"的问题。试问到底是两马齐鸣，难舍难分，还是人已萧然而去，只闻萧萧马鸣，更加意味深远悠长，仿佛余音在耳，久久不绝呢？我觉得两马更像"教坊犹奏别离歌"，不如一马"黯然销魂者，唯别而已矣"。还有"萧萧"二字，第一种译文说是难舍难分，马犹如此，人何以堪！第二种却重复了adieu（再见），这是不是"从心所欲"，将马拟人，"逾矩"了呢？我觉得译诗要使读者"知之，好之，乐之"。如果读者理解了原诗的内容，喜欢译诗的表达方式，读来感到乐趣，那么，"从心所欲"的翻译就不算"逾矩"，甚至可能成为"青出于蓝而胜于蓝"的译文。这样一来，译文就可以说是在和原文竞赛，看哪种形式更能表达原文的内容了。

真与美的矛盾可以说是科学与艺术的矛盾。自然，科学和艺术也有统一的时候，那翻译的问题不大。我和科学家杨振宁1938年在西南联大是同学，60年后，我们在清华大学会面，他问我有没有翻译晏几道的《鹧鸪天》"从别后，忆相逢"，我就给他看"歌尽桃花扇影风"的英译文，他说不对，他记得是"扇底风"。在我看来，"扇底风"是实写，"扇影风"是想象，这就是真与美的矛盾，可以看出科学和艺术的不同。

《杨振宁文选》英文本序言中引用了两句杜甫的名诗"文章千古事，得失寸心知"，振宁的英译文是：

A piece of literature is meant for the millennium.

But its ups and downs are known already in the author' s heart.

译文精确，是典型的科学家风格，但是音节太多，不宜入诗；如果要按艺术风格来译，可以翻译如下：

A poem may long, long remain.

Who knows the poet' s loss and gain!

A poem lasts a thousand years.

Who knows the poet' s smiles and tears!

比较一下三种译文，"文章"二字，第一种译得最正确；但杜甫并没有写过多少文章，他说的是"文"，指的是"诗"，所以第二、三种就译成poem了。"千古"二字，也是第一种最精确，第三种说"千年"，也算正确，第二种只说long（长久），就太泛了。"千古事"是流传千古的事，以意美而论，是第一种译得好；以音美和形美而论，却是第二、三种更合音律。"得失"二字，第二种译得最形似，但是并不明确；第一种译成ups and downs，更注意文章的客观作用；第三种译成笑和泪，更强调主观的感受。"寸心知"三字，第一种理解为作者有自知之明，第二、三种却理解为有谁知诗人之心了。

从李白、杜甫诗的译例看来，可以说科学派的译文更重"三似"：形似、意似、神似；艺术派的译文更重"三美"：意美、音美、形美。科学派常用对等的译法；艺术派则常用"三化"的译法：等化、浅化、深化。科学派的目的是使读者知之；艺术派则认为"知之"是低标准，高标准应该是"三之"：知之、好之、乐之。一般说来，诗是具有意美、音美、形美的文字，就是英国诗人柯尔律治（Coleridge）说的 the best words in the best order（见《英诗格律及自由诗》扉页，下同）。美国诗人弗洛斯特（Frost）却认为诗是"说一指二"的（saying one thing and meaning another）。这就是说，原诗是最好的文字，译成对等的文字，却不一定是最好的诗句，这时就要舍"对等"而求"最好"，也就是要发挥译语的优势，即充分利用译语最好的表达方式，而不是对等的表达方式。如"得失"的对等词是 gain and loss，但 ups and downs 或 smiles and tears 却是更好的表达方式。换句话说，在原文说一指一的时候，对等的译文不但形似，而且意似，甚至可以神似；如果原文说一指二，那形似或等化的译文就不可能神似，应该试用浅化或深化的译法，才有可能传达原诗的意美、音美、形美。总而言之一句话，就是要用再创的译法，例如把"得失"说成"啼笑"。这种"再创"不是内容等于形式，或一加一等于二的科学方法，而是内容大于形式，一加一大于二的艺术方法。所以我认为文学翻译，尤其是译诗，不是一种科学，而是一种艺术。从某种意义上来讲，文学翻译甚至可以看成是译语之间或译语和原语之间的竞赛，看哪种译文更能表达原语的内容。其实，这种竞赛在人类文化史上是不断进行的。如三千年前的特洛伊战争，经过多少行吟诗人竞相歌唱，最后荷马取得胜利。三四百年前，查普曼、蒲伯等诗人把荷马史诗译成英文，这是新的竞赛，又取得了新的胜利。从更广泛的意义来说，有一些莎士比亚的作品也是英语和原语的竞赛，例如《哈姆雷特》原是丹麦的故事，《罗密欧与朱丽叶》是威尼斯的故事，但是莎士比亚的英语赛过了原语的传说。到了17世纪，德莱顿把莎士比亚的《安东尼与克莉奥佩特拉》改写成《一切为了爱情》，这又是在和莎士比亚竞赛，当时的贵族观众认为胜过莎剧，后世的平民观众却认为不如莎剧宏伟。不管谁胜谁负，或者难分高下，这不都是竞赛吗？而人类的文化就在不断的竞赛中不断前进了。

《唐诗三百首》是中国文化的精粹。早在1929年，美国就出版了宾纳（Bynner）与中国学者江亢虎合作翻译的译本，基本上用的是艺术译法。到1973年，台北又出版了英国译者静霓·韩登（Innes Herdan）的译本，基本上用的是科学译法。但是两种译本都没有用韵，不能传达唐诗的意美、音美、形美。到1987年，香港才出版我和陆佩弦、吴钧陶等合译的《唐诗三百首新译》，基本上是韵文，得到国内外的好评和批评。如《记钱锺书先生》341页上说：《唐诗》及《翻译的艺术》"二书如羽翼之相辅，星月之交辉，足征非知者不能行，非行者不能知"。菲律宾《联合日报》1994年2月3日评论说："《唐诗三百首》中许译一百多首，炉火纯青；其他译者，多数译法与他相似，程度参差。"因此，我觉得香港版《唐诗三百首》有修订甚至重译的必要。

1994年英国企鹅图书公司出版了我英译的《中国不朽诗三百首》，美国宾夕法尼亚大学顾毓琇教授读后说："历代诗、词、曲译成英文，且能押韵自然，功力过人，实为有史以来第一。"（见1997年5月23日《信息报》）同年，湖南出版社《楚辞》英译本得到墨尔本大学美国学者好评，说是"当算英美文学里的一座高峰"（见1998年版 *Vanished Springs* 封底）。1992年外文出版社出了《西厢记》英译本，英国智慧女神出版社说："在艺术性和吸引力方面，可以和莎士比亚的《罗密欧与朱丽叶》媲美。"（见《中国图书商报》1999年8月31日《书评月刊》）

中国人英译的中国古典文学，怎么能成为英美文学的高峰，甚至可以和莎士比亚媲美呢？钱锺书先生说得好："非知者不能行，非行者不能知。"在我看来，"知"就是理论，"行"就是实践。因为我有了几十年的实践经验，把中国古典文学十大名著译成了英、法两种韵文，因此，我把中国学派的文学翻译理论总结成了十个字："美化之艺术，创优似竞赛。"

所谓"美",指的是意美、音美、形美。"三美",这是根据鲁迅在《自文字至文章》一文中所说的:"意美以感心,一也;音美以感耳,二也;形美以感目,三也。"不过鲁迅说的是写文章,我把他的理论应用到文学翻译上来了。所谓"化",是根据钱锺书提出的:"文学翻译的最高理想是'化'。"不过我把"化"字扩大为等化、浅化、深化"三化"了。所谓"之",是根据孔子在《论语》中说的:"知之者不如好之者,好之者不如乐之者。"我把知之、好之、乐之应用于文学翻译,就提出了"三之"论。至于"艺术"二字,那是根据朱光潜提出的:"'从心所欲,不逾矩'是一切艺术的成熟境界。"简单说来,"三美"是文学翻译的本体论,"三化"是方法论,"三之"是目的论,"艺术"是认识论。总体来说,就是"美化之艺术"。

我又从郭沫若提出的"好的翻译等于创作"中取了一个"创"字,从傅雷提出的"重神似不重形似"中再取一个"似"字,从我自己提出的"发挥译语优势"中取出一个"优"字,加上"竞赛"二字,就成了"创优似竞赛"。"优"是"三美"合而为一的本体论,"创"是"三化"合而为一的方法论,"似"是"三之"合而为一的目的论,"竞赛"是包含在"艺术"中的认识论。这就是中国学派的文学翻译理论。

世界上有十多亿人用中文，又有约十亿人用英文，所以中文和英文是世界上最重要的文字，中英互译是世界上最重要的翻译。中国有不少能互译的文学翻译家。"非行者不能知"，中国学派的文学翻译理论是今天世界上水平最高的理论，可以把文学翻译提高到创作的地位。这就是说，译著应该等于原作者用译语的创作，一流译者翻译出来的文句诗行，读起来和一流作家写出来的作品应该没有什么差别。

1
4

中国学派的翻译原则在20世纪初是严复提出的"信、达、雅"；到了20世纪末，大致可以分为"信、达、切"和"信、达、优"两派，基本上是直译派和意译派，或形似派和神似派。在我看来，"信、达、切"是文学翻译的低标准，如李白《送友人》的第一种英译；"信、达、优"是高标准，如第二种译文。但形似派有人不同意，认为"再创"的译文有损原作者的风格。什么是风格？这是一个仁者见仁、智者见智的问题。《文学翻译原理》96页上说，李白的风格是"飘逸"。但从《送友人》的两种译文看来，哪一种传达了"飘逸"的风格呢？从内容上来看，可以说两种译文都不能算是不"飘逸"的；从形式上来看，可以说第一种译文的字句更切合原文，而第二种译文则传达了原诗的意美、音美、形美，难道能说"三美"不符合原诗的风格吗？所以研究文学翻译理论，不能从抽象的"风格"概念出发，而要分析具体的实例，只要译文能使读者知之、好之、乐之，就不必多考虑作者的风格。罗曼·罗兰在《约翰·克里斯托夫》法文本1565页上说："作者有什么重要？只有作品才是真实的。"英国诗人艾略特（Eliot）更说过："个人的才智有限，文化的力量无穷。"（转引自《追忆逝水年华》43页）在我看来，这就是说，民族文化比个人风格重要得多，如果能对人类文化作出贡献，作者的风格应该是次要的。

法籍作家程纪贤在他的获奖作品《天一言》（*Le dit de Tianyi*）267页上说："艺术并不模仿自然，结果反倒迫使自然模仿艺术。"这话说得耐人寻味。思索一下，人类从四足有毛的爬行动物进化到两足无毛的直立动物，不就是自然模仿艺术（手艺）的过程吗？同样的道理，翻译开始模仿创作，最后创作反而模仿翻译，"五四"以来新文学的发展不就提供了范例吗？所以文学翻译应该发展为创作的范例，这就是和原作竞赛，甚至超越原作，提高人类的文化。

这本汉英对照《唐诗三百首》就是我用"再创"法重译的选集，所选的篇目和流行的《唐诗三百首》有所不同，主要是我喜欢的并能译成韵文的作品。希望这个新译本和我英译的《楚辞》《西厢记》一样，能使国外读者"知之，好之，乐之"，能使中国文学走向世界，走向21世纪，使新世纪的文化更加光辉灿烂。

荣获诺贝尔奖的几十位科学家1988年在巴黎发表宣言说："人类要继续生存下去，就必须回过头来学习孔子的智慧。"在我看来，孔子的智慧主要表现在"礼乐之治"或"己所不欲，勿施于人"的"礼治"上，这从热爱和平、热爱人生、热爱自然的唐诗中也可以看出。孔子是"圣之时者"，结合时代，"回过头来学习孔子的智慧"，我认为应该把"礼治"发展为"天下为公，人尽其才"的"理治"。其实，我国提出的和平共处五项原则，就是"己所不欲，勿施于人"发展到今天的国际政治原则。而"知之、好之、乐之"三之论和"从心所欲，不逾矩"的艺术，正是孔子的"礼乐"应用于文学翻译的理论。希望孔子的智慧、唐诗的智慧，能丰富21世纪的全球文化，使全世界都能享受和平、繁荣、幸福的生活。

许渊冲

1999年9月于北京大学

目录

CONTENTS

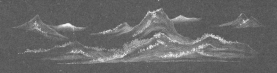

● 虞世南　YU SHINAN

　002　蝉
　004　咏萤

● 孔绍安　KONG SHAO'AN

　007　落叶

● 王绩　WANG JI

　010　野望

● 寒山　HAN SHAN

　013　杳杳寒山道

● 上官仪　SHANGGUAN YI

　016　早春桂林殿应诏

● 王勃　WANG BO

　019　送杜少府之任蜀州
　021　滕王阁

● 杨炯　YANG JIONG

　024　从军行

● 骆宾王　LUO BINWANG

　027　咏蝉

● 韦承庆　WEI CHENGQING

　030　南行别弟

● 宋之问　SONG ZHIWEN

　033　渡汉江

● 沈佺期　SHEN QUANQI

　036　杂诗三首（其三）

● 贺知章　HE ZHIZHANG

　039　咏柳
　041　回乡偶书二首

● 陈子昂　CHEN ZI'ANG

　044　登幽州台歌
　046　送东莱王学士无竞

● 张九龄　ZHANG JIULING

　049　望月怀远
　051　赋得自君之出矣

● 张旭　ZHANG XU

　054　山行留客

● 李隆基　LI LONGJI

　057　经邹鲁祭孔子而叹之

● 张若虚　ZHANG RUOXU

　060　春江花月夜

● 王湾 WANG WAN

066　次北固山下

● 王翰 WANG HAN

069　凉州词

● 王之涣 WANG ZHIHUAN

072　登鹳雀楼
074　凉州词

● 孟浩然 MENG HAORAN

077　留别王维
079　过故人庄
081　春晓
083　宿建德江

● 李颀 LI QI

086　古从军行

● 王昌龄 WANG CHANGLING

089　从军行七首（二首）
092　出塞
094　西宫秋怨
096　闺怨
098　芙蓉楼送辛渐

● 祖咏 ZU YONG

101　终南望余雪

● 王维 WANG WEI

104　送别
106　渭川田家
108　山居秋暝
110　终南山
112　观猎
114　汉江临泛
116　使至塞上
118　孟城坳
120　鹿柴
122　竹里馆
124　鸟鸣涧
126　山中送别
128　杂诗（其二）
130　相思
132　山中
134　秋夜曲
136　九月九日忆山东兄弟
138　送元二使安西
140　送沈子归江东

● 刘眘虚 LIU SHENXU

143　阙题

● 李白 LI BAI

146　峨眉山月歌
148　望庐山瀑布
150　望天门山
152　长干行
156　金陵酒肆留别
158　夜下征虏亭
160　静夜思
162　黄鹤楼送孟浩然之广陵

164　长相思
166　蜀道难
172　行路难
175　春思
177　长门怨
179　子夜吴歌·秋歌
181　将进酒
185　月下独酌四首（其一）
187　戏赠杜甫
189　梦游天姥吟留别
196　苏台览古
198　越中览古
200　越女词五首（其五）
202　山中问答
204　自遣
206　独坐敬亭山
208　宣州谢朓楼饯别校书
　　　叔云
210　送友人
212　秋浦歌十七首（其十五）
214　赠汪伦
216　早发白帝城
218　宿五松山下荀媪家
220　临终歌

● 崔颢　CUI HAO

223　黄鹤楼
225　长干曲（二首）

● 常建　CHANG JIAN

228　题破山寺后禅院

● 高适　GAO SHI

231　燕歌行

236　别董大

● 储光羲　CHU GUANGXI

239　钓鱼湾

● 刘长卿　LIU CHANG QING

242　逢雪宿芙蓉山主人
244　送灵澈上人

● 张谓　ZHANG WEI

247　早梅

● 杜甫　DU FU

250　望岳
252　兵车行
257　赠李白
259　饮中八仙歌
263　前出塞九首（其六）
265　自京赴奉先县咏怀
　　　五百字（节选）
267　月夜
269　春望
271　哀江头
275　羌村三首（其一）
277　赠卫八处士
281　石壕吏
285　梦李白二首（其一）
287　月夜忆舍弟
289　病马
291　蜀相
293　江村
295　客至
297　春夜喜雨

299　茅屋为秋风所破歌
303　赠花卿
305　戏为六绝句（其二）
307　闻官军收河南河北
309　绝句
311　旅夜书怀
313　八阵图
315　秋兴八首（其一）
317　登高
319　江汉
321　登岳阳楼
323　江南逢李龟年

● 岑参　CEN SHEN

326　白雪歌送武判官归京
330　走马川行奉送封大夫
　　　出师西征
334　山房春事二首（其二）
336　逢入京使

● 贾至　JIA ZHI

339　初至巴陵与李十二白、
　　　裴九同泛洞庭湖三首
　　　（其二）

● 刘方平　LIU FANGPING

342　月夜
344　春怨

● 司空曙　SIKONG SHU

347　江村即事
349　留卢秦卿

● 钱起　QIAN QI

352　归雁

● 顾况　GU KUANG

355　宫词五首（其二）

● 张继　ZHANG JI

358　枫桥夜泊

● 韩翃　HAN HONG

361　寒食

● 韦应物　WEI YINGWU

364　秋夜寄邱员外
366　滁州西涧

● 耿湋　GENG WEI

369　秋日

● 卢纶　LU LUN

372　塞下曲（四首）

● 李益　LI YI

377　喜见外弟又言别
379　宫怨
381　夜上受降城闻笛
383　江南曲

● 戎昱 RONG YU

　386　移家别湖上亭

● 雍裕之 YONG YUZHI

　389　江边柳

● 韩愈 HAN YU

　392　八月十五夜赠张功曹
　396　左迁至蓝关示侄孙湘

虞世南

YU
SHINAN

作者简介

虞世南（558—638），字伯施，越州余姚县（今浙江宁波）人，书法家、文学家、诗人、政治家，"凌烟阁二十四功臣"之一。

曾仕陈、隋二代。唐贞观年间，历任著作郎、秘书少监、秘书监等职。他性情刚烈，直言敢谏，深得李世民敬重，时称"德行、忠直、博学、文词、书翰"五绝。谥号"文懿"，陪葬昭陵。

善书法，与欧阳询、褚遂良、薛稷合称"初唐四大家"。有诗文集，散佚不全。

蝉

垂緌^①饮清露^②，流响^③出疏^④桐。
居高声自远，非是藉^⑤秋风。

① 垂緌：古人结在额下的帽缨下垂部分，蝉的头部伸出的触须，形状与其有
　 些相似。
② 清露：纯净的露水。古人以为蝉是喝露水生活的，其实是刺吸植物的汁液。
③ 流响：指连续不断的蝉鸣声传得很远。
④ 疏：开阔、稀疏。
⑤ 藉：凭借。

To the Cicada

Though rising high, you drink but dew;

Yet your voice flows from sparse plane trees.

Far and wide there's none but hears you;

You need no wings of autumn breeze.

咏萤^①

的皪^②流光^③小，飘飖^④弱翅轻。

恐畏^⑤无人识，独自暗中明。

① 萤：一种昆虫，身体黄褐色，触角丝状，腹部末端有发光的器官，能发出带绿色的光。白天伏在草丛里，夜晚飞出来。种类很多，通称萤火虫。

② 的皪：的历，指小粒明珠的光点，灵巧微弱的样子。

③ 流光：闪烁流动的光芒。

④ 飘飖：飘飘摇摇，很不稳定的样子。

⑤ 畏：怕。

To the Firefly

Flickering, you shed a green light;

Wafting weak wings, you flit in flight.

Being afraid to be unknown,

In the darkness you gleam alone.

KONG SHAO'AN

孔绍安

作者简介

孔绍安（约577—622），越州山阴（今浙江绍兴）人。孔奂次子，孔子三十二代孙。

少与兄孔绍新俱以文词知名。年十三，陈亡，入隋，徙居京兆鄠县，闭门读书，诵古文集数十万言。外兄虞世南叹异之。与词人孙万寿为忘年之好，时人称为"孙孔"。大业末，为监察御史。李渊讨贼河东，孔绍安为监军。李渊受禅，孔绍安自洛阳间行来奔，拜内史舍人，赐赉甚厚。尝因侍宴应诏咏石榴诗云"只为时来晚，开花不及春"为人称颂。寻诏撰《梁史》，未就而卒。有文集五十卷传世。

落叶

早秋惊落叶，飘零似客心^①。

翻飞未肯下，犹言惜^②故林。

① 客心：漂泊他乡的游子的心情。
② 惜：此处指舍不得。

Falling Leaves

In early autumn I'm sad to see falling leaves;

They're dreary like a roamer's heart which their fall grieves.

They twist and twirl as if struggling against the breeze;

I seem to hear them cry,

"We will not leave our trees."

王 绩

WANG JI

作者简介

王绩（约589—644），字无功，号东皋子，绛州龙门（今山西河津）人。隋唐大臣，大儒王通的弟弟。

隋末举孝廉，授秘书省正字，因不乐在朝，乞署外职，除六合县丞。面对天下大乱，弃官还乡。武德初年，待诏门下省。贞观初年，因病去职，躬耕于东皋山（今山西省河津市东皋村），自号"东皋子"。贞观十八年（644年）去世，时年五十六岁。

个性简傲，嗜酒，能饮五斗，自作《五斗先生传》，撰《酒经》《酒谱》。其诗近而不浅，质而不俗，真率疏放，有旷怀高致，直追魏晋风骨。

野望

东皋^①薄暮^②望，徙倚^③欲何依^④？

树树皆秋色^⑤，山山唯落晖^⑥。

牧人驱犊^⑦返，猎马带禽^⑧归。

相顾无相识，长歌怀采薇^⑨。

---

① 东皋：地名，今山西河津，诗人隐居的地方。

② 薄暮：傍晚。薄，迫近。

③ 徙倚：徘徊，来回地走。

④ 依：归依。

⑤ 秋色：一作"春色"。

⑥ 落晖：落日。

⑦ 犊：小牛，此处指牛群。

⑧ 禽：鸟兽，此处指猎物。

⑨ 采薇：薇，是一种植物。相传周武王灭商后，伯夷、叔齐不愿做周的臣子，在首阳山上采薇而食，最后饿死。古时"采薇"代指隐居生活。

A Field View

At dusk with eastern shore in view,

I stroll but know not where to go.

Tree on tree tinted with autumn hue,

Hill on hill steeped in sunset glow.

The shepherd drives his herd homebound;

The hunter loads his horse with game.

There is no connoisseur around;

I can but sing of hermits' name.

寒山

HAN SHAN

作者简介

　　寒山，生卒年、字与号均不详，长安（今陕西西安）人，唐代著名诗僧。出身于官宦人家，多次投考不第，后出家，三十岁后隐居于浙东天台山。

　　他经常在山林间题诗作偈，其诗通俗，表现山林逸趣与佛教出世思想，蕴含人生哲理，讥讽时态，同情贫民。他曾经一度被世人冷落，20世纪后，其诗越来越多地被世人接受并广泛流传。

杳杳寒山道

杳杳^①寒山^②道，落落^③冷涧^④滨。

啾啾常有鸟，寂寂更无人。

淅淅^⑤风吹面，纷纷雪积身。

朝朝不见日，岁岁不知春。

---

① 杳杳：幽暗状。

② 寒山：始丰县（今浙江天台县西）天台山有寒暗二岩，寒山即寒岩，乃诗
人所居。

③ 落落：冷清寂静的样子。

④ 涧：指的是山间流水的沟，或者小溪。

⑤ 淅淅：象声词，形容风声。一作"碛碛"。

Long, Long the Pathway to Cold Hill

Long, long the pathway to Cold Hill;

Drear, drear the waterside so chill.

Chirp, chirp, I often hear the bird;

Mute, mute, nobody says a word.

Gust by gust winds caress my face;

Flake on flake snow covers all trace.

From day to day the sun won't swing;

From year to year I know no spring.

SHANG GUAN YI

上官仪

作者简介

上官仪（608—665），字游韶，陕州陕县（今河南陕州）人，唐代宰相、诗人，才女上官婉儿的祖父。

早年曾出家为僧，后以进士及第，历任弘文馆直学士、秘书郎、起居郎、秘书少监、太子中舍人。他是初唐著名御用文人，常为皇帝起草诏书，并开创"绮错婉媚"的上官体诗风。

龙朔二年（662年），上官仪拜相，授为西台侍郎、同东西台三品。麟德元年十二月（665年1月），因为唐高宗起草废后诏书，得罪了武则天，被诬陷谋反，下狱处死。唐中宗年间，因上官婉儿受中宗宠信，追赠为中书令、秦州都督，追封楚国公。

早春桂林殿应诏

步辇^①出披香，清歌临太液^②。

晓树流莺满，春堤芳草积。

风光翻露文，雪华上空碧。

花蝶来未已，山光暖将夕。

---

① 步辇：帝王所乘坐的代步工具，原称辇，秦以后去掉轮子，改由人抬，故称步辇。

② 太液：即太液池，位于唐代长安大明宫的北部，是唐代最重要的皇家池苑。

Early Spring in Laurel Palace

The royal cab leaves palace hall

For poolside garden mid sweet songs.

The trees are loud with orioles' call;

On vernal shore grass grows in throngs.

The breeze can write with morning dew;

'Neath blue sky flowers bloom like snow.

Butterflies come now and anew;

The hills are warmed by evening glow.

王

勃

WANG BO

作者简介

王勃（649—676），字子安，绛州龙门（今山西河津）人。唐代文学家，与杨炯、卢照邻、骆宾王并称"初唐四杰"。

聪敏好学，六岁能文，下笔流畅，被赞为"神童"。九岁时，读秘书监颜师古注《汉书》，作《指瑕》十卷，以纠正其错。十六岁时，幽素科试及第，授朝散郎、沛王（李贤）府文学。写作《檄英王鸡文》，坐罪免官。游览巴蜀山川景物，创作大量诗文。

擅长五律和五绝，提倡表现浓郁的情感与壮大的气势，并在骈文上有很大成就。现存诗八十余首，有代表作《送杜少府之任蜀州》《滕王阁序》等。

送杜少府① 之② 任蜀州③

城阙辅三秦④，风烟望五津⑤。

与君离别意，同是宦游人⑥。

海内⑦存知己，天涯⑧若比邻⑨。

无为⑩在歧路⑪，儿女共沾巾⑫。

---

① 少府：唐人称县尉为少府。杜少府其人不详。

② 之：到、往。

③ 蜀州：今四川省崇州市。

④ 城阙辅三秦：城阙，即城楼，指唐代京师长安城。辅三秦，一作"俯西
　秦"。辅，护卫。三秦，指长安城附近的关中之地，即今陕西省潼关以西
　一带。秦朝末年，项羽破秦，把关中分为三区，分别封给三个秦国的降将，
　所以称三秦。这句是倒装句，意思是三秦之地护卫着京师长安城。

⑤ 五津：五津，指岷江的白华津、万里津、江首津、涉头津、江南津五个渡
　口。此处泛指蜀地。

⑥ 宦游人：为仕官而远游四方的人。

⑦ 海内：四海之内。古代人认为我国疆土四周环海，所以称天下为四海之内。

⑧ 天涯：天边，此处比喻极远的地方。

⑨ 比邻：近邻。古代五家相连为比，《周礼·地官·大司徒》："令五家为比，
　使之相保。"唐制，四家为邻。

⑩ 无为：无须、不必。

⑪ 歧路：岔路，古人送行常在大路分岔处告别。

⑫ 沾巾：泪水沾湿衣服和腰带，意思是挥泪告别。

Farewell to Prefect Du

You'll leave the town walled far and wide

For mist-veiled land by riverside.

I feel on parting sad and drear,

For both of us are strangers here.

If you have friends who know your heart,

Distance cannot keep you apart.

At crossroads where we bid adieu,

Do not shed tears as women do!

滕王阁 ①

滕王高阁临江②渚③，佩玉鸣鸾④罢歌舞。

画栋朝飞南浦⑤云，珠帘暮卷西山⑥雨。

闲云潭影日悠悠⑦，物换星移⑧几度秋。

阁中帝子⑨今何在？槛⑩外长江空自流。

---

① 滕王阁：故址位于今江西南昌赣江滨，江南三大名楼之一。

② 江：指赣江。

③ 渚：江中小洲。

④ 佩玉鸣鸾：身上佩戴的玉饰、响铃。

⑤ 南浦：地名，在南昌市西南。浦，水边或河流入海的地方（多用于地名）。

⑥ 西山：南昌市名胜。一名南昌山、厌原山、洪崖山。

⑦ 日悠悠：每日无拘无束地游荡。

⑧ 物换星移：形容时代的变迁、万物的更替。物，四季的景物。

⑨ 帝子：指滕王李元婴。

⑩ 槛：栏杆。

Prince Teng's Pavilion

By riverside towers Prince Teng's Pavilion proud,

But gone are cabs with ringing bells and stirring strain.

At dawn its painted beams bar the south-flying cloud;

At dusk its up rolled screens reveal western hills' rain.

Leisurely clouds hang over still water all day long;

Stars move from spring to autumn in changeless sky.

Where is the prince who once enjoyed here wine and song?

Beyond the rails the silent river still rolls by.

杨炯

YANG
JIONG

作者简介

杨炯（650—693），字令明，华州华阴（今陕西华阴）人。唐代文学家，唐左光禄大夫杨初曾孙，与王勃、卢照邻、骆宾王并称"初唐四杰"。

聪敏博学，文采出众。显庆四年（659年）进士及第，授弘文馆待制。上元三年（676年）参加制举，补为校书郎。后任崇书馆学士，迁詹事司直。垂拱二年（686年）贬为梓州司法参军。如意元年（692年）迁盈川县令。如意二年（693年）卒于任上。

善写散文，尤擅诗歌。现存诗三十余首，在内容和艺术风格上以突破齐梁"宫体诗风"为特色，在诗歌发展史上起到承前启后的作用。

从军行①

烽火②照西京，心中自不平③。

牙璋辞凤阙④，铁骑绕龙城⑤。

雪暗凋旗画⑥，风多杂鼓声。

宁为百夫长⑦，胜作一书生。

0
2
4

---

① 从军行：乐府旧题，属《相和歌辞·平调曲》，题材大多为边塞军旅战争。

② 烽火：古代边防报警的信号。

③ 不平：难以平静。

④ "牙璋"句：牙璋，调兵的符牒。两块合成，朝廷和主帅各执其半，嵌合处呈齿状，故名。此处指代奉命出征的将帅。凤阙，汉武帝所建的建章宫的圆阙上有鎏金铜凤凰，故称凤阙。后来常用作帝王宫阙的泛称。

⑤ "铁骑"句：铁骑，精锐的骑兵，指唐军。绕，围。龙城，汉时匈奴大会祭天之处，故址位于今蒙古国鄂尔浑河东侧。这里泛指敌方要塞、据点。

⑥ "雪暗"句：大雪弥漫，落满军旗，使旗帜上的图案暗淡失色。凋，原意是草木枯败凋零，此指失去了鲜艳的色彩。

⑦ 百夫长：周朝兵制以百人为一队，队长称"百夫长"。后世泛指下级武官。

I Would Rather Fight

The beacon fires spread to the capital;

My agitated mind can't be calmed down.

By royal order to leave palace hall;

Our armored steeds besiege the Dragon Town.

Darkening snow damages our banners red;

with the howling wind mingle our drumbeats.

I'd rather fight at a hundred men's head

Than pore over books without performing feats.

骆宾王

LUO
BINWANG

作者简介

  骆宾王（约640—684以后），字观光，婺州义乌（今浙江）人。唐代诗人，与王勃、杨炯、卢照邻合称"初唐四杰"。

  出身寒微，少有才名。仪凤三年（678年）任侍御史，因事下狱，遇赦而出。调露二年（680年）出任临海县丞，坐事免官。光宅元年（684年）跟随英国公徐敬业起兵讨伐武则天，撰写《讨武曌檄》。徐敬业败亡后，骆宾王结局不明，或说被乱军所杀，或说遁入空门。

  诗歌辞采华赡，格律谨严。长篇如《帝京篇》，五七言参差转换，讽时与自伤兼而有之；短篇如《于易水送人》，二十字中，悲凉慷慨，余情不绝。有《骆宾王文集》传世。

咏蝉

西陆^①蝉声唱，南冠^②客思深。

那堪^③玄鬓影^④，来对白头吟^⑤。

露重飞难进，风多响易沉^⑥。

无人信高洁，谁为表予心。

---

① 西陆：指秋天。《隋书·天文志》："日循黄道东行，一日一夜行一度，三百六十五日有奇而周天。行东陆谓之春，行南陆谓之夏，行西陆谓之秋，行北陆谓之冬。"

② 南冠：指囚犯。《左传·成公九年》："晋侯观于军府，见钟仪，问之曰：'南冠而系者谁也？'有司对曰：'郑人所献楚囚也。'"钟仪，南方楚国人，戴楚冠，故曰"南冠"。后世遂以之代指囚犯。此诗中作者以此自喻。

③ 那堪：怎能忍受得了。那，一作"不"。

④ 玄鬓影：指蝉。古代妇女将鬓发梳为蝉翼之状，称之蝉鬓。崔豹《古今注》："魏文帝宫人莫琼树始制蝉鬓，缥缈如蝉。"玄，黑色。此处以玄鬓称蝉，比喻自己正当盛年。

⑤ 白头吟：乐府曲名。《乐府诗集》解题说是鲍照、张正见、虞世南诸作，皆自伤清直却遭诬谤。白头，诗人自指。当时骆宾王不足四十岁，因身处狱中而以白头自况，极言烦虑之深重。此两句意谓，自己正当玄鬓之年，却来默诵《白头吟》那样哀怨的诗句。

⑥ 沉：沉没，掩盖。

The Cicada

Of autumn the cicada sings;

In prison I'm worn out with care.

How can I bear its blue-black wings

Which remind me of my grey hair?

Heavy with dew it cannot fly;

Drowned in the wind, its song's not heard.

Who would believe its spirit high?

Could I express my grief in word?

WEI CHENGQING

韦承庆

作者简介

　　韦承庆（640—706），字延休，河内郡阳武县（今河南原阳）人。唐朝武周时期宰相，纳言韦思谦之子。

　　个性谨畏，事亲笃孝。进士及第，授乌程县令，累迁中书舍人，屡进谠言。转吏部侍郎，铨授平允。长安年间，拜中书侍郎、同平章事。神龙革命，依附于幸臣张易之，坐罪流放岭表。韦后掌权后，召为员外秘书少监，兼修国史，封上柱国、扶阳县子。神龙二年（706年）迁黄门郎，未拜而卒，追赠礼部尚书，谥号为"温"。著有文集六十卷，已佚。

南行别弟

澹澹①长江水，悠悠②远客③情。

落花相与恨，到地一无声④。

---

① 澹澹：水波微微荡漾的样子。

② 悠悠：绵长深远的样子。

③ 远客：诗人自指。

④ "落花"二句：用花落无声比喻临别时相对无语。此二句即景寓情，与刘长卿《别严士元》诗文中"闲花落地听无声"构思相同，抒发宦途失意后和友人分别。

Parting with My Younger Brother

The long, long river coolly flows;

My parting sorrow endless grows.

Our grief is shared by falling blooms;

In their silence our sorrow looms.

宋之问

SONG ZHIWEN

作者简介

宋之问（656—712），字延清，又名少连，汾州（今山西汾阳）人。唐代诗人，与陈子昂、李白、孟浩然、卢藏用、司马承祯、王适、毕构、王维、贺知章称为"仙宗十友"。

上元二年（675年）进士。得武则天赏识，累转尚方监丞、左奉宸内供奉。趋附张易之兄弟，坐贬泷州参军。后几经辗转，先天元年（712年）八月，唐玄宗李隆基即位后，被赐死于徙所。

诗多歌功颂德之作，文辞华丽，自然流畅，对律诗定型颇有影响。

渡汉江①

岭外②音书断，经冬复历春。

近乡情更怯，不敢问来人。

---

① 汉江：水名，是长江的一条支流，此处指襄阳附近的一段汉水。
② 岭外：这里指五岭以南的地区。五岭由大庾岭、越城岭、骑田岭、萌渚岭、都庞岭组成，是位于广东、广西和江西、湖南交界处的一座山脉，是长江与珠江的分水岭。

Crossing River Han

I longed for news on the frontier

From day to day, from year to year.

Now nearing home, timid I grow;

I dare not ask what I would know.

沈佺期

SHEN QUANQI

作者简介

沈佺期（656—715），字云卿，相州内黄（今河南安阳）人，唐代诗人，与宋之问齐名，称"沈宋"。

上元二年（675年）进士及第。长安中，累迁通事舍人，预修《三教珠英》，转考功郎给事中。坐交张易之，流驩州。稍迁台州录事参军。神龙中，召见，拜起居郎，修文馆直学士，历中书舍人，太子少詹事。开元初卒。

善属文，尤长七言之作。建安后，讫江左，诗律屡变，至沈约、庾信，以音韵相婉附，属对精密，及沈佺期与宋之问，尤加靡丽。回忌声病，约句准篇，如锦绣成文，学者宗之，号为"沈宋"。语曰："苏李居前，沈宋比肩。"原有集十卷，已散佚。

杂诗三首（其三）

闻道黄龙戍^①，频年不解兵。

可怜闺里月，长在汉家营。

少妇今春意，良人昨夜情。

谁能将旗鼓，一为取龙城^②。

---

① 黄龙戍：即黄龙，位于今辽宁开原市，此处指边地。
② 龙城：地名，今蒙古国境内，此处借指敌方要地。

The Garrison at Yellow Dragon Town

'Tis said at Yellow Dragon Town

For years war has gone up and down.

Alas! At home wives watch the moon

Seen in the camp by men alone.

What would a young wife think in spring?

What dream last night did her man bring?

O, who with flags and drums could go

To take the town and beat the foe?

贺知章

HE ZHIZHANG

作者简介

　　贺知章（659—744），字季真，晚年自号"四明狂客""秘书外监"，越州永兴（今浙江杭州萧山）人。唐代诗人、书法家。

　　少时以诗文知名，不仅诗文精佳，且书法品位颇高，尤擅草隶。他为人旷达不羁，好酒，有"清谈风流"之誉，晚年尤纵。

　　与张若虚、张旭、包融并称"吴中四士"；与李白、李适之等谓"醉八仙"；又与陈子昂、卢藏用、宋之问、王适、毕构、李白、孟浩然、王维、司马承祯并称为"仙宗十友"。其诗文以绝句见长，除祭神乐章、应制诗外，其写景、抒怀之作风格独特，清新潇洒，其中《咏柳》《回乡偶书》等脍炙人口，千古传诵。作品大多散佚，《全唐诗》录其诗十九首。

咏柳 ①

碧玉 ② 妆 ③ 成一树高，万条垂下绿丝绦 ④。

不知细叶谁裁出，二月春风似剪刀。

---

① 诗题一作"柳枝词"。

② 碧玉：碧绿色的玉，此处借指春天的柳叶碧绿鲜嫩。

③ 妆：装饰，打扮。

④ 丝绦：丝带，此处用以形容柳条。

The Willow

The slender beauty's dressed in emerald all about;

A thousand branches droop like fringes made of jade.

But do you know by whom these slim leaves are cut out?

The wind of early spring is sharp as scissor blade.

回乡偶书^① 二首

一

少小离家老大回，乡音无改鬓毛衰^{cuī}^②。

儿童相见不相识，笑问客从何处来。

二

离别家乡岁月多，近来人事半消磨^③。

惟有门前镜湖^④水，春风不改旧时波。

---

① 偶书：偶然写的诗。偶，偶然，不经意，说明此诗是随见所得、随见所感。
② 鬓毛衰：指人的年纪大了，鬓发稀疏脱落。此时贺知章回乡时已年逾八十。
③ 消磨：逐渐消失、消除。
④ 镜湖：湖泊名，位于今浙江省绍兴市会稽山的北麓，方圆三百余里。贺知章的故乡就在镜湖边。

Home-Coming

I

I left home young and not till old do I come back,

Unchanged my accent, my hair no longer black.

The children whom I meet do not know who am I,

"Where do you come from, sir?" they ask with

beaming eye.

II

Since I left my homeland so many years have passed;

So much has faded away and so little can last.

Only in Mirror Lake before my oldened door

The vernal wind still ripples waves now as before.

陈子昂

CHEN ZI'ANG

作者简介

陈子昂（661—702），字伯玉，梓州射洪（今四川遂宁）人。唐代文学家、诗人，初唐诗文革新人物之一。因曾任右拾遗，后世称"陈拾遗"。

幼而聪颖，少而任侠，文明元年（684年）举进士，以上书论政得到女皇武则天重视，授麟台正字。后升右拾遗，直言敢谏，曾因"逆党"反对武后而株连下狱。曾两度从军边塞，对边防事务颇有远见。圣历元年（698年），因父老解官回乡，不久父死。他在居丧期间，权臣武三思指使射洪县令罗织罪名，加以迫害，最终冤死狱中。

存诗共一百多首，其诗风骨峥嵘，寓意深远，苍劲有力。其中最有代表性的有《登幽州台歌》《登泽州城北楼宴》和组诗《感遇诗三十八首》《蓟丘览古赠卢居士藏用七首》等。

登幽州台^①歌

前不见古人^②，后不见来者^③。

念天地之悠悠^④，独怆然^⑤而涕^⑥下！

---

① 幽州台：即黄金台，又称蓟北楼，故址位于今北京市大兴区，是燕昭王为
　招纳天下贤士而建。幽州，古十二州之一，现今北京市。
② "前不"句：前，过去。古人，古代那些能够礼贤下士的圣君。
③ "后不"句：后，未来。来者，后世那些重视人才的贤主。
④ 悠悠：形容时间的久远和空间的广大。
⑤ 怆然：凄伤的样子。
⑥ 涕：古时指眼泪。

On the Tower at Youzhou

Where are the great men of the past

And where are those of future years?

The sky and earth forever last;

Here and now I alone shed tears.

送东莱①王学士无竞②

宝剑千金买，平生未许人。

怀君万里别，持赠结交亲。

孤松宜晚岁③，众木爱芳春④。

已矣将何道⑤，无令白首新。

---

① 东莱：西汉郡名，位于今山东莱州市。
② 王学士无竞：无竞即王无竞，字仲烈，东莱人，性情刚烈耿直，不肯奉迎权贵，仕途坎坷，屡遭贬谪。学士，官名，皇帝身边的文学侍从。
③ 晚岁：一年将尽的时候。
④ 芳春：春天，春季。
⑤ 将何道：还有什么可说的呢？

Parting Gift

The sword that cost me dear,

To none would I confide.

Now you are to leave here,

Let it go by your side.

Trees delight in spring day;

The pine loves wintry air.

What more need I to say?

Don't add to your grey hair!

张九龄

ZHANG JIULING

作者简介

　　张九龄（673—740），字子寿，号博物，韶州曲江（今广东韶关）人。唐开元名相、政治家、文学家、诗人。

　　开元盛世的最后名相。举止优雅，风度不凡。富有远见卓识，忠耿尽职，秉公守则，直言敢谏，选贤任能，不徇私枉法，不附权贵，为"开元之治"作出了积极贡献。

　　积极发展五言古诗，诗风清淡，以素练质朴的语言，寄托深远的人生慨望，对扫除唐初所沿袭的六朝绮靡诗风，贡献尤大。著有《曲江集》，被誉为"岭南第一人"。

望月怀远 ①

海上生明月，天涯共此时。

情人②怨遥夜，竟夕③起相思。

灭烛怜光满④，披衣觉露滋。

不堪盈手赠，还寝梦佳期⑤。

---

① 怀远：怀念远方的亲人。

② 情人：多情的人，指作者自己。一说指亲人。

③ 竟夕：终夜，通宵，一整夜。

④ "灭烛"句：吹熄油灯仍然感受到月光的盈满霞美，当一个人静静地在屋子里面享受月光，便生出一种"怜"的感觉。怜，爱。光满，月光照射充盈的样子。

⑤ "不堪"二句：月华虽好但是不能盈手相赠，不如进入梦乡寻觅佳期。

Looking at the Moon and Longing for One Far Away

Over the sea grows the moon bright;

We gaze on it far, far apart.

Lovers complain of long, long night;

They rise and long for the dear heart.

Candles blown out, fuller is light;

My coat put on, I'm moist with dew.

As I can't hand you moonbeams white,

I go to bed to dream of you.

赋得^① 自君之出矣^②

自君之出矣，不复理残机^③。

思君如满月，夜夜减^④清辉^⑤。

---

① 赋得：凡摘取古人成句为题之诗，题首多冠以"赋得"二字。本诗属乐府诗《杂曲歌辞》。

② 君之出矣：夫君离家。之，助词，无实际意义。出，出行。矣，了。

③ 理残机：理会残破的织布机。

④ 减：减弱，消减。

⑤ 清辉：皎洁的月光。

Since My Lord from Me Parted

Since my lord from me parted,

I've left unused my loom.

The moon wanes, broken-hearted

To see my growing gloom.

张旭

ZHANG XU

作者简介

张旭（685—759），字伯高，一字季明，苏州吴县（今江苏苏州）人，唐代书法家，擅长草书，喜欢饮酒，世称"张颠"，与怀素并称"颠张醉素"，与贺知章、张若虚、包融并称"吴中四士"，又与贺知章等人并称"饮中八仙"，其草书则与李白的诗歌、裴旻的剑舞并称"三绝"。

在书法方面，张旭勤于观察客观事物，善于将客观的自然物象与个人的主观情感结合起来。在继承前人书法成就的同时并加以创新而使得自身的狂草艺术在盛唐时期达到了一个高峰。

山行^①留客

山光物态弄春晖，莫为轻阴^②便拟归^③。

纵使晴明无雨色，入云^④深处亦沾衣。

---

① 山行：一作"山中"。
② 轻阴：阴云。
③ 便拟归：就打算回去。
④ 云：此处指雾、烟霭。

To a Guest in the Hills

On all things in the hills spring sheds a golden light.

Do not go back when some dark rain clouds come in sight!

Even on a fine day when the sun's shining bright,

Your gown will moisten still in the thick of clouds white.

李隆基

LI
LONGJI

作者简介

李隆基（685—762），唐高宗李治与武则天之孙，唐睿宗李旦第三子，故又称李三郎，母窦德妃。唐代在位时间最长的皇帝（712—756在位）。

在位前期，注意拨乱反正，任用姚崇、宋璟等贤相，励精图治，开创了唐朝的极盛之世——开元盛世。但是在位后期逐渐怠慢朝政、宠信奸臣，宠爱杨贵妃，加上政策失误和重用安禄山等塞外民族将领试图来稳定唐王朝的边疆，结果导致了后来长达八年的"安史之乱"，为唐朝由盛转衰埋下伏笔。天宝十五载（756年）太子李亨即位，尊其为太上皇。

宝应元年（762年）病逝，谥号"至道大圣大明孝皇帝"，庙号"玄宗"。清朝为避讳康熙帝之名玄烨，多称其为"唐明皇"，另有尊号"开元圣文神武皇帝"。

经邹鲁祭孔子而叹之

夫子①何为者②，栖栖③一代中。

地犹鄹zōu氏邑④，宅即鲁王宫。

叹凤嗟身否pǐ⑤，伤麟怨道穷⑥。

今看两楹奠⑦，当与梦时同⑧。

---

① 夫子：此处是对孔子的敬称。

② 何为者：何为乎，为什么这样。

③ 栖栖：忙碌不安的样子，指孔子四方奔走。

④ 鄹氏邑：指鄹人的城邑。鄹，春秋时鲁地，今山东曲阜县东南。孔子出生于此，后迁曲阜。

⑤ "叹凤"句：《论语·子罕》载："子曰：凤鸟不至，河不出图，吾已矣夫。"意思是凤至象征圣人出而受瑞，今凤凰既不至，故孔子遂有身不能亲见圣之叹。身否，指生不逢时。否，不畅，不幸。

⑥ "伤麟"句：麟，瑞兽，象征太平盛世。相传孔子见人捕获了麟，曾大为悲痛地说："噫，天丧予！""吾道穷矣！"

⑦ 两楹奠：指人死后灵柩停放于两楹之间，意指祭祀的庄严隆重。两楹，指殿堂的中间。楹，堂前直柱。奠，致祭。

⑧ "当与"句：孔子说他曾经夜梦自己坐于两柱之间受人祭奠，他的梦于今天实现了。

Sacrifice to Confucius

How much have you done, O, my sage,

All for the good of all the ages!

Your offspring lives still on this land;

Your house and temple still there stand.

The phoenix deplored your sad state;

The unicorn foretold your fate.

We offer sacrifice to you,

For once you dreamed it was your due.

张若虚

ZHANG RUOXU

作者简介

张若虚（约670—约730），扬州（今江苏扬州）人，唐代诗人，与贺知章、张旭、包融并称为"吴中四士"。

其诗描写细腻，音节和谐，清丽开宕，富有情韵，在初唐诗风的转变中有重要地位。但受六朝柔靡诗风影响，常露人生无常之感。诗作大部散佚，《全唐诗》仅存两首，其一为《春江花月夜》，乃千古绝唱，是一篇脍炙人口的名作，有"以孤篇压倒全唐"之誉；闻一多评价《春江花月夜》是"诗中的诗，顶峰中的顶峰"。另一首诗是《代答闺梦还》。

春江花月夜

春江潮水连海平，海上明月共^①潮生。

滟滟^②随波千万里，何处春江无月明。

江流宛转绕芳甸^③，月照花林皆似霰^④。

空里流霜^⑤不觉飞，汀^⑥上白沙看不见。

江天一色无纤尘，皎皎空中孤月轮。

江畔何人初见月？江月何年初照人？

人生代代无穷已，江月年年望相似。

不知江月待何人，但见长江送流水。

---

① 共：一起。
② 滟滟：水波闪动的样子。
③ 甸：郊野。
④ 霰：雪珠。
⑤ 流霜：形容月光洁白如霜。古人以为霜和雪一样，都是飞动的。
⑥ 汀：沙滩，水边平地。

白云一片去悠悠，青枫^⑧浦上不胜愁。

谁家今夜扁舟子^⑨？何处相思明月楼？

可怜楼上月裴回，应照离人妆镜台。

玉户^⑩帘中卷不去，捣衣砧^⑪上拂还来。

此时相望不相闻，愿逐月华流照君。

鸿雁长飞光不度^⑫，鱼龙潜跃水成文^⑬。

昨夜闲潭梦落花，可怜春半不还家。

江水流春去欲尽，江潭落月复西斜。

斜月沉沉藏海雾，碣石潇湘^⑭无限路。

不知乘月几人归，落月摇情满江树。

061

---

⑧ 青枫：暗用《楚辞·招魂》中"湛湛江水兮上有枫，目极千里兮伤春心"的意思。

⑨ 扁舟子：指飘荡在外的游子。

⑩ 玉户：形容楼阁华丽，以玉石镶嵌。

⑪ 捣衣砧：捶衣服用的石板。

⑫ 度：飞越。

⑬ 文："纹"，波纹。

⑭ 碣石潇湘：泛指天南地北。碣石，山名，原为河北省乐亭县西南的大碣石山，现已沉落海中。潇湘，潇湘二水在湖南零陵县合流后称作潇湘。

The Moon over the River on a Spring Night

In spring the river rises as high as the sea,

And with the river's tide uprises the moon bright.

She follows the rolling waves for ten thousand Li;

Where'er the river flows, there overflows her light.

The river winds around the fragrant islet where

The blooming flowers in her light all look like snow.

You cannot tell her beams from hoar frost in the air,

Nor from white sand upon Farewell Beach below.

No dust has stained the water blending with the skies;

A lonely wheel-like moon shines brilliant far and wide.

Who by the riverside did first see the moon rise?

When did the moon first see a man by riverside?

Many generations have come and passed away;

From year to year the moons look alike, old and new.

We do not know tonight for whom she sheds her ray,

But hear the river say to its water adieu.

Away, away is sailing a single cloud white;

On Farewell Beach are pining away maples green.

Where is the wanderer sailing his boat tonight?

Who, pining away, on the moonlit rails would lean?

Alas! The moon is lingering over the tower;

It should have seen her dressing table all alone.

She may roll curtains up, but light is in her bower;

She may wash, but moonbeams still remain on the stone.

She sees the moon, but her husband is out of sight;

She would follow the moonbeams to shine on his face.

But message-bearing swans can't fly out of moonlight,

Nor letter-sending fish can leap out of their place.

He dreamed of flowers falling o'er the pool last night;

Alas! Spring has half gone, but he can't homeward go.

The water bearing spring will run away in flight;

The moon over the pool will sink low.

In the mist on the sea the slanting moon will hide;

It's a long way from northern hills to southern streams.

How many can go home by moonlight on the tide?

The setting moon sheds over riverside trees but dreams.

王 湾

WANG
WAN

作者简介

王湾（693—751），号为德，唐代诗人，洛阳（今河南洛阳）人。

玄宗先天年间（约712年）进士及第，授荥阳县主簿。后由荥阳主簿受荐编书，参与集部的编撰辑集工作，书成之后，因功授任洛阳尉。

其诗以歌咏江南山水为主，《次北固山下》是最著名的一篇。尤其其中"海日生残夜，江春入旧年"两句，得到当时的宰相张说的极度赞赏，并亲自书写悬挂于宰相政事堂上，这两句诗中表现的那种壮阔高朗的景象对盛唐诗坛产生了重要的影响。

次^①北固山下

客路青山^②外，行舟绿水前。

潮平两岸阔，风正一帆悬。

海日生残夜^③，江春入旧年^④。

乡书^⑤何处达？归雁洛阳边。

---

① 次：旅途中暂时停宿，此处是停泊的意思。

② 青山：指北固山，位于今江苏省镇江市。

③ "海日"句：海日，即海上的旭日。生，升起。残夜，夜晚将尽。

④ "江春"句：江春，江上的春天。入，到。

⑤ 乡书：家信。

Passing by the Northern Mountains

My boat goes by green mountains high,

And passes through the river blue.

The banks seem wide at the full tide;

A sail with ease hangs in soft breeze.

The sun brings light born of last night;

New spring invades old year which fades.

Where can I send word to my friend?

Homing wild geese, fly westward please!

王翰

WANG
HAN

作者简介

王翰（687—726），字子羽，并州晋阳（今山西太原）人，唐代边塞诗人，与王昌龄同时期。

性格豪爽，无拘无束，常与文人志士结交，杜甫诗中以"李邕求识面，王翰愿卜邻"之句赞叹王翰。

其诗题材大多吟咏沙场少年、玲珑女子以及欢歌饮宴等，表达对人生短暂的感叹和及时行乐的旷达情怀。

凉州词

葡萄美酒夜光杯^①，欲饮琵琶^②马上催^③。

醉卧沙场君莫笑，古来征战几人回？

---

① 夜光杯：用白玉制成的酒杯，倒入酒后，放在月光下，杯中会闪闪发亮，因此得名。此处指华贵而精美的酒杯。
② 琵琶：此处指作战时用来发出号角声时用的。
③ 催：催人出征，又解鸣奏助兴。

Starting for the Front

With wine of grapes the cups of jade would glow at night;

Drinking to pipa songs, we are summoned to fight.

Don't laugh if we lay drunken on the battleground!

How many warriors ever came back safe and sound?

WANG ZHIHUAN

王之涣

作者简介

王之涣（688—742），字季凌，祖籍并州晋阳（今山西太原）。唐代诗人。

慷慨有大略，倜傥有异才。以门荫入仕，授衡水主簿。后受人诬谤，拂衣去官。天宝元年（742年）补文安县尉，清白处世，理政公平。

精于文章，善于写诗，多被引为歌词。尤善五言诗，以描写边塞风光为胜，代表作有《登鹳雀楼》《凉州词二首》等。

登鹳雀楼^①

白日^②依山尽，黄河入海流。

欲穷^③千里目^④，更^⑤上一层楼。

---

① 鹳雀楼：位于今山西省永济市，始建于北周，下临黄河。传说常有鹳雀在此停留，故有此名。

② 白日：太阳。

③ 穷：尽，使达到极点。

④ 千里目：意指眼界宽阔。

⑤ 更：再。

On the Stork Tower

The sun along the mountain bows;

The Yellow River seawards flows.

You will enjoy a grander sight

By climbing to a greater height.

凉州词①

黄河远上白云间，一片孤城万仞②山。

羌笛③何须怨杨柳④，春风不度玉门关⑤。

---

① 凉州词：又作《出塞》。《凉州歌》的唱词，不是诗题，是盛唐时流行的一种曲调名。开元年间，陇右节度使郭知运搜集了一批西域的曲谱，进献给唐玄宗，玄宗交给教坊翻成中国曲谱，并配上新的歌词演唱，以这些曲谱产生地的名称为曲调名。后来，许多诗人都喜欢这种曲调，为它填写新词，因此唐代许多诗人都写有《凉州词》。
② 万仞：形容山很高的意思。仞，古代的长度单位，一仞约为八尺。
③ 羌笛：古代羌人所制的一种管乐器，有两孔，属于横吹式管乐。
④ 杨柳：指《折杨柳曲》，是一种哀怨的曲调。古人常以杨柳喻送别情事。
⑤ 玉门关：关名，位于今甘肃省敦煌市区以西，是古代通往西域的要道。

Out of the Great Wall

The Yellow River rises to the white cloud;

The lonely town is lost amid the mountains proud.

Why should the Mongol flute complain no willows grow?

Beyond the Gate of Jade no vernal wind will blow.

MENG
HAORAN

孟浩然

作者简介

孟浩然（689—740），字浩然，号孟山人，襄州襄阳（今湖北襄阳）人，唐代著名的山水田园派诗人，世称"孟襄阳"。因他未曾入仕，又称之为"孟山人"。

四十岁时，游长安，应进士举不第。曾在太学赋诗，名动公卿，一座倾服，为之搁笔。开元二十五年（737年）张九龄招致幕府，后隐居。

其诗在艺术上有独特的造诣，大部分为五言短篇，多写山水田园和隐居的逸兴以及羁旅行役的心情。其中虽不无愤世嫉俗之词，而更多属于诗人的自我表现。后人把孟浩然与盛唐另一山水诗人王维并称为"王孟"，有《孟浩然集》三卷传世。

留别王维

寂寂^①竟何待，朝朝空自归。

欲寻芳草去^②，惜与故人违。

当路^③谁相假，知音世所稀。

只应守寂寞，还掩故园扉。

---

① 寂寂：安静，无人声。

② "欲寻"句：意为想归隐。芳草，古人常用来比喻有美德的人。

③ 当路：当政，指当权者。

Parting from Wang Wei

Lonely, lonely, what is there to hope for?

Day by day I come back without an end.

I would seek fragrant grass in native shore.

How I regret to part with my old friend!

I'm one whom those in high place would elude,

For there are few connoisseurs in the state.

I can but keep myself in solitude

And go back to close my old garden gate.

过^①故人庄

故人具^②鸡黍^③，邀我至田家。

绿树村边合^④，青山郭外斜。

开轩面场圃^⑤，把酒话桑麻。

待到重阳日，还来就^⑥菊花。

---

① 过：拜访。

② 具：准备。

③ 鸡黍：鸡和黄米饭，指农家待客的丰盛饭食。

④ "绿树"句：翠绿的树林围绕着村落。合，围绕、环抱。

⑤ 场圃：农家种植蔬菜或收放农作物的地方。后泛指庭园。

⑥ 就：靠近。此处指欣赏的意思。

Visiting an Old Friend's Cottage

My friends prepared chicken and rice;

I'm invited to his cottage hall.

Green trees surround the village nice;

Blue hills slant beyond city wall.

Windows open to field and ground;

Over wine we talk of crops of grain.

On Double Ninth Day I'll come round

For the chrysanthemums again.

春晓^①

春眠不觉晓，处处闻啼^②鸟。

夜来风雨声，花落知多少。

---

① 春晓：春天的早晨。晓，天刚亮的时候。

② 啼：人的啼哭或鸟兽的叫声，此处指鸟的啼叫声。

A Spring Morning

This spring morning in bed I'm lying,

Not to awake till birds are crying.

After one night of wind and showers,

How many are the fallen flowers!

宿建德江 ①

移舟②泊烟渚③，日暮客④愁⑤新。

野旷⑥天低树⑦，江清月近人⑧。

---

① 建德江：是新安江流经建德市（今浙江）西部的一段江水。

② 移舟：划动小船。

③ 烟渚：指江中雾气笼罩的小沙洲。烟，一作"幽"。

④ 客：指作者自己。

⑤ 愁：为思乡而忧思不堪。

⑥ 野旷：空阔远大的原野。野，原野。

⑦ 天低树：天幕低垂，好像和树木相连。

⑧ 月近人：倒映在水中的月亮好像在靠近人。

Mooring on the River at Jiande

My boat is moored near an isle in mist gray;

I'm grieved anew to see the parting day.

On boundless plain trees seem to touch the sky;

In water clear the moon appears so nigh.

李颀

LI QI

作者简介

　　李颀（？—757），字、号不详，唐代诗人。开元十三年（725年）中进士，曾任新乡县尉，后辞官归隐。

　　性格疏放超脱，厌薄世俗，一生交游很广，与王维、高适、王昌龄等著名诗人皆有来往，诗名颇高。其诗内容涉及较广，尤以边塞诗成就最大，奔放豪迈，慷慨悲凉，最著名的有《古从军行》《古意》《塞下曲》等。

古从军行①

白日登山望烽火，黄昏饮马傍交河②。

行人刁斗风沙暗③，公主琵琶④幽怨多。

野营⑤万里无城郭，雨雪纷纷连大漠。

胡雁哀鸣夜夜飞，胡儿⑥眼泪双双落。

闻道玉门犹被遮⑦，应将性命逐轻车⑧。

年年战骨埋荒外⑨，空见葡萄入汉家。

---

① 古从军行：《从军行》乃乐府旧题，这首诗是拟古，所以称《古从军行》。

② "黄昏"句：饮马，给马喂水。交河，古县名，位于今新疆维吾尔自治区中东部的吐鲁番市以西。

③ "行人"句：行人，行军之人。刁斗，古代军队用的铜器，白天用以煮饭，夜晚用来打更。

④ 公主琵琶：相传汉武帝时以江都王刘建女细君嫁乌孙国王昆莫，恐其途中烦闷，故弹琵琶以娱之。这句用此典故，写征途中听到的幽怨的琵琶声。

⑤ 野营：一作"野云"。

⑥ 胡儿：少数民族。

⑦ "闻道"句：遮，阻拦。据《汉书·李广利传》，汉武帝曾命令李广利攻大宛，欲至贰师城取良马，战不利，广利上书请撤兵回国，武帝大怒，发使遮玉门关，曰："军有敢入，斩之！"

⑧ "应将"句：意为只得豁出命追随将军去拼搏。逐，跟随。轻车，车将军的简称，此处代指将帅。

⑨ 荒外：极边远的地方。

Army Life

We climb up mountains to watch for beacon fires,

And water horses by riverside when day expires.

We beat the gong in sand-darkened land where wind blows

And hear the pipa tell the princess' secret woe.

There is no town for miles and miles but tents in rows;

Beyond the desert there's nothing but rain and snow.

The wild geese honk from night to night, that's all we hear;

We see but Tartar soldiers shedding tear on tear.

'Tis said we cannot go back through the Jade Gate Pass;

We'd risk our lives to follow war-chariots, alas!

The dead are buried in the desert year by year,

Only to bring back grapes from over the frontier.

WANG CHANGLING

王昌龄

作者简介

王昌龄（698—757），字少伯，唐代著名边塞诗人。

开元十五年（727年）进士及第，授校书郎，迁汜水县尉。参加博学宏辞科考试，因事被流放岭南。开元末年返回长安，授江宁县丞。安史之乱时，惨遭濠州刺史闾丘晓杀害。

与李白、高适、王维、王之涣、岑参等人交往深厚。其诗以七绝见长，尤以边塞诗最为著名，有"诗家夫子王江宁""七绝圣手王江宁"之称。存诗一百七十余首，有《王昌龄集》。

从军行七首（二首）

其四

青海[1]长云暗雪山[2]，孤城[3]遥望玉门关[4]。

黄沙百战穿[5]金甲，不破楼兰[6]终不还。

---

[1] 青海：指青海湖，位于今青海省西宁市。

[2] 雪山：此处指祁连山，因山巅终年积雪，故云。

[3] 孤城：一说为青海地区的一座城池，一说孤城即玉门关。两说都可通。今取后者，乃考虑到格律诗经常有为了格律谐整而把正常语序调整成非正常语序的情况。"孤城遥望"，或即为"遥望孤城"之调整。

[4] 玉门关：汉武帝时置，因西域输入玉石取道于此而得名。

[5] 穿：磨穿，磨破。

[6] 楼兰：汉时西域的鄯善国，位于今新疆维吾尔自治区鄯善县东南一带。西汉时，楼兰国与匈奴联合，屡次截杀汉朝派往西域的使臣。傅介子奉命前往，用计刺杀楼兰王，"遂持王首还诣阙，公卿、将军议者，成嘉其功。"（《汉书·傅介子传》）。此以楼兰泛指西北地区的敌人。

其五

大漠^⑦风尘日色昏，红旗半卷出辕门^⑧。

前军夜战洮河^⑨北，已报生擒吐谷浑^⑩。

---

⑦ 大漠：此泛指西北沙漠，非确指某处之沙漠。

⑧ 辕门：军营的大门。古代行军扎营时，一般用车环卫，出口处把两车的车
辕相对竖起，对立如门。

⑨ "前军"句：前军，指唐军的先头部队。洮河，黄河上游支流，位于今甘肃
省甘南藏族自治州境内，源出甘青两省边界西倾山东麓，东流到岷县折向
北，经临洮县到永靖县城附近入黄河。

⑩ 吐谷浑：晋代鲜卑族慕容氏的后裔，唐前期据有青海洮水西南等处，地势
险要，唐朝三次征讨均无功而返。后李靖挂帅，一改先前正面进攻的策略，
几十万唐军从青海甘肃交界的狭窄小路穿越，从吐谷浑身后发起攻击，一
举歼灭吐谷浑。一说王昌龄此诗即记此次大捷。一说此诗非实写，此处吐
谷浑乃只借指边境之敌而已。考察此次战役发生在唐太宗时期，而王昌龄
生活在武后、玄宗时期，所以后说为当。

Poems on Army Life

IV

Clouds on frontier overshadow mountains clad in snow;

A lonely town afar faces Pass of jade Gate.

Our golden armor pierced by sand, we fight the foe;

We won't come back till we destroy the hostile state.

V

The wind and sand in the desert have dimmed sunlight;

With red flags half unfurled we go through the camp gate.

North of River Tao, after nocturnal fight,

Our vanguards have captured the chief of hostile state.

出塞^①

秦时明月汉时关，万里长征人未还。

但使龙城^②飞将^③在，不教胡^④马度阴山^⑤。

---

① 出塞：乐府《横吹曲》旧题。唐人乐府中的《出塞》《前出塞》《后出塞》
《塞上曲》《塞下曲》等均由此演变而出。

② 龙城：汉时匈奴大会祭天之地，在今蒙古国境内，汉车骑将军卫青曾率兵
到此。有的版本作"卢城"或"陇城"。

③ 飞将：指汉名将李广。李广，甘肃天水人。《史记·李将军传》："（李）广
居右北平，匈奴闻之，号曰汉之飞将军。"此处可理解为两典合用，指古代
卫青、李广这样的守边名将，也可泛指一切良将。

④ 胡：指匈奴等北方部族。

⑤ 阴山：西起河套，绵亘于今内蒙古自治区境内，东与内兴安岭相接。汉时
匈奴常据此犯边。

On the Frontier

The moon still shines on mountain passes as of yore.

How many guardsmen of the Great Wall are no more!

If the Flying General were still there in command,

No hostile steeds would have dared to invade our land.

西宫秋怨

芙蓉^①不及美人妆，水殿风来珠翠香。
谁分含啼^②掩秋扇^③，空悬明月待君王^④。
fèn

---

① 芙蓉：指荷花。
② 谁分含啼：一作"却恨含情"。谁分，谁料。分，料，料想。
③ 秋扇：暗用班婕妤《怨歌行》"秋凉团扇"之典，形容女子失宠。
④ "空悬"句：语出司马相如《长门赋并序》："悬明月以自照兮，徂清夜于
洞房。"

A Neglected Beauty in the West Palace

The lotus bloom feels shy beside the lady fair;

The breeze across the lake takes fragrance from her hair.

An autumn fan cannot conceal her hidden love;

In vain she waits for her lord with the moon above.

闺怨^①

闺中少妇不知愁，春日凝妆^②上翠楼^③。

忽见陌头^④杨柳色，悔教^⑤夫婿觅封侯^⑥。

---

① 闺怨：少妇的幽怨。闺，女子卧室，借指女子，一般指少女或少妇。古人
　"闺怨"之作，一般是写少女的青春寂寞，或少妇的离别相思之情。以此题
　材写的诗称"闺怨诗"。
② 凝妆：盛妆，严妆。
③ 翠楼：翠，青色。古代显贵之家楼房多饰青色，这里因平仄要求用"翠"，
　且与女主人公的身份、与时令季节相应。
④ 陌头：路边。
⑤ 悔教：后悔让。
⑥ 觅封侯：觅，寻求。此处指从军建功封爵。

Sorrow of a Young Bride in Her Boudoir

The young bride in her boudoir does not know what grieves;

She mounts the tower, gaily dressed, on a spring day.

Suddenly seeing by roadside green willow leaves,

How she regrets her lord seeking fame far away!

芙蓉楼①送辛渐②

寒雨③连江④夜入吴⑤，平明⑥送客⑦楚山⑧孤。

洛阳亲友如相问，一片冰心在玉壶。

① 芙蓉楼：故址位于今江苏省镇江市西北角。
② 辛渐：王昌龄的朋友。这首诗是王昌龄在芙蓉楼送别辛渐去洛阳时所作。
③ 寒雨：秋雨。
④ 连江：满江，形容雨水很大。
⑤ 夜入吴：夜晚秋雨入镇江。镇江三国时属吴地，故说"夜入吴"。
⑥ 平明：天刚亮。
⑦ 客：指辛渐。
⑧ 楚山：指辛渐即将行经的楚地。

Farewell to Xin Jian at Lotus Tower

A cold rain dissolved in East Stream invades the night;

At dawn you'll leave the lonely Southern hills in haze.

If my friends in the North should ask if I'm all right,

Tell them I'm free from blame as ice in crystal vase.

祖咏

ZU YONG

作者简介

祖咏（699—746），字、号均不详，唐代诗人，洛阳（今河南洛阳）人。少有文名，擅长诗歌创作。

开元十二年（724年）进士及第，长期未授官。后入仕，又遭迁谪，仕途落拓，后归隐汝水一带。

诗多状景咏物，宣扬隐逸生活。其诗讲求对仗，亦带有诗中有画之色彩，与王维友善。王维在济州赠诗云："结交二十载，不得一日展。贫病子既深，契阔余不浅。"（《赠祖三咏》）其流落不遇的情况可知。

终南①望余雪

终南阴岭②秀，积雪浮云端。

林表③明霁色④，城中增暮寒。

① 终南：终南山，位于今陕西西安长安区境内，秦岭山脉中段，绵延两百余
　千米。
② 阴岭：山的北面为阴。终南山在长安之南，从长安望去，看到的是山北部。
③ 林表：树林的顶部。
④ 霁色：雨雪过后的阳光。霁，雨、雪后天气转晴。

Snow Atop the Southern Mountains

How fair the gloomy mountainside!

Snow-crowned peaks float above the cloud.

The forest's bright in sunset dyed,

With evening cold the town's overflowed.

王维

WANG WEI

作者简介

王维（701—761），字摩诘，号摩诘居士，河东蒲州（今山西运城）人。唐代诗人、画家。

出身河东王氏，开元九年（721年）中进士第，为太乐丞。历官右拾遗、监察御史、河西节度使判官。天宝年间，拜吏部郎中、给事中。安禄山攻陷长安时，被迫受伪职。长安收复后，被责授太子中允。唐肃宗乾元年间任尚书右丞，世称"王右丞"。

参禅悟理，精通诗书音画，以诗名盛于开元、天宝年间，尤长五言，多咏山水田园，与孟浩然合称"王孟"，因笃诚奉佛，有"诗佛"之称。书画特臻其妙，后人推其为南宗山水画之祖。存诗约四百首，重要诗作有《相思》《送别》《山居秋暝》等。北宋苏轼评云："味摩诘之诗，诗中有画；观摩诘之画，画中有诗。"

送别

下马饮君酒①，问君何所之②？

君言不得意，归卧南山陲③。

但④去莫复问，白云无尽时。

---

① 饮君酒：劝君饮酒。
② 何所之：去哪里。之，往。
③ "归卧"句归卧，隐居。南山，终南山，即秦岭，位于今陕西省西安市西
  南。陲，边缘。
④ 但：只。

At Parting

Dismounted, I drink with you

And ask what you've in view.

"I can't do what I will;

So I'll do what I will;

I'll ask you no more, friend,

Let clouds drift without end!"

渭川^①田家

斜阳^②照墟落^③，穷巷^④牛羊归。

野老^⑤念牧童^⑥，倚杖候荆扉^⑦。

雉雊^{zhìgòu}^⑧麦苗秀，蚕眠桑叶稀。

田夫荷^{hè}^⑨锄至，相见语依依。

即此羡闲逸，怅然吟式微^⑩。

---

① 渭川：一作"渭水"。渭水源于甘肃鸟鼠山，经陕西，流入黄河。
② 斜阳：一作"斜光"。
③ 墟落：村庄。
④ 穷巷：深巷。
⑤ 野老：村野老人。
⑥ 牧童：一作"僮仆"。
⑦ "倚杖"句：拄着拐杖在自家的柴门边等候。倚杖，靠着拐杖。荆扉，柴门。
⑧ 雉雊：野鸡鸣叫。《诗经·小雅·小弁》："雉之朝雊，尚求其雌。"
⑨ 荷：肩负的意思。
⑩ 式微：《诗经》篇名，其中有"式微，式微，胡不归"之句，表归隐之意。

Rural Scene by River Wei

The village lit by slanting rays,

The cattle trail on homeward ways.

See an old man for the herd wait,

Leaning on staff by wicker gate.

Pheasants call in wheat field with ease;

Silkworms sleep on sparse mulberries.

Shouldering hoe, two ploughmen meet;

They talk long, standing on their feet.

For this unhurried life I long,

Lost in singing "Home-going song".

山居^①秋暝^②

空山新雨后，天气晚来秋。

明月松间照，清泉石上流。

竹喧归浣女^③，莲动下渔舟。

随意春芳歇，王孙自可留^④。

① 山居：山中居所。
② 秋暝：秋天的傍晚。
③ "竹喧"句：竹喧，竹林中笑语喧哗。喧，喧哗。浣女，洗衣服的女子。浣，洗涤。
④ "王孙"句：王孙原指贵族子弟，后来也泛指隐居的人。而此句反用《招隐士》中的"王孙兮归来，山中兮不可久留"二句，王孙实为自指，反映出诗人对山居生活的留恋，隐含着对污浊官场的厌恶和洁身自好、毅然归隐的决心。留，居。

Autumn Evening in the Mountains

After fresh rain in mountains bare,

Autumn permeates evening air.

Among pine trees bright moonbeams peer;

Over crystal stones flows water clear.

Bamboos whisper of washer-maids;

Lotus stirs when fishing boat wades.

Though fragrant spring may pass away,

Still here's the place for you to stay.

终南山

太乙^①近天都^②，连山接海隅^③。

白云回望合，青霭^④入看无。

分野^⑤中峰变，阴晴众壑殊。

欲投人处^⑥宿，隔水问樵夫。

---

① 太乙：又名太一，秦岭之一峰。按经传所载，终南山一名太一，亦名终南。

② 天都：天帝所居。

③ 海隅：海边。终南山并不到海，此为夸张之词。

④ 青霭：山中的岚气。霭，云气。

⑤ 分野：古天文学名词。古人以天上的二十八个星宿的位置来区分中国境内
的地域，称之为分野，地上的每一个区域都对应星空的某一处分野。

⑥ 人处：有人烟的地方。

Mount Eternal South

The highest peak scrapes the sky blue;

It extends from hills to the sea.

When I look back, clouds shut the view;

When I come near, no mist I see.

Peaks vary in north and south side;

Vales differ in sunshine or shade.

Seeking a lodge where to abide,

I ask a woodman when I wade.

观猎

风劲角弓①鸣，将军猎渭城②。

草枯鹰眼疾③，雪尽马蹄轻。

忽过新丰市④，还归细柳营⑤。

回看射雕处⑥，千里暮云平⑦。

---

① 角弓：用兽角装饰的硬弓，使用动物的角、筋等材料制作而成的传统复合弓。

② 渭城：秦时咸阳城，汉改为渭城，位于今西安市西北，渭水北岸。

③ 眼疾：指目光敏锐。

④ 新丰市：位于今陕西省临潼区东北，是古代盛产美酒的地方。

⑤ 细柳营：位于今陕西省长安区，是汉代名将周亚夫屯军之地。此处借指打猎的将军所居营地。

⑥ 射雕处：借射雕处表达对将军的赞美。北齐斛律光精通武艺，曾射中一雕，人称"射雕都督"，此引用其事以赞美将军。

⑦ 暮云平：傍晚的云与大地连成一片。

Hunting

Louder than gusty winds twang horn-backed bows;

Hunting outside the town the general goes.

Keener over withered grass his falcons's eye,

Lighter on melted snow his steed trots by.

No sooner is New Harvest Market passed

Than he comes back to Willowy Camp at last.

He looks back where he shot down vultures bare

Only to find cloud on cloud spread o'er there.

汉江^①临泛

楚塞^②三湘^③接，荆门^④九派^⑤通。

江流天地外，山色有无中。

郡邑^⑥浮前浦^⑦，波澜动^⑧远空。

襄阳好风日^⑨，留醉与山翁^⑩。

---

① 汉江：即汉水，流经陕西、湖北等地，到汉口流入长江。汉江从襄阳城中流过，城池分成大大小小无数城郭（包括襄阳城门外的许多"瓮城"），一个个都像在眼前的水道两旁漂浮。

② 楚塞：楚国边境地带，此处指汉水流域，古为楚国辖区。

③ 三湘：湘水合漓水为漓湘，合蒸水为蒸湘，合潇水为潇湘，总称三湘。一说是湖南的湘潭、湘阴、湘乡合称三湘。古诗文中，三湘一般泛称今洞庭湖南北、湘江一带。

④ 荆门：山名，荆门山，位于今湖北宜都市西北的长江南岸。

⑤ 九派：原指长江的九条支流。相传大禹治水，开凿江流，使九派相通。此处指江西九江。

⑥ 郡邑：指汉水两岸的城镇。

⑦ 浦：水边。

⑧ 动：震动。

⑨ 好风日：一作"风日好"，风景天气好。

⑩ 山翁：一作山公，指山简，晋代竹林七贤之一山涛的幼子，西晋将领，镇守襄阳，有政绩，好酒，每饮必醉。此处借指襄阳地方官。一说是作者以山简自喻。

A View of the River Han

Three southern rivers rolling by,

Nine tributaries meeting here.

Their water flows from earth to sky;

Hills now appear, now disappear.

Towns seem to float on rivershore;

With waves horizons rise and fall.

Such scenery as we adore

Would make us drink and drunken all.

使至塞上 ①

单车②欲问边，属国③过居延④。

征蓬⑤出汉塞，归雁入胡天。

大漠孤烟直，长河落日圆。

萧关⑥逢候骑⑦，都护⑧在燕然⑨。

---

① 使至塞上：奉命出使边塞。使，出使。塞上，边塞之上。
② 单车：一辆车，此处形容出使的车仗简单、随从不多。
③ 属国：有几种说法。一种说法，汉代称那些仍旧保留原有国号的附属国为属国。另一种说法是，属国是官名"典属国"的简称，其职事是与少数民族交往，苏武归国后任此职。唐代则以其代指使臣，本诗指王维，当时王维以监察御史的身份出塞慰问得胜将士。
④ 居延：汉代居延县，汉末设县，属张掖郡，位于今内蒙古额济纳旗。《后汉书·郡国志》："凉州有张掖居延属国。"唐代称居延海。
⑤ 征蓬：蓬，草名，茎高尺余，叶如柳叶，开小白花，秋枯根拔，随风飘扬，因此又叫飞蓬。古人以征蓬、飘蓬比喻漂泊的旅人。此处为诗人自喻。
⑥ 萧关：今陇山关，位于今宁夏回族自治区固原市。汉朝与匈奴对抗时的要塞。汉文帝十四年，匈奴杀北地都尉入萧关。
⑦ 候骑：骑马的侦察兵。
⑧ 都护：唐代边疆设置都护府，都护府的长官为都护，负责辖区一切事务，这里指唐代将崔希逸。
⑨ 燕然：山名，即杭爱山，即今蒙古国境内杭爱山。汉车骑将军窦宪击破匈奴北单于，追击至燕然山，登山刻石记功而还，后世用于克敌制胜的典故。这里借用之。

On Mission to the Frontier

A single carriage goes to the frontier;

An envoy crosses northwest mountains high.

Like tumbleweed I leave the fortress drear;

As wild geese I come under Tartarian sky.

In boundless desert lonely smokes rise straight;

Over endless river the sun sinks round.

I meet a cavalier at the camp gate;

In northern fort the general will be found.

孟城坳^①

新家孟城口，古木余衰柳。

来者复为谁？空^②悲昔人^③有。

---

① 孟城坳：辋川风景点之一，有古城墙。坳，低洼的地方。

② 空：徒然地。

③ 昔人：过去的人。

The City Gate

I've moved in near the city gate

Where withered willow trees are left.

Should another move here too late,

Alas! Of trees he'd be bereft.

鹿柴^①

zhài

空山不见人，但闻^②人语响。

返景^③入深林，复照青苔上。

---

① 鹿柴：柴，通"寨"，栅栏。此为地名，是王维在辋川别业的胜景之一。

② 但闻：只听见。

③ 返景：夕阳返照的光。"景"，日光之影，古时同"影"。

The Deer Enclosure

In pathless hills no man's in sight,

But I still hear echoing sound.

In gloomy forest peeps no light,

But sunbeams slant on mossy ground.

竹里馆^①

独坐幽篁^{huáng}^②里，弹琴复长啸^③。

深林人不知，明月来相照。

---

① 竹里馆：辋川别业胜景之一。
② 幽篁：幽深茂密的竹林。
③ 啸：撮口发出悠长而清亮的声音。《晋书·阮籍传》载阮籍善长啸，入苏门山寻孙登，惊闻孙登之啸"若鸾凤之音，响乎岩谷"。魏晋以后，啸成为隐逸高士的一种风尚与标志。

The Bamboo Hut

Sitting among bamboos alone,

I play on lute and croon carefree.

In the deep woods where I'm unknown,

Only the bright moon peeps at me.

鸟鸣涧 ①

人闲 ②桂花 ③落，夜静春山空。

月出惊山鸟，时鸣 ④春涧中。

---

① 鸟鸣涧：鸟儿在山涧中鸣叫。

② 人闲：指没有人事活动打扰。闲，安静、悠闲，含有人声寂静的意思。

③ 桂花：此指木樨，有春花、秋花等不同品种，这里写的是春天开花的一种。

④ 时鸣：偶尔（时而）啼叫。时，时而，偶尔。

The Dale of Singing Birds

Sweet laurel blooms fall unenjoyed;

Vague hills dissolve into night void.

The moonrise startles birds to sing;

Their twitters fills the dale with spring.

山中送别

山中相送罢，日暮掩^①柴扉^②。

春草明年^③绿，王孙^④归不归？

---

① 掩：关闭。

② 柴扉：柴门。

③ 明年：一作"年年"。

④ 王孙：贵族的子孙，此处指送别的友人。

Parting in the Hills

I see off the hills my compeer;

At dusk I close my wicket door.

When grass turns green in spring next year,

Will my friend come with spring once more?

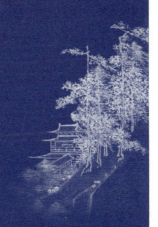

杂诗①（其二）

君自故乡来，应知故乡事。
来日②绮窗③前，寒梅④著花⑤未。

---

① 杂诗：不定题目的诗，写随时产生的零星感想和琐事。
② 来日：指动身前来的那天。
③ 绮窗：雕刻花纹的窗子。绮，有花纹的丝织品。
④ 寒梅：冬天开的梅花。
⑤ 著花：开花，开放。

Our Native Place

II

You come from native place;

What happened there you'd know.

Did mume blossoms in face

Of my gauze window blow?

相思①

红豆②生南国，春来发几枝？

愿③君多④采撷⑤，此物最相思。

---

① 唐人范摅《云溪友议》："明皇幸岷山，百官皆窜辱……唯李龟年奔迫江潭……龟年曾于湘中采访使筵上唱'红豆生南国，春来发几枝？愿君多采撷，此物最相思'，又唱'清风明月苦相思，荡子从戎十岁余。征人去日殷勤嘱，归雁来时数附书'。此辞皆王右丞所制，至今梨园唱焉。歌阕，合座莫不望南幸而惨然。"据此，安史之乱以前当已有此诗。此诗以家常语道出人间相思寄意之事，遂广为人们传诵。

② 红豆：相思木所结子，产于亚热带地区，古人又称其为相思子。唐李匡《资暇集》卷下："豆有圆而红，其首乌者，举世呼为相思子，即红豆之异名也。"李时珍《本草纲目》卷三十五："相思子生岭南，树高丈余，白色，其叶似槐，其花似皂荚，其荚似扁豆，其子大如小豆，半截红色，半截黑色，彼人以嵌首饰。"梁武帝《欢闻歌》："南有相思木，含情复同心。"

③ 愿：一作"劝"。

④ 多：一作"休"。

⑤ 撷：采摘。

Love Seeds

The red beans grow in southern land.

How many loads in spring the trees?

Gather them till full is your hand;

They would revive fond memories.

山中

荆溪①白石出，天寒红叶②稀。

山路元③无雨，空翠④湿人衣。

---

① 荆溪：长水，又名浐水、荆谷水，源出陕西蓝田县。《水经注·渭水》："长水出自杜县白鹿原，西北流，谓之荆溪。"一作"溪清"。
② 红叶：枫、槭一类的树叶，秋季经霜之后逐渐由绿变红。
③ 元：原来，本来。
④ 空翠：弥漫在空间的浓翠欲滴的山色。

In the Hills

White pebbles hear a blue stream glide;

Red leaves are strewn on cold hillside.

Along the path no rain is seen;

My gown is moist with drizzling green.

秋夜曲 ①

桂魄②初生秋露微，轻罗③已薄未更衣。

银筝夜久殷勤弄④，心怯空房⑤不忍归。

---

① 秋夜曲：属于乐府《杂曲歌辞》，是一首婉转含蓄的闺怨诗。

② 桂魄：传说月中有桂，故为月的别称。《尚书》注谓月轮无光之处为"魄"。
月魄是指月初或圆而始缺时不明亮的部分，亦泛指月亮、月光。

③ 轻罗：轻盈的丝织品，宜做夏装，此代指夏装。

④ 殷勤弄：频频弹拨。

⑤ 空房：意指独眠无伴。

Song of an Autumn Night

Chilled by light autumn dew beneath the crescent moon,

She has not changed her dress though her silk robe is thin.

Playing all night on silver lute an endless tune,

Afraid of empty room, she can't bear to go in.

九月九日忆山东兄弟①

独在异乡为异客，每逢佳节倍思亲。

遥知兄弟登高②处，遍插茱萸③少一人。

136

---

① 九月九日：即重阳节。古以九为阳数，故曰重阳。忆，想念。山东，指华山以东。

② 登高：重阳节风俗，重阳日要登高饮酒。

③ 茱萸：一种有香味的植物。《太平御览》引《风土记》："俗于此日，以茱萸气烈成熟，尚此日，折萸房以插头，言辟热气而御初寒。"古时人们认为重阳节插戴茱萸可以辟热驱寒、避灾克邪。

Thinking of My Brothers on Mountain-Climbing Day

Alone, a lonely stranger in a foreign land,

I doubly pine for my kinsfolk on a holiday.

I know my brothers would, with dogwood spray in hand,

Climb up the mountain and miss me so far away.

送元二①使②安西③

渭城④朝雨浥⁵轻尘，客舍青青柳色新。

劝君更尽一杯酒，西出阳关⑥无故人。

1
3
8

---

① 元二：王维好友，生平不详。
② 使：出使。
③ 安西：唐代的安西都护府，治所位于今新疆维吾尔自治区库车市。
④ 渭城：秦代首都咸阳，汉代改为渭城，位于今陕西西安市西北、渭水北岸。
⑤ 浥：润湿。
⑥ 阳关：位于今甘肃省敦煌市西南，玉门关南，为自古赴西北边疆的要道。

Seeing Yuan the Second off to the Northwest Frontier

No dust is raised on the road wet with morning rain;

The willows by the hotel look so fresh and green.

I invite you to drink a cup of wine again;

West of the Sunny Pass no more friends will be seen.

送沈子归江东 [1]

杨柳渡头行客稀，罟师 [2] 荡桨向临圻 [3]。

惟有相思似春色，江南江北送君归。

140

---

① 沈子：王维好友，生平事迹不详。归又作"之"。

② 罟师：渔人，此处指船夫。罟，打鱼用的网。

③ 临圻：近岸之地，此处指友人所去之地。

Seeing a Friend off to the East

At willow-shaded ferry passengers are few;

Into the eastward stream the boatman puts his oars.

Only my longing heart looks like the vernal hue;

It would go with you along northern and southern shores.

LIU SHENXU

刘眘虚

作者简介

刘眘虚（714—767），亦作慎虚，字全乙，亦字挺卿，号易轩，洪州新吴（今江西奉新）人，盛唐著名诗人。

八岁能文，二十岁中进士，二十二岁参加吏部宏词科考试，得中，初授左春坊司经局校书郎，为皇太子校勘经史；旋转崇文馆校书郎，为皇亲国戚的子侄们校勘典籍，均为从九品的小吏。

为人淡泊，脱略势利，壮年辞官归田，寄意山水，与孟浩然、王昌龄等诗人相友善，互唱和。他曾游江南西道洪州建昌县桃源里（今江西省靖安县水口乡桃源村），见此地山水秀美，民风淳厚，于是定居于此，构筑深柳读书堂，著书自娱。《唐诗三百首》上载的首句"道由白云尽"诗，就是写于此时此地。

阙题①

道由白云尽②，春③与青溪长。

时有落花至，远随流水香。

闲门④向山路，深柳读书堂。

幽映⑤每⑥白日，清辉照衣裳。

---

① 阙题："阙"通"缺"，即缺题。此诗原题在流传过程中遗失，后人在编诗时以"阙题"为名。
② "道由"句：山路从白云近处延伸过来，也即在尘境之外。道，道路。由，因为。
③ 春：春意，即诗中所说的花、柳。
④ 闲门：指门前清净、环境清幽，俗客不至的门。
⑤ 幽映：指"深柳"在阳光映照下的浓荫。
⑥ 每：每当。

A Scholar's Retreat

The pathway ends where rise clouds white;

Spring reigns as far as clear stream goes.

I oft see falling blooms in flight;

With endless waves their fragrance flows,

The path leads to the door oft shut;

A study's shaded by willow trees.

From dazzling sun is screened the hut;

Soft light is filtered by the breeze.

李白

LI BAI

作者简介

李白（701—762），字太白，号青莲居士，唐代伟大的浪漫主义诗人，被后人誉为"诗仙"，与杜甫并称为"李杜"，为与另两位诗人李商隐与杜牧即"小李杜"区别，李白与杜甫又合称"大李杜"。《新唐书》记载，李白为兴圣皇帝李暠九世孙，与李唐诸王同宗。

性格豪迈，热爱祖国山河，游踪遍及南北各地，写出大量赞美名山大川的壮丽诗篇。其诗既豪迈奔放，又清新飘逸，而且想象丰富，意境奇妙，语言轻快。尤以乐府、歌行及绝句成就为最高。有《李太白集》传世，代表作有《望庐山瀑布》《行路难》《蜀道难》《将进酒》等。

峨眉^①山月歌

峨眉山月半轮秋^②，影入平羌^③江水流。
夜发清溪^④向三峡^⑤，思君不见下渝州。

---

① 峨眉：峨眉山，位于今四川峨眉山市。
② 半轮秋：半圆的秋月。半轮，指月形如半个车轮。
③ 平羌：江名，即青衣江。源出四川芦山市，流经乐山市注入岷江。
④ 清溪：驿名，位于今四川犍为县。
⑤ 三峡：关于三峡众说纷纭。《峡程记》："三峡者，明月峡、巫山峡、广溪峡。"有人解释为三峡俱在巴东，大抵六七百里，巫山之下者为巫峡，巫峡之上为广溪峡，巫峡之下为西陵峡。另一说指长江瞿塘峡、巫峡、西陵峡，位于今重庆、湖北的交界处。

The Moon over Mount Brow

The crescent moon looks like old Autumn's golden brow;

Its deep reflection flows with limpid water blue.

I'll leave the town on Clear Stream for the Three Gorges now.

O Moon, how I miss you when you are out of view!

望庐山^①瀑布

日照香炉^②生紫烟^③，遥看瀑布挂前川^④。

飞流直下三千尺，疑是银河落九天^⑤。

148

---

① 庐山：又名匡山，位于今江西省九江市南，为著名风景区，历来有"匡庐奇秀甲天下"之称。
② 香炉：庐山上的香炉峰，因形状如香炉又有烟雾缭绕而得名。
③ 紫烟：紫色的烟气（香炉峰顶的烟气在阳光照射下呈紫色）。
④ 前川：香炉峰前的水流。一作"长川"。
⑤ 九天：传说天有九重，九天是天的最高层。此句极言瀑布落差之大。

The Waterfall in Mount Lu Viewed from Afar

The sunlit Censer Peak exhales incense-like cloud;

Like an upended stream the cataract sounds loud.

Its torrent dashes down three thousand feet from high

As if the Silver River fell from the blue sky.

望天门山①

天门中断楚江②开，碧水东流至此③回。

两岸青山④相对出⑤，孤帆一片日边来。

---

① 天门山：古称云梦山，又名玉屏山，位于安徽省和县与芜湖市长江两岸，在江南的叫东梁山（又称博望山），在江北的叫西梁山。两山隔江对峙，形同天设的门户，天门由此得名。

② 楚江：即长江。因为古代长江中游地带属于楚国，所以也叫楚江。

③ 至此回：意为东流的江水在这里转向北流。回，回旋，回转。指这一段江水由于地势险峻，水流方向有所改变，并更加汹涌。

④ 两岸青山：分别指东梁山和西梁山。

⑤ 出：突出，出现。

Mount Heaven's Gate Viewed from Afar

Breaking Mount Heaven's Gate, the great River rolls through;

Its east-flowing green billows, hurled back here, turn north.

From the two river banks thrust out the mountains blue;

Leaving the sun behind, a lonely sail comes forth.

长干行[①]

妾发初覆额，折花门前剧[②]。

郎骑竹马来，绕床[③]弄青梅。

同居长干里，两小无嫌猜。

十四为君妇，羞颜未尝开。

低头向暗壁，千唤不一回。

十五始展眉，愿同尘与灰。

常存抱柱[④]信，岂上望夫台[⑤]。

① 长干行：属乐府《杂曲歌辞》调名。长干，古金陵（今南京）里巷名，下文“长干里”同，系船民集居之地，故《长干曲》多抒发船家女子的感情。

② 剧：游戏。

③ 床：古代的一种坐具。

④ 抱柱：典出《庄子·杂篇·盗跖》，写尾生与一女子相约于桥下，女子未到而突然涨水，尾生守信而不肯离去，抱着柱子被水淹死。

⑤ 望夫台：在忠州南数十里。

十六君远行，瞿塘滟滪堆⑥。

五月不可触，猿声天上哀。

门前迟行迹，一一生绿苔。

苔深不能扫，落叶秋风早。

八月蝴蝶黄⑦，双飞西园草。

感此伤妾心，坐愁红颜老。

早晚下三巴⑧，预将书报家。

相迎不道远，直至长风沙⑨。

⑥ 滟滪堆：三峡之一瞿塘峡峡口的一块大礁石，农历五月涨水没礁，船只易触礁翻沉。

⑦ 蝴蝶黄：一作"蝴蝶来"。

⑧ 三巴：巴东、巴郡、巴西。汉献帝时分巴地为三郡。是今天重庆、夔州、合州一带。

⑨ 长风沙：位于今安徽省安庆市东长江边上。

Ballad of a Trader's Wife

My forehead barely covered by my hair,

Outdoors I plucked and played with flowers fair.

On hobby horse he came upon the scene;

Around the well we played with mumes still green.

We lived close neighbors on Riverside Lane,

Carefree and innocent, we children twain.

At fourteen years old I became his bride,

I often turned my bashful face aside.

Hanging my head, I'd look on the dark wall;

I would not answer his call upon call.

I was fifteen when I composed my brows;

To mix my dust with his were my dear vows.

Rather than break faith, he declared he'd die.

Who knew I'd live alone in tower high?

I was sixteen when he went far away,

Passing Three Gorges studded with rocks grey,

Where ships were wrecked when spring flood ran high.

Where gibbons' wails seemed coming from the sky.

Green moss now overgrows before our door;

His footprints, hidden, can be seen no more.

Moss can't be swept away, so thick it grows,

And leaves fall early when the west wind blows.

In yellow autumn butterflies would pass

Two by two in west garden over the grass.

The sight would break my heart and I'm afraid,

Sitting alone, my rosy cheeks would fade.

"O when are you to leave the western land?

Do not forget to tell me beforehand!

I'll walk to meet you and would not call it far

Even to go to Long Wind Beach where you are."

金陵^① 酒肆留别^②

风吹柳花满店香，吴姬压酒唤客尝^③。

金陵子弟来相送，欲行不行各尽觞^④。

请君试问^⑤东流水，别意与之谁短长？

---

① 金陵：今江苏省南京市。

② 留别：临别留诗给送行者。

③ "吴姬"句：吴姬，吴地的青年女子，这里指酒店中的侍女。压酒，压糟取酒。古时新酒酿熟，临饮时压糟取用。唤，一作"劝"，一作"使"。

④ "欲行"句：欲行，指诗人自己。不行，不走的人，即送行的人，指金陵子弟。尽觞，喝尽杯中的酒。觞，酒杯。

⑤ 试问：一作"问取"。

Parting at a Tavern in Jinling

The tavern's sweetened when wind blows in willow-down;

A southern maiden urges guests to taste her wine.

My dear young friends have come to see me leave the town;

They who stay drink their cups and I who leave drink mine.

O ask the river flowing to the east, I pray,

If he is happier to go than I to stay!

夜下征虏亭^①

船下广陵^②去，月明征虏亭。

山花如绣颊^③，江火似流萤^④。

158

---

① 征虏亭：东晋时征虏将军谢石所建，位于今江苏南京市。

② 广陵：郡名，位于今江苏扬州市一带。

③ 绣颊：涂过丹脂的女子面颊。这里借指岸上山花的娇艳。

④ "江火"句：江火，即江船上的灯火。流萤，飞动的萤火虫。

Passing by the Triumphal Tower at Night

My boat sails down to River Town.

The Tower's bright in the moonlight.

The flowers blow like cheeks aglow,

And lanterns beam as fireflies gleam.

静夜思①

床②前明月光，疑③是地上霜。

举头望明月，低头思故乡。

---

① 静夜思：安静的夜晚产生的思绪。
② 床：今传四种说法，指井台；井栏；"床"，即"窗"的通假字；取本义，即坐卧的器具。
③ 疑：好像。

Thoughts on a Tranquil Night

Before my bed a pool of light—

O can it be frost on the ground?

Looking up, I find the moon bright;

Bowing, in homesickness I'm drowned.

黄鹤楼^①送孟浩然之广陵^②

故人^③西辞^④黄鹤楼，烟花^⑤三月下^⑥扬州。

孤帆远影碧空尽^⑦，唯见长江天际流。

162

---

① 黄鹤楼：位于今湖北省武汉市蛇山黄鹄矶上。传说三国时期的费祎于此登
　仙乘黄鹤而去，故称黄鹤楼。
② 广陵：今江苏省扬州市。
③ 故人：指孟浩然。
④ 西辞：因黄鹤楼在广陵之西，孟浩然由西去东，所以说"西辞"。
⑤ 烟花：指艳丽、绚烂的春天景物。
⑥ 下：顺流向下而行。
⑦ 碧空尽：消失在碧蓝的天际。尽，尽头，消失了。碧空，一作"碧山"。

Seeing Meng Haoran off at Yellow Crane Tower

My friend has left the west where the Yellow Crane Towers

For River Town green with willows and red with flowers.

His lessening sail is lost in the boundless blue sky,

Where I see but the endless River rolling by.

长相思①

长相思，在长安。

络纬②秋啼金井阑③，微霜凄凄簟④色寒。

孤灯不明思欲绝，卷帷望月空长叹。

美人如花隔云端！

上有青冥⑤之高天，下有渌水⑥之波澜。

天长路远魂飞苦，梦魂不到关山难。

长相思，摧心肝！

---

① 长相思：属乐府《杂曲歌辞》，常以"长相思"三字开头和结尾。
② 络纬：虫名，又名蟋蟀、纺织娘、促织。
③ 金井阑：意思是井栏的木石美丽，价值如金玉。井阑，井上的栏杆。
④ 簟：竹席。
⑤ 青冥：天空。《楚辞》："据青冥而摅虹兮。"
⑥ 渌水：清澈的水。

Endless Longing

I long for one in all at royal capital.

The autumn cricket wails beside the golden rails.

Light frost mingled with dew, my mat looks cold in hue.

My lonely lamp burns dull, of longing I would die;

Rolling up screens to view the moon, in vain I sigh.

My flowerlike Beauty is high up as clouds in the sky.

Above, the boundless heaven spreads its canopy screen;

Below, the endless river rolls its billows green.

My soul can't fly over sky so vast nor streams so wide;

In dreams I can't go through mountain pass to her side.

We are so far apart; the longing breaks my heart.

蜀道难

噫吁嚱^{xī}，危乎高哉！

蜀道之难，难于上青天！

蚕丛及鱼凫^①，开国何茫然。

尔来四万八千岁，不与秦塞通人烟。

西当太白^②有鸟道，可以横绝峨眉巅。

地崩山摧^③壮士死，然后天梯石栈相钩连。

上有六龙^④回日之高标^⑤，下有冲波逆折之回川。

黄鹤之飞尚不得过，猿猱^{náo}欲度愁攀援。

青泥^⑥何盘盘，百步九折萦岩峦。

---

① 蚕丛及鱼凫：古蜀国两位国王的名字。

② 太白：太白山，又名太乙山，秦岭峰名，位于今陕西。

③ 摧：崩塌。

④ 六龙：神话中替太阳驾车的羲和，每天赶着六条龙在天上从东行到西。

⑤ 高标：最高峰，指蜀道中可作一方之标识的最高峰。

⑥ 青泥：青泥岭，为唐入蜀要道，位于今甘肃省徽县南，陕西省略阳县北。
《元和郡县志》："悬崖万仞，山多云雨，行者屡逢泥淖，故号青泥岭。"

扪参历井^⑦仰胁息，以手抚膺坐长叹。

问君西游何时还？畏途巉岩不可攀。

但见悲鸟号古木，雄飞雌从绕林间。

又闻子规^⑧啼夜月，愁空山，

蜀道之难，难于上青天，使人听此凋朱颜。

连峰去天不盈尺，枯松倒挂倚绝壁。

飞湍瀑流争喧豗，砯崖转石万壑雷。

其险也如此，嗟尔远道之人，胡为乎来哉！

剑阁^⑨峥嵘而崔嵬，一夫当关，万夫莫开。

1
6
7

---

⑦ 扪参历井：形容山势高峻，道路险阻。参、井，皆星宿名。参是蜀的分野，井是秦的分野（古人认为地上某地区与天上某星宿相应，分成若干界域，叫分野）。扪，用手摸。
⑧ 子规：杜鹃鸟。据《华阳国志·蜀志》，古有蜀王杜宇，号望帝，后禅位出奔，其时子规鸟鸣。蜀人因思念杜宇，故觉此鸟鸣悲切。
⑨ 剑阁：四川省剑阁县北七里大、小剑山间的一座雄关，即剑门关。西晋张载《剑阁铭》："一夫荷戟，万夫趑趄。形胜之地，非亲勿居。"

所守或匪亲，化为狼与豺。

朝避猛虎，夕避长蛇，

磨牙吮血，杀人如麻。

锦城虽云乐，不如早还家。

蜀道之难，难于上青天，侧身西望长咨嗟[10]！

---

[10] 咨嗟：叹息。

Hard is the Road to Shu

Oho! Behold! How steep! How high!

The road to Shu is harder than to climb to the sky.

Since the two pioneers

Put the kingdom in order,

Have passed forty-eight thousand years,

And few have tried to pass its border.

There's a bird track o'er Great White Mountain to the west,

Which cuts through Mountain Eyebrows by the crest.

The crest crumbled,five serpent-killing heroes slain,

Along the cliffs a rocky path was hacked then.

Above stand peaks too high for the sun to pass o'er;

Below the torrents run back and forth,churn and roar.

Even the Golden Crane can't fly across;

How to climb over,gibbons are at a loss.

What tortuous mountain path Green Mud Ridge faces!

Around the top we turn nine turns each hundred paces.

Looking up breathless,I can touch the stars nearby;

Beating my breast,I sink aground with long,long sigh.

When will you come back from this journey to the west?

How can you climb up dangerous path and mountain crest,

Where you can hear on ancient trees but sad birds wail

And see the female birds fly,followed by the male?

And hear home-going cuckoos weep

Beneath the moon in mountains deep?

The road to Shu is harder than to climb to the sky,

On hearing this,your cheeks would lose their rosy dye.

Between the sky and peaks there is not a foot's space,

And ancient pines hang,head down,from the cliff's surface,

And cataracts and torrents dash on boulders under,

Roaring like thousands of echoes of thunder.

So dangerous these places are,

Alas!Why should you come here from afar?

Rugged is the path between the cliffs so steep and high,

Guarded by one

And forced by none.

Disloyal guards would turn wolves and pards.

Man-eating tigers at day-break

And at dusk blood-sucking long snake.

One may make merry in the Town of Silk,I know,

But I would rather homeward go.

The road to Shu is harder than to climb the sky,

I'd turn and westward look with long,long sigh.

行路难^①

金樽^②清酒斗十千^③，玉盘^④珍羞^⑤直万钱。

停杯投箸^⑥不能食，拔剑四顾心茫然。

欲渡黄河冰塞川，将登太行^⑦雪满山。

---

① 行路难：古乐府《杂曲歌辞》调名，内容多写世路艰难和离别悲伤之意，多以"君不见"开头。原诗有三首，这是第一首。
② 金樽：古代盛酒的器具，以金为饰。
③ 斗十千：一斗值十千钱，此处形容酒价昂贵。
④ 玉盘：玉制的盘子。
⑤ 珍羞：精美的食品。羞，同"馐"。
⑥ 投箸：丢下筷子。箸，筷子。
⑦ 太行：山名，即太行山。

闲来垂钓碧溪上^⑧，忽复乘舟梦日边^⑨。

行路难！行路难！多歧路^⑩，今安在？

长风破浪^⑪会有时，直挂云帆^⑫济^⑬沧海^⑭！

---

⑧ "闲来"句：垂钓碧溪上，据《史记·齐太公世家》记载，吕尚（姜太公）曾在渭水边垂钓，后来遇到周文王，被重用。此句表示诗人自己对从政仍有期待，下句同。碧，一作"坐"。

⑨ 乘舟梦日边：传说伊尹在受商汤重用前，曾梦见自己乘船经过日月旁边。

⑩ 歧路：岔路。

⑪ 长风破浪：比喻远大抱负得以实现。据《宋书·宗悫传》载：宗悫少年时，叔父宗炳问他的志向，他说："愿乘长风破万里浪。"

⑫ 云帆：高高的船帆。船在海里航行，因天水相连，船帆好像出没在雨雾之中。

⑬ 济：渡过。

⑭ 沧海：大海。

Hard is the Way of the World

Pure wine in golden cup costs ten thousand coins, good!

Choice dish in a jade plate is worth as much, nice food!

Pushing aside my cup and chopsticks, I can't eat;

Drawing my sword and looking round, I hear my heart beat.

I can't cross Yellow River: ice has stopped its flow;

I can't climb Mount Taihang: the sky is blind with snow.

I poise a fishing pole with ease on the green stream

Or set sail for the sun like the sage in a dream.

Hard is the way. Hard is the way.

Don't go astray! Whither today?

A time will come to ride the wind and cleave the waves;

I'll set my cloud-like sail to cross the sea which raves.

春思

燕草^①如碧丝，秦桑^②低绿枝。

当君怀归日，是妾断肠时。

春风不相识，何事入罗帏^③？

1
7
5

---

① 燕草：指燕地的草。燕，当年是戍边之地，位于今河北北部。
② 秦桑：秦地的桑树。秦，系征夫们的家乡，位于今陕西一带。
③ 罗帏：丝织的帘帐。

A Faithful Wife Longing for Her Husband in Spring

Northern grass looks like green silk thread,

Western mulberries bend their head.

When you think of your home on your part,

Already broken is my heart.

Vernal wind, instruder unseen,

O how dare you part my bed screen!

长门怨 ①

桂殿长愁不记春 ②，黄金四屋 ③ 起秋尘。

夜悬明镜 ④ 青天上，独照长门宫里人。

---

① 长门怨：古乐府题。据《乐府解题》记载："《长门怨》者，为陈皇后作也。
　后退居长门宫，愁闷悲思。……相如为作《长门赋》。……后人因其《赋》
　而为《长门怨》。"陈皇后，即汉武帝的皇后，小名阿娇。汉武帝小时曾说：
　"若得阿娇作妇，当作金屋贮之。"
② "桂殿"句：桂殿，指长门殿。不记春，犹不记年，言时间之久长。
③ 四屋：四壁。
④ 明镜：指月亮。

Sorrow of the Long Gate Palace

Does Laurel Bower where grief reigns remember spring?

On the four golden walls the dusts of autumn cling.

The night holds up a mirror bright in the azure sky

To show the fair on earth as lonely as on high.

子夜吴歌·秋歌

长安一片月①，万户捣衣声②。

秋风吹不尽③，总是玉关④情。

何日平胡虏，良人⑤罢⑥远征。

---

① 一片月：一片皎洁的月光。
② "万户"句：万户，即千家万户。捣衣，把衣料放在石砧上用棒槌捶击，使衣料绵软以便裁缝；将洗过头次的脏衣放在石板上捶击，去浑水，再清洗。
③ 吹不尽：吹不散。
④ 玉关：玉门关，位于今甘肃省敦煌，此处代指丈夫戍边之地。
⑤ 良人：古时妇女对丈夫的称呼。
⑥ 罢：结束。

Ballads of Four Seasons

Moonlight is spread all over the capital.

The sound of beating clothes far and near

Is brought by autumn wind which can't blow all

The longings away for far-off frontier.

When can we vanquish the barbarian foe

So that our men no longer into battle go?

将进酒 ^{qiāng} ①

君不见②黄河之水天上来，奔流到海不复回。

君不见高堂③明镜悲白发，朝如青丝暮成雪。

人生得意须尽欢，莫使金樽空对月。

天生我材必有用，千金散尽还复来。

烹羊宰牛且为乐，会须④一饮三百杯。

岑夫子，丹丘生⑤，将进酒，杯莫停。

与君歌一曲，请君为我倾耳听。

---

① 将进酒：乐府旧题，属《鼓吹曲·铙歌》，内容多写饮酒放歌的情感。将，请。

② 君不见：你没有看见。这是乐府诗中常用的套语。君，多为泛指。

③ 高堂：高大的厅堂。一说父母，又说床头。

④ 会须：应该，应当。

⑤ 岑夫子，丹丘生：指岑勋、元丹丘，两人均为李白好友。

钟鼓 馔玉^⑥不足贵，但愿长醉不复醒。

古来圣贤皆寂寞，唯有饮者留其名。

陈王^⑦昔时宴平乐^⑧，斗酒十千恣欢谑。

主人^⑨何为言少钱，径须沽取对君酌。

五花马^⑩，千金裘^⑪，

呼儿将出换美酒，与尔同销万古愁。

---

⑥ 钟鼓馔玉：代指豪门富贵。钟鼓，富贵人家宴会中奏乐使用的乐器。馔玉，"玉馔"的倒文，喻精美的饮食。

⑦ 陈王：三国魏曹植，他是曹操的第三个儿子，生前曾为陈王，去世后谥号"思"，因此又称陈思王。

⑧ 宴平乐：曹植《名都篇》："归来宴平乐，美酒斗十千。"平乐，即平乐观，汉宫阙名，为汉代富豪显贵的娱乐场所，旧址位于今河南省洛阳市附近。

⑨ 主人：诗人自称。

⑩ 五花马：唐人喜将骏马鬃毛修剪成瓣用来装饰，修剪成五瓣者被称为"五花马"。一说于阗向唐进贡的一种有五色毛发的西域马种。

⑪ 千金裘：价值千金的皮衣。裘，皮衣。

Invitation to Wine

Do you not see the Yellow River come from the sky,

Rushing into the sea and ne'er come back?

Do you not see the mirrors bright in chambers high

Grieve o'er your snow-white hair though once it was

silk-black?

When hopes are won, oh! Drink your fill in high delight,

And never leave your wine-cup empty in moonlight!

Heaven has made us talents, we're not made in vain.

A thousand gold coins spent, more will turn up again.

Kill a cow, cook a sheep and let us merry be,

And drink three hundred cupfuls of wine in high glee!

Dear friends of mine,

Cheer up, cheer up!

I invite you to wine.

Do not put down your cup!

I will sing you a song, please hear,

O hear! Lend me a willing ear!

What difference will rare and costly dishes make?

I only want to get drunk and never to wake.

How many great men were forgotten through the ages?

But great drinkers are more famous than sober sages.

The Prince of Poets feast'd in his palace at will,

Drank wine at ten thousand a cask and laughed his fill.

A host should not complain of money he is short,

To drink with you I will sell things of any sort.

My fur coat worth a thousand coins of gold

And my flower-dappled horse may be sold

To buy good wine that we may drown the woes age-old.

月下独酌①四首（其一）

花间一壶酒，独酌无相亲。

举杯邀明月，对影成三人②。

月既③不解④饮，影徒随我身。

暂伴月将⑤影，行乐须及春。

我歌月徘徊，我舞影零乱。

醒时同交欢⑥，醉后各分散。

永结无情⑦游，相期邈云汉⑧。

---

① 独酌：一个人饮酒。
② 成三人：明月和我以及我的影子恰是三人。
③ 既：且。
④ 不解：不懂，不理解。
⑤ 将：和。
⑥ 同交欢：一起欢乐。
⑦ 无情：忘却世情。
⑧ "相期"句：约定在天上相见。期，约会。邈云汉，一作"碧岩畔"。邈，遥远。云汉，银河，这里指遥天仙境。

Drinking Alone Under the Moon

I

Among the flowers, from a pot of wine

I drink without a companion of mine.

I raise my cup to invite the Moon who blends

Her light with my shadow and we're three friends.

The Moon does not know how to drink her share;

In vain my shadow follows me here and there.

Together with them for the time I stay,

And make merry before spring's spent away.

I sing and the Moon lingers to hear my song;

My Shadow's a mess while I dance along.

Sober, we three remain cheerful and gay;

Drunken, we part and each may go his way.

Our friendship will outshine all earthly love;

Next time we'll meet beyond the stars above.

戏赠①杜甫

饭颗山②头逢杜甫，顶戴笠子③日卓午④。

借问别来太瘦生⑤，总为⑥从前作诗苦⑦。

---

① 戏赠：开玩笑的话。实际上，这表现了至交之间的真情实话。

② 饭颗山：山名，相传在长安一带。"饭颗山头"一作"长乐坡前"。长乐坡也在长安附近。

③ 笠子：用竹箬或棕皮等编成的笠帽，用来御雨遮阳。

④ 日卓午：指正午太阳当头。

⑤ "借问"句：借问，即为请问的意思。太瘦生，消瘦、瘦弱，生为语助词，唐时习语。

⑥ 总为：怕是为了。

⑦ 作诗苦：杜甫曾自言："为人性僻耽佳句，语不惊人死不休。"此处指的正是杜甫一丝不苟的创作精神。

Joking With Du Fu

On top of Hill of Boiled Rice I met with Du Fu,

Who in the noonday sun wore a hat of bamboo.

Pray, how could you have grown so thin since we did part?

Is it because the verse-composing wrung your heart?

梦游天姥^{mǔ}吟留别 ①

海客谈瀛洲②，烟涛微茫信难求③。

越人④语天姥，云霞明灭或可睹。

天姥连天向天横⑤，势拔五岳掩赤城⑥。

天台四万八千丈，对此欲倒东南倾。

---

① 天姥山，位于今绍兴新昌县东，东接天台山。传说曾有登此山者听到天姥
  （老妇）歌谣之声，故名。唐玄宗天宝三年，李白在长安受到权贵的排挤被
  放出京。次年，他经由东鲁（今山东）南游越州（今绍兴），写下这首描绘
  梦中游历天姥山的诗，留给东鲁的朋友，所以也题作《梦游天姥山别鲁东
  诸公》。
② “海客”句：海客，浪迹海上之人。瀛洲，传说中的东海仙山。
③ “烟涛”句：烟涛，波涛渺茫，远看像烟雾笼罩的样子。微茫，景象模糊不
  清。信，实在。难求，难以寻访。
④ 越人：指浙江绍兴一带的人。
⑤ 向天横：遮住天空。横，遮蔽。
⑥ “势拔”句：山势超过五岳，遮掩住了赤城。拔，超出。赤城，山名，位于
  今浙江天台，为天台山的南门，土色皆赤。

我欲因之梦吴越，一夜飞度镜湖⑦月。

湖月照我影，送我至剡溪⑧。

谢公宿处今尚在，渌⑨水荡漾清⑩猿啼。

脚著谢公屐⑪，身登青云梯。

半壁见海日⑫，空中闻天鸡。

千岩万转路不定，迷花倚石忽已暝⑬。

熊咆龙吟殷岩泉⑭，栗深林兮惊层巅⑮。

云青青⑯兮欲雨，水澹澹兮生烟。

⑦ 镜湖：即鉴湖，在绍兴，唐朝最有名的城市湖泊。

⑧ 剡溪：水名，位于今浙江绍兴，曹娥江上游。

⑨ 渌：清澈。

⑩ 清：这里是凄清的意思。

⑪ 谢公屐：指谢灵运穿的那种木屐，是谢灵运游山时穿的一种特制木鞋。

⑫ "半壁"句：上到半山腰就见到从海上升起的太阳。

⑬ "迷花"句：迷恋着花，依靠着石，不觉得天色已经晚了。暝：夜晚。

⑭ "熊咆"句：熊在怒吼，龙在长鸣，震荡着山山水水，岩中的泉水在震响。殷源泉，即源泉殷。殷，此处作动词用，震响。

⑮ "栗深"句：使深林战栗，使层巅震惊。

⑯ 青青：黑沉沉的。

列缺[17]霹雳，丘峦崩摧。

洞天石扉，訇然中开[18]。

青冥[19]浩荡不见底，日月照耀金银台[20]。

霓为衣兮风为马，云之君[21]兮纷纷而来下。

虎鼓瑟兮鸾回车[22]，仙之人兮列如麻。

忽魂悸以魄动，恍[23]惊起而长嗟。

---

[17] 列缺：闪电。列，通"裂"，分裂。缺，指云的缝隙。电光从云中决裂而
出，故称"列缺"。

[18] "洞天"句：仙府的石门，訇的一声从中间打开。洞天，神仙所居的洞府，
意谓洞中别有天地。石扉，即石门。訇然，形容声音很大。

[19] 青冥：天空。

[20] 金银台：金银筑成的宫阙，指神仙居住的地方。

[21] 云之君：云里的神仙。

[22] 鸾回车：鸾鸟驾着车。鸾，传说中凤凰一类的鸟。回，回旋、运转。

[23] 恍：恍然，猛然。

惟觉时之枕席，失向来之烟霞^㉔。

世间行乐亦如此，古来万事东流水。

别君去兮何时还？

且放白鹿青崖间，须行即骑访名山^㉕。

安能摧眉折腰^㉖事权贵，使我不得开心颜！

192

㉔ "失向"句：刚才梦中所见的烟雾云霞都不见了。向来，原来。烟霞，指前
文所写的仙境。

㉕ "且放"两句：暂且把白鹿放在青青的山崖间，等到要走的时候就骑上它去
访问名山。须，等待。

㉖ 摧眉折腰：低头弯腰，即卑躬屈膝。摧眉，即低眉。陶渊明曾叹"吾不能
为五斗米折腰，拳拳事乡里小人邪"。

惟觉时之枕席，失向来之烟霞[24]。

世间行乐亦如此，古来万事东流水。

别君去兮何时还？

且放白鹿青崖间，须行即骑访名山[25]。

安能摧眉折腰[26]事权贵，使我不得开心颜！

192

---

[24] "失向"句：刚才梦中所见的烟雾云霞都不见了。向来，原来。烟霞，指前文所写的仙境。

[25] "且放"两句：暂且把白鹿放在青青的山崖间，等到要走的时候就骑上它去访问名山。须，等待。

[26] 摧眉折腰：低头弯腰，即卑躬屈膝。摧眉，即低眉。陶渊明曾叹"吾不能为五斗米折腰，拳拳事乡里小人邪"。

Mount Skyland Ascended in a Dream——A Song of Farewell

Of fairy isles seafarers speak,

'Mid dimming mist and surging waves, so hard to seek.

Of Skyland southerners are proud,

Perceivable through fleeting or dispersing cloud.

Mount Skyland threatens heaven, massed against the sky,

Surpassing the Five Peaks and dwarfing Mount Red Town.

Mount Heaven's Terrace, five hundred thousand feet high,

Nearby to the southeast, appears crumbled down.

Longing in dreams for Southern Land, one night

I flew o'er Mirror Lake in moonlight.

My shadow's followed by moonbeams

Until I reach Shimmering Streams.

Where Hermitage of Master Xie can still be seen,

And clearly gibbons wail o'er rippling water green.

I put Xie's pegged boot

Each on one foot,

And scale the mountain ladder to blue cloud.

On eastern cliff I see

Sunrise at sea,

And in mid-air I hear sky cock crow loud.

The footpath meanders' mid a thousand crags in the vale,

I'm lured by rocks and flowers when the day turns pale.

Bears roar and dragons howl and thunders the cascade;

Deep forests quake and ridges tremble: they're afraid.

From dark, dark cloud comes rain;

On pale, pale waves mists plane.

Oh! Lightning flashes

And thunder rumbles;

With stunning crashes

Peak on peak crumbles.

The stone gate of a fairy cavern under

Suddenly breaks asunder.

So blue, so deep, so vast appears an endless sky,

Where sun and moon shine on gold and silver terraces high.

Clad in the rainbow, riding on the wind,

The Lords of Clouds descend in a procession long,

Their chariots drawn by phoenix disciplined,

And tigers playing for them a zither song,

Row upon row, like fields of hemp, immortals throng.

Suddenly my heart and soul stirred,

I awake with a long, long sigh.

I find my head on pillow lie

And fair visions gone by.

Likewise all human joys will pass away

Just as east-flowing water of olden day.

I'll take my leave of you, not knowing for how long,

I'll tend a white deer among

The grassy slopes of the green hill

So that I may ride it to famous mountains at will.

How can I stoop and bow before the men in power

And so deny myself a happy hour!

苏台①览古

旧苑②荒台杨柳新，菱歌③清唱④不胜春。

只今惟有西江月，曾照吴王宫里人⑤。

196

---

① 苏台：即姑苏台，位于今江苏省苏州市姑苏山上。
② 旧苑：指苏台。苑，园林。
③ 菱歌：东南水乡百姓采菱时所唱的民歌。
④ 清唱：形容歌声婉转清亮。
⑤ 吴王宫里人：指吴王夫差宫廷里的嫔妃。

The Ruined Wu Palace

Deserted garden, crumbling terrace, willows green,

Sweet notes of lotus songs cannot revive old spring.

All are gone but the moon over West River that's seen

The ladies fair who won the favor of the king.

越中^①览古

越王勾践^②破吴归，义士还家尽锦衣。

宫女如花满春殿，只今惟有鹧鸪^③飞。

1
9
8

---

① 越中：春秋时越国领地。隋初将会稽郡改为越州，唐代沿用越州名，即今
浙江绍兴。

② 勾践：春秋越国君王，曾被同时期的吴国所灭。后来勾践卧薪尝胆，发愤
图强，终于在被灭的二十年后又灭掉吴国。

③ 鹧鸪：产于我国南部，形似雉，体大如鸠。古人称它的鸣叫声为"钩辀格
磔"，其叫声凄厉，极像"行不得也哥哥"，所以古人常借其抒逐客流人之
情，描绘荒芜凄凉之景。

The Ruined Capital of Yue

The king of Yue returned, having destroyed the foe;

His loyal men came home, with silken dress aglow.

His palace thronged with flower-like ladies fair;

Now we see but a flock of partridges flying there.

越女词五首（其五）

镜湖^①水如月，耶溪女似雪。

新妆荡新波，光景^②两奇绝。

---

① 镜湖：一名鉴湖、庆湖，位于今浙江省绍兴市会稽山。

② 景：同"影"。

Song of the Southern Maiden

V

The waves of Mirror Lake look like moonbeam;

The maiden's fair as snow on waterside.

Her rippling dress vies with the rippling stream;

We know not which by which is beautified.

山中问答

问余何意栖①碧山②，笑而不答心自闲③。

桃花流水窅然④去，别有天地非人间。

---

① 栖：停留，居住。
② 碧山：一说指青翠苍绿的小山。一说指山下桃花岩，李白读书处，位于今湖北安陆。
③ 自闲：悠闲自得。闲，安然，泰然。
④ 窅然：远去的样子。窅，深邃、深远。

A Reply

I dwell among green hills and someone asks me why;

My mind care free, I smile and give him no reply.

Peach petals fallen on running water pass by;

This is an earthly paradise beneath the sky.

自遣

对酒不觉暝^①，落花盈我衣。

醉起步^②溪月，鸟还人亦稀^③。

---

① 暝：暮色昏暗。

② 步：漫步。

③ 稀：稀少。

Solitude

I'm drunk with wine

And with moonshine,

With flowers fallen o'er the ground

And o'er me the blue-gowned.

Sobered, I stroll along the stream

Whose ripples gleam.

I see no bird

And hear no word.

独坐敬亭山①

众鸟高飞尽②，孤云独去闲③。

相看两不厌④，只有敬亭山。

---

① 敬亭山：位于今安徽宣城市。
② 尽：无，没有。
③ 独去闲：独去，独自去。闲，形容云彩飘来飘去，悠闲自在的样子。
④ 两不厌：两是诗人和敬亭山。厌，满足。

Sitting Alone in Face of Peak Jingting

All birds have flown away, so high;

A lonely cloud drifts on, so free.

Gazing on Mount Jingting,

Nor I am tired of him, nor he of me.

宣州谢朓楼① 饯别校书叔云②

弃我去者，昨日之日不可留。

乱我心者，今日之日多烦忧。

长风万里送秋雁，对此可以酣高楼。

蓬莱③文章建安骨④，中间小谢⑤又清发。

俱怀逸兴壮思飞，欲上青天揽明月。

抽刀断水水更流，举杯消愁愁更愁。

人生在世不称意，明朝散发⑥弄扁舟⑦。

---

① 谢朓楼：南齐诗人谢朓做宣城太守时所建，又称谢公楼、北楼，唐末改名叠嶂楼，位于今安徽宣城市。

② 校书叔云：李云曾为秘书省校书郎，唐人同姓者常相互攀连亲戚，李云当较李白长一辈，但不一定是近亲。

③ 蓬莱：汉时称中央政府的著述藏书处东观为道家蓬莱山，唐人用以代指秘书省。

④ 建安骨：汉献帝建安时代的诗文慷慨多气，史称建安风骨。

⑤ 小谢：谢朓，与其先辈谢灵运分别称大、小谢。

⑥ 散发：古人平时都是用簪子束发，并戴上帽子。散发则是不束发、不戴帽，指避世隐居。

⑦ 弄扁舟：扁舟，小船。越亡吴后，范蠡"乘扁舟浮于江湖"，后世便以弄扁舟喻避世隐遁。

Farewell to Uncle Yun, Imperial Librarian, at Xie Tiao's Pavilion in Xuancheng

What left me yesterday

Can be retained no more;

What troubles me today

Is the times for which I feel sore.

In autumn wind for miles and miles the wild geese fly.

Let's drink in face of this in the pavilion high!

Your writing's forcible like ancient poets while

Mine is in Junior Xie's clear and spirited style.

Both of us have an ideal high;

We would reach the moon in the sky.

Cut running water with a sword, it will faster flow;

Drink wine to drown your sorrow, it will heavier grow.

If we despair of all human affairs,

Let us roam in a boat with loosened hairs!

送友人

青山横北郭^①，白水^②绕东城。

此地一^③为别，孤蓬^④万里征^⑤。

浮云游子意^⑥，落日故人情。

挥手自兹^⑦去，萧萧^⑧班马^⑨鸣。

① 郭：古代在城外修筑的一种外墙。

② 白水：清澈的水。

③ 一：助词，加强语气。

④ 蓬：又名"飞蓬"，一种植物，干枯后根株断开，遇风飞旋。此处喻指远行
的朋友。

⑤ 征：远行。

⑥ "浮云"句：此处用典，以浮云飘飞无定喻游子四方漂游。曹丕《杂诗》：
"西北有浮云，亭亭如车盖。惜哉时不遇，适与飘风会。吹我东南行，行行
至吴会。"浮云，飘动的云。游子，离家远游的人。

⑦ 兹：指这里、此处。

⑧ 萧萧：马的呻吟嘶叫声。

⑨ 班马：离群的马，此处指载人远离的马。班，分别、离别，一作"斑"。

Farewell to a Friend

Blue mountains bar the northern sky;

White river girds the eastern town.

Here is the place to say goodbye;

You'll drift like lonely thistledown.

With floating cloud you'll float away;

Like parting day I'll part from you.

You wave your hand and go your way;

Your steed still neighs, "Adieu, adieu!"

秋浦歌十七首（其十五）

白发三千丈，缘①愁似个长②。

不知明镜里，何处得秋霜③？

---

① 缘：因为。
② 个：这样。
③ 秋霜：指白发。

My White Hair

XV

Long, long is my whitening hair;

Long, long is it laden with care.

I look into my mirror bright:

From where comes autumn frost so white?

赠汪伦①

李白乘舟将欲行，忽闻岸上踏歌②声。

桃花潭③水深千尺，不及汪伦送我情。

---

① 汪伦：李白在桃花潭结识的朋友，性格豪爽。

② 踏歌：唐代广为流行的民间歌舞形式，一边唱歌，一边用脚踏地打着拍子。

③ 桃花潭：水潭名，位于今安徽泾县西南。

To Wang Lun

I, Li Bai, sit in a boat about to go,

When suddenly on shore your farewell songs overflow.

However deep the Lake of Peach Blossoms may be,

It's not so deep, O Wang Lun, as your love for me.

早发^① 白帝城^②

朝辞白帝彩云间^③，千里江陵^④一日还。

两岸猿声啼不住^⑤，轻舟已过万重山^⑥。

2
1
6

---

① 发：启程。
② 白帝城：位于今重庆市奉节县白帝山上。
③ "朝辞"句：朝，早晨。白帝，白帝城。辞，告别。彩云间，因白帝城在白帝山上，地势高耸，从山下江中仰望，仿佛其耸入云间。
④ 江陵：今湖北荆州市。从白帝城到江陵约一千二百里，其间包括七百里三峡。
⑤ 啼不住：不停地鸣叫。啼，鸣、叫。住，停息。
⑥ 万重山：层层叠叠的山，形容有许多山。

Leaving the White Emperor Town at Dawn

Leaving at dawn the White Emperor crowned with cloud,

I've sailed a thousand miles through canyons in a day.

With monkeys' sad adieus the riverbanks are loud;

My skiff has left ten thousand mountains far away.

宿五松山①下荀媪②家

我宿五松下，寂寥无所欢。

田家秋作苦③，邻女夜舂寒④。

跪进雕胡饭⑤，月光明素盘。

令人惭漂母⑥，三谢⑦不能餐⑧。

---

① 五松山：位于今安徽省铜陵市。

② 媪：妇人。

③ "田家"句：田家，农家。秋作，秋天的劳作。苦，劳作之苦，也指心中的悲苦。

④ 夜舂寒：夜间舂米寒冷。舂，将谷物等倒进器具进行捣碎破壳。此句中的寒与上句苦对应，既指农家劳动辛苦，亦指家境贫寒。

⑤ "跪进"句：古人席地而坐，上半身挺直，坐在足跟上。雕胡，即菰，俗称茭白。秋天结小圆柱形的果实，叫作菰米。用菰米做饭，香甜可口，古人将其当作美食。

⑥ "令人"句：惭，惭愧。漂母，在水边漂洗丝絮的妇人。《史记·淮阴侯列传》载：汉时韩信少时穷困，在淮阴城下钓鱼，一洗衣老妇见他饥饿，便给他饭吃。后来韩信助刘邦平定天下，功高封楚王，以千金报答漂母。此诗以漂母比荀媪。

⑦ 三谢：多次推辞。

⑧ 不能餐：惭愧得吃不下。

Passing One Night in an Old Woman's Hut at the Foot of Mount Five Pines

I lodge under the five pine trees;

Lonely, I feel not quite at ease.

Peasants work hard in autumn old;

Husking rice at night, the maid's cold.

Wild rice is offered on her knees;

The plate in moonlight seems to freeze.

I'm overwhelmed with gratitude.

Do I deserve the hard-earned food?

临终歌

大鹏飞兮振八裔^①，中天^②摧^③兮力不济。

馀风^④激兮万世，游扶桑^⑤兮挂^⑥左袂^⑦。

后人得^⑧之传此，仲尼亡兮谁为出涕^⑨。

---

① 裔：边远的地方。
② 中天：半空中。
③ 摧：摧折。
④ 馀风：遗风。馀，通"余"。
⑤ 扶桑：神话传说中的大树，这里指皇帝。
⑥ 挂：喻腐朽势力阻挠。
⑦ 左袂：左衽。汉服传统习俗，死者穿衣用左衽，示"不复解"。此句指诗人幻想自己与大鹏合为一体，挂于扶桑枝上而死。
⑧ 得：得知，即得知大鹏夭折半空。
⑨ "仲尼"句：此处用孔子泣麟的典故。鲁国抓获一条麒麟，孔子认为麒麟出非其时，世道将乱，遂大哭。

On Death Bed

When flies the roc, he shakes the world.

In mid-air his weakened wings are furled.

The wind he's raised still stirs the sea,

He hangs his left wing on sun-side tree.

Posterity mine, hear, O, hear!

Confucius dead, who'll shed a tear?

崔颢

CUI HAO

作者简介

崔颢（704—754），汴州（今河南开封）人，唐代著名诗人。

唐开元十一年（723年）进士及第，官至太仆寺丞。天宝年间，为司勋员外郎。秉性耿直，才思敏捷，其作品激昂豪放，气势宏伟，早期诗作多写闺情和妇女生活，诗风较轻浮，反映上层统治阶级生活的侧面，后期以边塞诗为主，诗风雄浑奔放，反映边塞的慷慨豪迈、戎旅之苦。

最为人称道的是《黄鹤楼》，曾使李白叹服。据说李白为之搁笔，曾有"眼前有景道不得，崔颢题诗在上头"的赞叹。

黄鹤楼 [①]

昔人已乘黄鹤去，此地空余黄鹤楼。

黄鹤一去不复返，白云千载空悠悠。

晴川 [②] 历历汉阳树，芳草萋萋鹦鹉洲 [③]。

日暮乡关何处是？烟波 [④] 江上使人愁。

[①] 黄鹤楼：因处汉水与长江交接处的武昌黄鹤山而得名。黄鹤山，《齐谐志》中记载，仙人王子安乘黄鹤路过此地而得名。

[②] 晴川：晴天中的汉水。川，河道。

[③] 鹦鹉洲：位于今湖北省武汉市武昌区。据《后汉书》记载，东汉末年黄祖担任江夏太守时，在此大宴宾客，有人献上鹦鹉，故此地称鹦鹉洲。

[④] 烟波：朦胧得看不清的江波，像被烟雾笼罩着一样。

Yellow Crane Tower

The sage on yellow crane was gone amid clouds white.

To what avail is Yellow Crane Tower left here?

Once gone, the yellow crane will not on earth alight;

Only white clouds still float in vain from year to year.

By sunlit river trees can be counted one by one;

On Parrot Islet sweet green grass grows fast and thick.

Where is my native land beyond the setting sun?

The mist-veiled waves of River Han make me homesick.

长干曲①（二首）

一

君家何处住，妾住在横塘②。
停船暂借问③，或恐是同乡。

二

家临九江④水，来去九江侧。
同是长干人，生小⑤不相识。

① 长干曲：《长干曲》一共四首，这里选取第一首和第二首。长干，地名，位于金陵（今江苏南京）。
② 横塘：地名，位于今南京西南麒麟门外，与长干相近。
③ 借问：打听事情的客气的说法。船家女直率，才问罢郎家何处，不及回答，便自言横塘人。
④ 九江：原指长江浔阳一段，此泛指长江。
⑤ 生小：从小。

Songs On The River

I. The Woman's Song

Where are you coming from?

On the shore I've my home.

Will you rest on your oar?

Are we from the same shore?

II. The Man's Song

I dwell by riverside,

And sail on river wide.

We live on the same shore,

Not knowing it before.

常　建

CHANG JIAN

作者简介

常建（708—765），字少府，唐代诗人。

开元十五年（727年）与王昌龄同榜进士，长仕宦不得意，来往山水名胜，长期过着漫游生活。后移家隐居鄂渚。天宝中，曾任盱眙尉。

其诗以田园、山水为主要题材，风格接近王维、孟浩然一派，意境清迥，语言洗练自然，艺术上有独特造诣。

题破山寺^①后禅院

清晨入古寺，初日照高林。

曲径通幽处^②，禅房^③花木深。

山光悦鸟性，潭影空人心^④。

万籁^⑤此^⑥俱寂，但余^⑦钟磬^⑧音。

---

① 破山寺：即兴福寺，位于今江苏省常熟市西北虞山上。为南朝齐邑人郴州刺史倪德光舍宅所建。
② "曲径"句：曲径，一作"竹径"，又作"一径"。通，一作"遇"。幽，幽静。
③ 禅房：僧人居住修行的地方。
④ "潭影"句：潭水空明清澈，临潭照影，令人俗念全消。
⑤ 万籁：各种声音。籁，从孔穴里发出的声音，此处泛指声音。
⑥ 此：在此，即在后禅院。
⑦ 但余：只留下。一作"惟余"，又作"唯闻"。
⑧ 钟磬：指钟、磬之声。磬，古代用玉或金属等制成的曲尺形的打击乐器。

A Buddhist Retreat Behind Broken-Mountain Temple

I come to the old temple at first light;

Only tree-tops are steeped in sunbeams bright.

A winding footpath leads to deep retreat;

The abbots cell is hid' mid flowers sweet.

In mountain's aura flying birds feel pleasure;

In shaded pool a carefree mind finds leisure.

All worldly noises are quieted here;

I only hear temple bells ringing clear.

高 适

GAO SHI

作者简介

高适（704—765），字达夫，沧州渤海县（今河北景县）人。唐代中期名臣、边塞诗人，安东都护高侃之孙。

天宝八载（749年）进士及第，授封丘县尉。投靠河西节度使哥舒翰，担任掌书记。拜左拾遗，转监察御史，辅佐哥舒翰把守潼关。天宝十五载（756年），护送唐玄宗进入成都，擢谏议大夫。出任淮南节度使，讨伐永王李璘叛乱。讨伐安史叛军，解救睢阳之围，历任太子詹事、彭蜀二州刺史、剑南东川节度使。广德二年（764年），入为刑部侍郎、左散骑常侍，册封渤海县侯。永泰元年（765年）去世，追赠礼部尚书，谥号为"忠"。

其诗笔力雄厚，气势奔放。与岑参、王昌龄、王之涣合称"边塞四诗人"，有《高常侍集》二十卷。

燕歌行①

开元二十六年，客有从御史大夫张公②出塞而还者，作《燕歌行》以示适，感征戍之事，因而和焉。

汉家烟尘在东北③，汉将辞家破残贼。

男儿本自重横行④，天子非常赐颜色⑤。

① 燕歌行：属乐府《相和歌·平调曲》。
② 张公：指河北节度副使张守珪。开元二十三年（735年），张守珪因为与契丹作战立功拜为辅国大将军兼御史大夫。开元二十六年（738年），其部将假借张之命，与叛余党战，先胜后败。张不据实上报，反而贿赂去调查情况的牛仙童。事败，张被贬。
③ "汉家"句：汉家即汉朝，代指唐朝，唐代诗人在诗文中经常借汉说唐。烟尘，烽烟战尘，代指敌人入侵。
④ 横行：纵横驰骋，无可阻挡。
⑤ 赐颜色：赐予荣耀。

摐(chuāng)金伐鼓下榆关⑥，旌旆(jīngpèi)逶迤碣石间⑦。

校尉羽书飞瀚海⑧，单于猎火照狼山⑨。

山川萧条极边土⑩，胡骑凭陵⑪杂风雨。

战士军前半死生⑫，美人帐下⑬犹歌舞。

大漠穷秋塞草腓(féi)⑭，孤城落日斗兵稀。

身当恩遇恒轻敌，力尽关山未解围。

⑥ "摐金"句：摐，撞击。金，军中乐器，指钲（zhēng）一类的铜制打击乐器。伐鼓，击鼓。下，往，直奔。榆关，即山海关。

⑦ "旌旆"句：旌旆，旌是竿头饰羽的旗，旆是末端状如燕尾的旗，此处皆泛指各种旗帜。逶迤，弯曲延伸的样子。碣石，山名。

⑧ "校尉"句：校尉，武官名，仅次于将军。羽书，插有鸟羽毛的紧急军函。瀚海，大漠，此处指内蒙古自治区西拉木伦河上游一带的沙漠。

⑨ "单于"句：单于，匈奴首领，也泛指北方少数民族首领。猎火，打猎时点燃的火光。古代游牧民族出征前，常举行大规模校猎作为军事演习。狼山，位于今内蒙古自治区。

⑩ 极边土：临边境的尽头。极，穷尽。

⑪ 凭陵：仗势侵犯。

⑫ 半死生：形容伤亡惨重。

⑬ 帐下：指将帅的营帐。

⑭ 腓：衰败，枯萎。一作"衰"。

铁衣[15]远戍辛勤久，玉箸[16]应啼别离后。

少妇城南欲断肠，征人蓟北[17]空回首。

边庭飘飖那可度[18]。绝域[19]苍茫更何有。

杀气三时作阵云[20]，寒声一夜传刁斗[21]。

相看白刃血纷纷，死节从来岂顾勋[22]。

君不见沙场征战苦，至今犹忆李将军[23]。

---

[15] 铁衣：指远征战士。

[16] 玉箸：白色的筷子，此处形容思妇的眼泪。

[17] 蓟北：唐蓟州治所在渔阳（今天津蓟州），此处泛指东北边地。

[18] "边庭"句：边庭，边疆。飘飖，此处形容边地局势紧张。度，越过。

[19] 绝域：极僻远的地方。

[20] "杀气"句：三时，指晨、午、晚，即一整天。阵云，战云，即战场上象征杀气的云。

[21] 刁斗：军中的一种煮饭、夜里报更的两用铜器。

[22] "死节"句：死节，此指为保卫国家而死。顾勋，顾及个人功勋。

[23] 李将军：汉代李广，他骁勇善战、身先士卒、爱惜士兵。

Song of the Northern Frontier

A cloud of smoke and dust spreads over northeast frontier;

To fight the remnant foe our generals leave the rear.

Brave men should go no matter where beneath the sky;

The emperor bestows on them his favor high.

To the beat of drums and gongs through Elm Pass they go;

Round Mount Stone Tablet flags serpentine row on row.

But urgent orders speed over the Sea of Sand:

Mount Wolf aflame with fires set by the Tartar band.

Both hills and streams are desolate on border plain;

The Tartar horsemen flurry like the wind and rain.

Half of our warriors lie killed on the battleground,

While pretty girls in camp still sing and dance their round.

Grass withers in the desert as autumn is late;

At sunset few men guard the lonely city gate.

Imperial favor makes them hold the foemen light;

Their town is under siege, though they've fought with their
might.

In coats of mail they've served so long on the frontiers;

Since they left home their wives have shed streams of
impearled tears.

In southern towns the women weep with broken heart;

In vain their men look southward, still they're far apart.

The northern front at stake, how can they go away?

On borders vast and desolate, how can they stay?

All day a cloud of slaughter mounts now and again;

All night the boom of gongs is heard to chill the plain.

Each sees the other's sword bloodstained in the hard strife.

Will they care for reward when they give up their life?

Do you not know the bitterness of fighting with the foe?

Can they forget General Li sharing their weal and woe?

别董大①

千里黄云白日曛②，北风吹雁雪纷纷。

莫愁前路无知己，天下谁人不识君。

236

---

① 董大：董庭兰，唐代著名音乐家。因其在兄弟中排行第一，故称"董大"。
② "千里"句：黄云，天上的乌云，在阳光下，乌云是暗黄色，所以叫黄云。白日曛，指太阳暗淡无光；曛，昏暗，夕阳西沉时的黄昏景象。

Farewell to a Lutist

Yellow clouds spread for miles

And miles have veiled the day;

The north wind blows down snow and wild geese fly away.

Fear not you've no admirers as you go along.

There is no connoisseur on earth but loves your song.

储光羲

CHU GUANGXI

作者简介

储光羲（706—763），润州延陵（今江苏丹阳延陵）人，唐代田园山水诗派代表诗人之一。

开元十四年（726年）举进士，授冯翊县尉，转汜水、安宣、下邽等地县尉。因仕途失意，遂隐居终南山。后复出任太祝，世称储太祝，官至监察御史。安史之乱中，叛军攻陷长安，被俘，迫受伪职。乱平，自归朝廷请罪，被系下狱，有《狱中贻姚张薛李郑柳诸公》诗，后贬谪岭南。江南储氏多为光羲公后裔，尊称为"江南储氏之祖"。

其诗风格朴实，生活气息比较浓厚。《四库全书总目》中，对他的诗评价为"源出陶潜，质朴之中，有古雅之味，位置于王维、孟浩然间，殆无愧色"。

钓鱼湾

垂钓绿湾春，春深杏花乱^①。

潭清疑水浅，荷动知鱼散。

日暮待情人^②，维舟^③绿杨岸。

---

① "春深"句：春意浓郁。乱，纷繁的样子。
② 情人：即志同道合的人。
③ 维舟：系船停泊。维，系。

The Fishing Bay

You may fish in late spring by lakeside green

Where apricot blossoms are running riot.

The lake seems shallow for its water's clean;

You see dispersed fish disturb lotus quiet.

You may wait at dusk for one you adore

And moor your boat by willow-shaded shore.

刘长卿

LIU ZHANGQING

作者简介

刘长卿（726—790），字文房，唐代诗人。宣城（今安徽）人，后迁居洛阳，河间（今河北）为其郡望。

唐玄宗天宝年间进士。唐肃宗至德年间任监察御史、苏州长洲县尉，唐代宗大历年间任转运使判官，知淮西、鄂岳转运留后，又被诬再贬睦州司马。因刚而犯上，两度迁谪。唐德宗建中年间，官终随州刺史，世称刘随州。

工于诗，长于五言，自称"五言长城"，有代表作《逢雪宿芙蓉山主人》。

逢^①雪宿芙蓉山主人^②

日暮苍山远^③，天寒白屋^④贫。

柴门闻犬吠，风雪夜归人。

---

① 逢：遇，遇上。

② 芙蓉山主人：芙蓉山，各地以芙蓉命山名者甚多，这里大约是指湖南桂阳或宁乡的芙蓉山。主人，指留诗人借宿者。

③ 苍山远：青山在暮色中影影绰绰，显得很遥远。苍，青色。

④ 白屋：未加装饰的简陋的茅草房，通常指贫苦人家。

Seeking Shelter in Lotus Hill on a Snowy Night

At sunset hillside village still seems far;

Cold and deserted the thatched cottages are.

At wicket gate a dog is heard to bark;

With wind and snow I come when night is dark.

送灵澈上人①

苍苍竹林寺②，杳杳③钟声晚。

荷笠④带夕阳，青山独归远。

2
4
4

---

① 灵澈上人：中唐时期一位著名诗僧，俗姓杨，出家后号灵澈，字源澄，会稽（今浙江绍兴）人。上人，对僧人的敬称。

② "苍苍"句：苍苍即深青色。竹林寺，位于今江苏省镇江市丹徒。

③ 杳杳：深远处。

④ 荷笠：背着斗笠。荷，负、背。

Seeing off a Recluse

Green, green the temple amid bamboos,

Late, late bell rings out the evening.

Alone, he's lost in mountains blue,

With sunset his hat is carrying.

张谓

ZHANG WEI

作者简介

张谓，生卒年不详，字正言，河内（今河南沁阳）人，唐代诗人。

天宝二载（743年）登进士第，乾元中为尚书郎，大历年间潭州刺史，后官至礼部侍郎，三典贡举。

其诗词精意深，讲究格律，诗风清正，多饮宴送别之作。代表作中以《早梅》为最著名，《唐诗三百首》各选本多有辑录。

早梅

一树寒梅①白玉条，迥临村路傍溪桥②。

不知③近水花先发，疑是经冬雪未销④。

---

① 寒梅：梅花。因其凌寒开放，故称。
② "迥临"句：迥，远。村路，乡间小路。傍，靠近。
③ 不知：一作"应缘"。应缘，犹言大概是。
④ "疑是"句：经冬即经过冬天。一作"经春"。销，通"消"，融化，此处指冰雪融化。

Early Mume Blossoms

Like belts of white jade the cold-proof mume branches look,

Beside the pathway near the bridge over a brook.

If you don't know riverside blossoms early blow,

You would take them for last winter's unmelted snow.

杜甫

DU FU

作者简介

杜甫（712—770），字子美，自号少陵野老，河南府巩县（今河南巩义）人。唐代伟大的现实主义诗人，与李白合称"李杜"。为了与另两位诗人李商隐与杜牧即"小李杜"区别，杜甫与李白又合称"大李杜"。

他于少年时代曾先后游历吴越和齐赵，其间曾赴洛阳应举不第。天宝六载（747年），在长安应试，落第。天宝十载（751年），向皇帝献赋，得玄宗赏识，但未得官职。天宝十四载（755年），安史之乱爆发，潼关失守，先后辗转多地。乾元二载（759年）弃官入川，虽然躲避了战乱，生活相对安定，但仍然心系苍生，胸怀国事。大历五年（770年）冬病逝。

其诗兼备多种风格，普遍具有"沉郁"的特点，多有意象，炼字精到，有"建筑美"，在中国古典诗歌中的影响非常深远，被后世尊称为"诗圣"。他的诗被称为"诗史"。

望岳

岱宗①夫如何？齐鲁青未了②。

造化钟神秀③，阴阳④割昏晓。

荡胸生层云，决眦⑤入归鸟。

会当⑥凌⑦绝顶，一览众山小。

---

① 岱宗：指东岳泰山。泰山别名岱，为五岳之首，故又名岱宗。
② "齐鲁"句：齐鲁，古代齐鲁两国以泰山为界，泰山之北为古齐地，之南为
　　古鲁地。青未了，指郁郁苍苍的山色无边无际，没有尽头。了，尽。
③ "造化"句：造化，天地，大自然。钟，集中，聚集。神秀，指山色的
　　奇丽。
④ 阴阳：山北为阴，山南为阳。意指泰山横天蔽日，山南向阳而天色明亮，
　　山北背阴而天色晦暗。
⑤ 决眦：眼角裂开。眦，眼角。
⑥ 会当：一定要。
⑦ 凌：登上。

Gazing on Mount Tai

O peak of peaks, how high it stands!

One boundless green overspreads two States.

A marvel done by Nature's hands,

Over light and shade it dominates.

Clouds rise therefrom and lave my breast;

I stretch my eyes to see birds fleet.

I will ascend the mountain's crest;

It dwarfs all peaks under my feet.

兵车行

车辚辚，马萧萧，行人弓箭各在腰。

耶①娘妻子②走相送，尘埃不见咸阳桥。

牵衣顿足拦道哭，哭声直上干③云霄。

道旁过者问行人，行人但云点行频④。

或从十五北防河，便至四十西营田⑤。

去时里正⑥与裹头⑦，归来头白还戍边。

边庭流血成海水，武皇⑧开边意未已。

---

① 耶：同"爷"，父亲。

② 妻子：妻子和儿女。

③ 干：犯，冲。

④ 点行频：多次点兵出征。

⑤ 营田：戍边的士卒，兼从事垦荒工作。

⑥ 里正：里长。唐制，百户为一里，里有里正，管户口、赋役等事。

⑦ 与裹头：古以皂罗三尺裹头作头巾。因应征者年龄还小，故由里正替他裹头。

⑧ 武皇：指汉武帝刘彻，历史上他以开疆拓土著称。此处暗喻唐玄宗。

君不闻汉家山东二百州⑨，千村万落生荆杞。

　　纵有健妇把锄犁，禾生陇亩无东西。

　　况复秦兵耐苦战，被驱不异犬与鸡。

　　　　长者虽有问，役夫敢申恨？

　　　　且如今年冬，未休关西卒⑩。

　　　　县官⑪急索租，租税从何出？

　　　　信知生男恶，反是生女好。

生女犹得嫁比邻⑫，生男埋没随百草。

　　君不见青海头，古来白骨无人收。

新鬼烦冤旧鬼哭，天阴雨湿声啾啾。

---

⑨ 山东二百州：指华山以东的广大土地。

⑩ 关西卒：指应征出发的秦地士卒。

⑪ 县官：指官府。

⑫ 比邻：近邻。

Song of the Conscripts

Chariots rumble And horses grumble.

The conscripts march with bow and arrows at the waist.

Their fathers, mothers, wives and children come in haste

To see them off; the bridge is shrouded in dust they've

raised.

They clutch at their coats, stamp the feet and bar the way;

Their grief cries loud and strikes the cloud straight, straight

away.

An onlooker by roadside asks an enrollee.

"The conscription is frequent," only answers he.

Some went north at fifteen to guard the rivershore,

And were sent west to till the land at forty.

The elder bound their young heads when they went away;

Just home, they're sent to the frontier though their hair's

gray.

The field on borderland becomes a sea of blood;

The emperor's greed for land is still at high flood.

Have you not heard

Two hundred districts east of the Hua Mountains lie,

Where briers and brambles grow in villages far and nigh?

Although stout women can wield the plough and the hoe,

Thorns and weeds in the east as in the west o'ergrow.

The enemy are used to hard and stubborn fight;

Our men are driven just like dogs or fowls in flight.

You are kind to ask me.

To complain I'm not free.

In winter of this year

Conscription goes on here.

The magistrates for taxes press.

How can we pay them in distress?

If we had known sons bring no joy,

We would have preferred girl to boy.

A daughter can be wed to a neighbor, alas!

A son can only be buried under the grass?

Have you not seen on borders green

Bleached bones since olden days unburied on the plain?

The old ghosts weep and cry, while the new ghosts

complain;

The air is loud with screech and scream in gloomy rain.

赠李白

秋来相顾尚飘蓬①，未就②丹砂③愧葛洪④。

痛饮狂歌空度日，飞扬跋扈⑤为谁雄。

---

① 飘蓬：常用来比喻行踪飘忽不定。

② 未就：没有成功。

③ 丹砂：即朱砂。道教认为炼砂成药，服之可以延年益寿。

④ 葛洪：东晋著名医药学家，著有《肘后方》，书中最早记载一些传染病如天花、恙虫病症候及诊治。

⑤ 飞扬跋扈：不守常规，狂放不羁。此处贬词褒义用。

To Li Bai

When autumn comes, you're drifting still like thistledown

You try to find the way to heaven, but you fail.

In singing mad and drinking dead your days you drown.

O when will fly the roc?

O when will leap the whale?

饮中八仙歌

知章骑马似乘船，眼花落井水底眠。

汝阳三斗始朝天，道逢麴车口流涎，恨不移封向酒泉^①。

左相日兴费万钱，饮如长鲸吸百川，衔杯乐圣称避贤^②。

宗之潇洒美少年，举觞白眼望青天，皎如玉树临风前^③。

---

① "汝阳"三句：汝阳即汝阳王李琎，唐玄宗的侄子。朝天，朝见天子，此谓李琎痛饮后才入朝。麴车，酒车。移封，改换封地。酒泉，郡名，位于今甘肃酒泉，相传那里"城下有金泉，泉味如酒"，故名酒泉。

② "左相"三句：左相即指左丞相李适之，后为李林甫排挤罢相。长鲸，鲸鱼，古人以为鲸鱼能吸百川之水，此处用来形容李适之的酒量之大。圣，酒的代称。李适之罢相后，作诗云："避贤初罢相，乐圣且衔杯。为问门前客，今朝几个来？"此处指李适之虽然罢相，但仍豪饮如昔。

③ "宗之"三句：宗之即崔宗之，吏部尚书崔日用之子，袭父封为齐国公，也是李白的朋友。觞，大酒杯。白眼，晋阮籍能作青白眼，青眼看朋友，白眼视俗人。玉树临风，崔宗之风姿秀美，故以玉树为喻。

苏晋长斋绣佛前，醉中往往爱逃禅④。

李白斗酒诗百篇，长安市上酒家眠。

天子呼来不上船，自称臣是酒中仙。

张旭三杯草圣传，脱帽露顶王公前，挥毫落纸如云烟⑤。

焦遂五斗方卓然⑥，高谈雄辩惊四筵。

④ "苏晋"二句：苏晋，开元进士，曾为户部和吏部侍郎。长斋，长期斋戒。
  绣佛，画的佛像。逃禅，这里指不守佛门戒律。佛教戒饮酒，苏晋长斋信
  佛，却嗜酒，故曰"逃禅"。

⑤ "张旭"三句：张旭，苏州吴县（今江苏苏州）人，唐代著名书法家，善草
  书，时人称为"草圣"。脱帽露顶，写张旭狂放不羁的醉态。据说张旭每当
  大醉，常呼叫奔走，索笔挥洒，甚至以头濡墨而书。醒后自视手迹，以为
  神异，不可复得。世称"张颠"。

⑥ "焦遂"句：焦遂，布衣之士，平民，以嗜酒闻名，事迹不详。卓然，神采
  焕发的样子。

Songs of Eight Immortal Drinkers

Zhizhang feels dizzy on his horse as in a boat.

Should he fall into the well, asleep there he should float.

Prince Lian would go to court after drinking three jars;

His mouth would water, seeing wine-transporting cars.

He would have as his fief the Spring of Wine in dreams.

Left Minister buys wine with thousand coins by day,

He would drink like a whale a hundred streams,

Dismissed now, he would drink impure wine as he may.

Without restraint, Zongzhi is a gallant young guy.

Like one of the jade trees standing in vernal breeze.

The Buddhist Su Jin should neither drink nor eat the meat,

But drunk, to run away from Buddha he is fleet.

Li Bai would turn sweet nectar into verses fine;

Drunk in the capital, he'd lie in shops of wine.

Even imperial summons proudly he'd decline,

Saying immortals could not leave the drink divine.

In cursive writing Zhang Xu's worthy of his fame.

After three drinks he bares his head before lord and dame,

And splashes cloud and mist on paper as with flame.

Jiao Sui is sober after drinking jar on jar;

His eloquence astonishes guests near and far.

前出塞九首（其六）

挽弓当挽强，用箭当用长。

射人先射马，擒贼先擒王。

杀人亦有限^①，列国自有疆^②。

苟^③能制^④侵陵^⑤，岂在多杀伤？

① 亦有限：也应该有个限度。

② 自有疆：本来应该有个疆界。疆，边界。

③ 苟：如果。

④ 制：制止。

⑤ 侵陵：侵犯，侵略。

Song Of The Frontier

VI

The bow you carry should be strong;

The arrows you use should be long.

Shoot before a horseman his horse;

Capture the chief to beat his force!

Slaughter shan't go beyond its sphere;

Each State should guard its own frontier.

If an invasion is repelled,

Why shed more blood unless compelled?

自京赴奉先县咏怀五百字（节选）

朱门酒肉臭，路有冻死骨①。

荣枯②咫尺异，惆怅③难再述。

---

① "朱门"两句：为全诗诗眼。臭，通"嗅"，意为气味。

② 荣枯：繁荣、枯萎。此喻朱门的豪华生活和路边冻死的尸骨。

③ 惆怅：此言感慨、难过。

On the Way from the Capital to Fengxian (Excerpt)

The mansions burst with wine and meat;

The poor die frozen on the street.

Woe stands within an inch of weal.

Distressed, can I tell what I feel?

月夜

今夜鄜^{fū}州^①月，闺中^②只独看^{kān}。

遥怜小儿女，未解忆长安。

香雾云鬟^{huán}湿，清辉玉臂寒^③。

何时倚虚幌^④，双照泪痕干。

---

① 鄜州：位于今陕西省富县。彼时杜甫的家属在鄜州的羌村，杜甫在长安。
② 闺中：此指妻子。
③ "香雾"两句：写想象中妻独自久立，望月怀人的形象。香雾，雾本来没有香气，香气从涂有膏沐的云鬟中散发出来，故称。云鬟，古代妇女的环形发髻，此处指女子头发蓬松的样子。
④ 虚幌：轻薄透明的帷帐。幌，帷幔。

A Moonlit Night

On the moon over Fuzhou which shines bright,

Alone you would gaze in your room tonight.

I'm grieved to think our little children dear

Too young to yearn for their old father here.

Your cloudlike hair is moist with dew, it seems;

Your jade-white arms would feel the cold moonbeams.

O when can we stand by the window side,

Watching the moon with our tear traces dried?

春望

国破^①山河在，城春草木深。

感时花溅泪，恨别鸟惊心。

烽火^②连三月，家书抵^③万金。

白头搔更短，浑^④欲不胜簪^⑤。

---

① 国破：指国都长安被叛军占领。破，沦陷。
② 烽火：战火。
③ 抵：值，相当。
④ 浑：简直。
⑤ 不胜簪：不能别上发簪。

Spring View

On war-torn land streams flow and mountains stand;

In vernal town grass and weeds are overgrown.

Grieved over the years, flowers make us shed tears;

Hating to part, hearing birds breaks our heart.

The beacon fire has gone higher and higher;

Words from household are worth their weight in gold.

I cannot bear to scratch my grizzled hair;

It grows too thin to hold a light hairpin.

哀江头

少陵野老①吞声哭，春日潜行曲江曲②。

江头宫殿锁千门，细柳新蒲为谁绿。

忆昔霓旌下南苑③，苑中万物生颜色④。

昭阳殿里第一人⑤，同辇随君侍君侧。

辇前才人带弓箭，白马嚼啮⁽ⁿⁱè⁾⑥黄金勒⑦。

① 少陵野老：杜甫祖籍长安杜陵，少陵是汉宣帝许皇后的陵墓，杜甫曾在少陵附近居住过，故自称。
② 曲江曲：曲江的隐曲角落之处。曲江，长安城南著名的风景区。
③ "忆昔"句：霓旌，此处指皇帝的旌旗。南苑，指曲江东南的芙蓉苑，因其在曲江之南，故称。
④ 生颜色：焕发生机。
⑤ 昭阳殿里第一人：此处指杨贵妃。昭阳殿，汉代宫殿名。
⑥ 啮：咬。
⑦ 黄金勒：用黄金做的衔勒。勒，马衔的嚼口。

翻身向天仰射云，一笑正坠双飞翼。

明眸皓齿今何在？血污游魂归不得[8]。

清渭[9]东流剑阁[10]深，去住彼此无消息。

人生有情泪沾臆，江水江花岂终极！

黄昏胡骑尘满城，欲往城南望城北。

---

[8] 归不得：指马嵬坡兵变，杨贵妃被缢死。

[9] 清渭：渭水。

[10] 剑阁：大剑山，位于今四川省广元市剑阁县，是由长安入蜀的必经之道。

Lament along the Winding River

Old and deprived, I swallow tears on a spring day;

Along Winding River in stealth I go my way.

All palace gates and doors are locked on river shore;

Willows and reeds are green for no one to adore.

I remember rainbow banners streamed at high tide

To Southern Park where everything was beautified.

The first lady of the Sunny Palace would ride

In the imperial chariot by the emperor's side.

The horsewomen before her bore arrows and bow;

Their white steeds champed at golden bits on the front row.

One archer, leaning back, shot at cloud in the sky;

One arrow brought down two winged birds from on high.

Where are the first lady's pearly teeth and eyes bright?

Her spirit, blood-stained, could not come back from the height.

Far from Sword Cliff, with River Wei her soul flew east;

The emperor got no news from her in the least.

A man who has a heart will wet his breast with tears.

Would riverside grass and flowers not weep for years?

At dusk the rebels' horses overrun the town;

I want to go upward, but instead I go down.

羌村三首（其一）

峥嵘①赤云西，日脚下平地。

柴门鸟雀噪，归客千里至。

妻孥②怪我在③，惊定还拭泪。

世乱遭飘荡，生还偶然遂④。

邻人满墙头，感叹亦歔欷⑤。

夜阑⑥更秉烛，相对如梦寐。

---

① 峥嵘：山高峻的样子，这里形容天空中云层重叠。
② 妻孥：妻子和儿女。
③ 怪我在：杜甫的妻子此前虽已接到杜甫的信，明知杜甫未死，但对于他的
   突然出现，仍不免惊疑发愣，所以说"怪我在"。
④ 遂：如愿。
⑤ 歔欷：感叹的样子。
⑥ 夜阑：夜深。

Coming Back To Giang Village

I

Like rugged hills hangs gilt-edged cloud;

The sunset sheds departing ray.

The wicket gate with birds is loud

When I come back from far away.

At my appearance starts my wife;

Then calming down, she melts in tears.

Happy, I come back still in life,

While people drift in bitter years.

My neighbors look over the wall;

They sigh and from their eyes tears stream.

When night comes, candles light the hall;

We sit face to face as in dream.

赠卫八处士 ①

人生不相见，动如参^{shēn}与商②。

今夕复何夕，共此灯烛光。

少壮能几时，鬓发各已苍。

访旧半为鬼③，惊呼热中肠④。

焉知二十载，重上君子堂。

昔别君未婚，儿女忽成行^{háng}⑤。

---

① 卫八处士：名字和生平事迹已不可考。八，是处士的排行。处，指隐居不
　仕的人。
② "动如"句：动如，就像此起彼落的。参、商，二星名。商星居于东方卯位
　（上午五点到七点），参星居于西方酉位（下午五点到七点），一出一没，永
　不相见，故以为比。
③ "访旧"句：意谓彼此打听故旧亲友，竟已死亡一半。访旧，一作"访问"。
④ "惊呼"句：有两种理解，一为，见到故友的惊呼，使人内心感到热乎乎
　的；二为，意外的死亡，使人惊呼怪叫以至心中感到火辣辣的难受。惊呼，
　一作"呜呼"。
⑤ 成行：指儿女众多。

怡然敬父执⑥，问我来何方。

问答乃未已⑦，驱儿罗酒浆。

夜雨剪春韭⑧，新炊间^{jiàn}黄粱⑨。

主称⑩会面难，一举累⑪十觞。

十觞亦不醉，感子故意长⑫。

明日隔山岳⑬，世事两茫茫⑭。

---

⑥ "父执"：执是接的借字，接友，即常相接近之友，意为父亲的友人。

⑦ 乃未已：还未等说完。

⑧ "夜雨"句：与郭林宗冒雨剪韭招待好友范逵的故事有关。林宗自种畦圃，友人范逵夜至，自冒雨剪韭，作汤饼以供之。

⑨ "新炊"句：新炊，刚煮的新鲜饭。"间"，掺和的意思。黄粱，即黄米。

⑩ 主：即卫八。称，说。

⑪ 累：接连。

⑫ 故意长：老朋友的情谊深长。

⑬ 山岳：指西岳华山。此句是说明天便要分手。

⑭ "世事"句：世事，包括社会和个人。两茫茫，指明天分手后，命运如何，便彼此都不相知了，极言会面之难。这时大乱未定，故杜甫有此感觉。据末两句推测，这首诗应是饮酒当晚写成的。

For Wei The Eighth

How rarely together friends are!

As Morning Star with Evening Star.

O what a rare night is tonight?

Together we share candlelight.

How long can last our youthful years?

Grey hair on our temples appears.

We find half of our friends departed.

How can we not cry broken-hearted!

After twenty years, who knows then,

I come into your hall again.

Unmarried twenty years ago,

Now you have children in a row.

Seeing their father's friend at home,

They're glad to ask where I come from.

Our talk has not come to an end,

When wine is offered to the friend.

They bring leeks cut after night rain

And millet cooked with new grain.

The host says, "It is hard to meet.

Let us drink ten cups of wine sweet!"

Ten cupfuls cannot make me drunk,

For deep in your love I am sunk.

Mountains will divide us tomorrow.

O What can we foresee but sorrow!

石壕吏

暮投石壕村[①]，有吏夜捉人。

老翁逾墙走[②]，老妇出门看。

吏呼一何怒[③]！妇啼一何苦。

听妇前致词[④]：三男邺城戍[⑤]。

一男附书至，二男新战死。

存者且偷生，死者长已矣！

室中更无人，惟有乳下孙[⑥]。

① "暮投"句：投，投宿。石壕村，现名干壕村，位于今河南省三门峡市。

② 走：跑，此处指逃跑。

③ "吏呼"句：呼，诉说，叫喊。一何，何其、多么。怒，恼怒，凶猛，粗
暴，此处指凶狠。

④ 前致词：指老妇走上前去（对差役）说话。前，上前，向前。致，对……说。

⑤ 邺城戍：邺城，即相州，位于今河南安阳。戍，防守，此处指服役。

⑥ 乳下孙：正在吃奶的孙子。

有孙母未去⑦，出入无完裙。

老妪力虽衰，请从吏夜归⑧。

急应河阳役⑨，犹得备晨炊⑩。

夜久语声绝，如闻泣幽咽。

天明登前途，独⑪与老翁别。

---

⑦ 去：离开，此处指改嫁。

⑧ "请从"句：请允许我跟随你连夜赶回营去。请，请求。从，跟从，跟随。

⑨ "急应"句：赶快到河阳去服役。应，响应。河阳，今河南孟州，当时唐王朝官兵与叛军在此对峙。

⑩ "犹得"句：犹得，还能够。得，能够。备，准备。晨炊，早饭。

⑪ 独：唯独、只有。

The Pressgang at Stone Moat Village

I seek for shelter at nightfall.

What is the pressgang coming for?

My old host climbs over the wall;

My old hostess answers the door.

How angry is the sergeant's shout!

How bitter is the woman's cry!

I hear what she tries to speak out.

"I'd three sons guarding the town high.

One wrote a letter telling me

That his brothers were killed in war.

He'll keep alive if he can be;

The dead have passed and are no more.

In the house there is no man left,

Except my grandson in the breast.

Of his mother, of all bereft;

She can't come out, in tatters dressed.

Though I'm a woman weak and old,

I beg to go tonight with you,

That I may serve in the stronghold

And cook morning meals as my due."

With night her voices fade away;

I seem to hear still sob and sigh.

At dawn again I go my way

And only bid my host goodbye.

梦李白二首（其一）

死别已吞声，生别常恻恻①。

江南瘴疠地，逐客无消息②。

故人入我梦，明我长相忆。

君今在罗网，何以有羽翼？

恐非平生魂③，路远不可测。

魂来枫林④青，魂返关塞黑⑤。

落月满屋梁，犹疑照颜色⑥。

水深波浪阔，无使蛟龙得。

---

① "死别"二句：吞声，极端悲恸，哭不出声来。恻恻，悲痛。此二句互文。

② "江南"二句：瘴疠，疾疫。古代称江南为瘴疠之地。逐客，被放逐的人，此处指李白。

③ "恐非"句：疑心李白死于狱中或道路。

④ 枫林：李白放逐的西南之地多枫林。

⑤ "魂返"句：关塞，杜甫流寓的秦州之地多关塞。李白的魂来魂往都是在夜间，所以说"青""黑"。

⑥ 颜色：此处指容貌。

Dreaming of Li Bai

I

We stifle sobs on parting with the dead;

On parting with the living, tears are shed.

You're exiled to miasmic Southern shore.

How can you not send us news any more?

Last night you came into my dream anew;

This shows how long I am thinking of you.

Now you are caught in net and bound with strings.

How can you free yourself with bound-up wings?

I fear it was not your soul I did dream.

Could it go such long way o'er mount and stream?

When it came, green would maple forests loom;

When it went, dark mountains were left in gloom.

The setting moon on rafters sheds its light;

I seem to see your beaming face as bright.

O monstrous billows where water is deep,

Don't wake up monsters and dragons asleep!

月夜忆舍弟

戍鼓^①断人行，边秋^②一雁声。

露从今夜白，月是故乡明。

有弟皆分散，无家问死生。

寄书长^③不达，况乃未休兵^④。

---

① 戍鼓：戍楼上的更鼓。戍，驻防。
② 边秋：秋天的边境。
③ 长：一直，老是。
④ "况乃"句：况乃，何况是。未休兵，战争还没有结束。

Thinking of My Brothers on a Moonlit Night

War drums break people's journey drear;

A swan honks on autumn frontier.

Dew turns into frost since tonight;

The moon viewed from home is more bright.

I've brothers scattered here and there;

For our life or death none would care.

Letters can't reach where I intend;

Alas! The war's not come to an end.

病马

乘尔亦已久，天寒关塞深^①。

尘中老尽力，岁晚病伤心^②。

毛骨岂殊众^③？驯良犹至今。

物微意不浅，感动一沉吟^④。

---

① "乘尔"二句：此二句指这匹马和自己患难相依已久。尔，指马。关塞，边
　关；边塞。深，远、险。

② "尘中"二句：在风尘中奔波，老了还在为我尽力，当岁晚天寒之时，身上
　有疾病，使人伤心。老尽力，尽力一生，年老而力衰。

③ 岂殊众：岂，难道。殊众，不同于众。

④ "物微"二句：马之为物虽微，可是与人的情分很深厚，使我不禁为之感动
　而沉吟起来。沉吟，忧思。

To My Sick Horse

You have been ridden long

Through cold, deep mountain pass.

In dust you toil along,

Sick at year's end, alas!

Is your coat not the same

As others? Meek till now,

You're dearer than your frame.

Can I not be moved? How?

蜀相①

丞相祠堂②何处寻？锦官城外柏森森③。

映阶碧草自春色，隔叶黄鹂空好音。

三顾频烦天下计④，两朝⑤开济老臣心。

出师未捷身先死⑥，长使英雄泪满襟。

---

① 蜀相：三国时期蜀国的丞相诸葛亮，字孔明，山东琅琊（今山东临沂）人，曾辅佐刘备建立蜀国，使三国鼎立局面得以形成。

② 丞相祠堂：《三国志·蜀书》中记载，诸葛亮去世后被葬于定军山上，因山为坟，蜀后主赐谥爵为"忠武侯"，后来又为他立了祠堂，成为"武侯祠"，位于今成都。

③ "锦官"句：锦官城，成都的别称。柏森森，柏树茂盛繁密的样子。

④ "三顾"句：刘备三顾茅庐访诸葛亮，诸葛亮由此出山，此处指这一典故。天下计，指的是诸葛亮《隆中对》中所说东连孙权、北抗曹操、西取刘璋的计划。

⑤ 两朝：刘备、刘禅父子两朝。

⑥ "出师"句：《三国志·蜀书》记载，诸葛亮在刘备去世后，曾出祁山伐魏，想要成就"北定中原，兴复汉室"的大业，但是六出祁山，大业未竟，反而身患重疾，在五丈原军中去世。

Temple of the Premier of Shu

Where is the famous premier's temple to be found?

Outside the Town of Brocade with cypresses around.

In vain before the steps spring grass grows green and long,

And amid the leaves golden orioles sing their song.

Thrice the king visited him for the State's gains and pains;

He served heart and soul the kingdom during two reigns.

But he died before he accomplished his career.

How could heroes not wet their sleeves with tear on tear!

江村

清江①一曲②抱村流，长夏③江村事事幽。

自去自来梁上燕，相亲相近水中鸥。

老妻画纸为棋局，稚子④敲针作钓钩。

但有故人供禄米，微躯⑤此外更何求？

---

① 清江：清澈的江水，指浣花溪。江，指锦江，岷江的支流，在成都西郊的一段称浣花溪。
② 曲：曲折。
③ 长夏：长长的夏日。
④ 稚子：幼小的孩子。
⑤ 微躯：微贱的身体。这是诗人的一种谦辞。

The Riverside Village

See the clear river wind by the village and flow!

We pass the long summer by riverside with ease.

The swallows freely come in and freely out go;

The gulls on water snuggle each other as they please.

My wife draws lines on paper to make a chessboard;

My son bends a needle into a fishing hook.

Ill, I need only medicine I can afford.

What else do I want for myself in my humble nook?

客至 [1]

舍南舍北皆春水，但见群鸥日日来 [2]。

花径不曾缘客扫，蓬门 [3] 今始为君开。

盘飧（sūn）市远无兼味，樽酒家贫只旧醅（pēi） [4]。

肯 [5] 与邻翁相对饮，隔篱呼取 [6] 尽余杯 [7]。

---

① 客至：客指崔明府。明府，县令的美称。

② "舍南"二句：舍，家。但见，只见。此句意为平时交游很少，只有鸥鸟不嫌弃，日日皆能与之相见。

③ 蓬门：用蓬草编成的门户，表达房子的简陋。

④ "盘飧"二句：市远，离市集远。兼味，多种美味佳肴。无兼味，谦言菜少。樽，酒器。旧醅，隔年的陈酒。古人好饮新酒，杜甫以家贫无新酒而深感歉意。

⑤ 肯：能否允许，这是向客人征询。

⑥ 呼取：叫，招呼。

⑦ 余杯：余下来的酒。

For a Guest

North and south of my cottage winds spring water green;

I see but flocks of gulls coming from day to day.

The footpath strewn with fallen blooms is not swept clean;

My wicket gate is opened but for you today.

Far from market, I can afford but simple dish;

Being not rich, I've only old wine for our cup.

To drink together with my neighbor if you wish,

I'll call him o'er the fence to finish the wine up.

春夜喜雨

好雨知①时节，当春乃发生②。

随风潜入夜，润物细无声。

野径③云俱黑，江船火独明。

晓看红湿处，花重锦官城④。

---

① 知：懂得。本诗中可解作适应的意思。
② 发生：萌发，指的是植物的生长。
③ 野径：田野小道，乡间小路。
④ "花重"句：花重，花因沾了雨水，显得饱满沉重的样子。锦官城，位于四
　　川成都。成都盛产蜀锦，诗人做过主持织锦的官，故曰。

Happy Rain on a Spring Night

Good rain knows its time right;

It will fall when comes spring.

With wind it steals in night;

Mute, it wets everthing.

Over wild lanes dark cloud spreads;

In boat a lantern looms.

Dawn sees saturated reds;

The town's heavy with blooms.

茅屋为秋风所破歌

八月秋高^①风怒号^{háo}，卷我屋上三重^{chóng}茅。

茅飞渡江洒江郊，高者挂罥^{juàn}长林梢^②，下者飘转沉塘坳^{ào③}。

南村群童欺我老无力，忍能对面为盗贼^④。

公然抱茅入竹去，唇焦口燥呼不得^⑤，归来倚杖自叹息。

俄顷^{qǐng⑥}风定云墨色，秋天漠漠向昏黑。

---

① 秋高：秋深。

② "高者"句：挂罥，挂着，挂住。罥，挂。长，高。

③ 塘坳：低洼积水的地方，即池塘。塘，一作"堂"。坳，水边低地。

④ "忍能"句：竟忍心这样当面做"贼"。忍能，忍心如此。对面，当面。为，做。

⑤ 呼不得：喝止不住。

⑥ 俄顷：不久，一会儿，顷刻之间。

布衾⁷多年冷似铁，娇儿恶卧踏里裂⁸。

床头屋漏无干处，雨脚如麻未断绝。

自经丧乱⁹少睡眠，长夜沾湿何由彻⁰！

安得广厦千万间⑪，大庇天下寒士俱欢颜⑫！

风雨不动安如山。

呜呼⑬！

何时眼前突兀⑭见⑮此屋，吾庐独破受冻死亦足⑯！

---

⑦ 布衾：布制的被子。衾，被子。
⑧ "娇儿"句：孩子睡相不好，把被里都蹬坏了。恶卧，睡相不好。
⑨ 丧乱：战乱，指安史之乱。
⑩ 何由彻：如何才能挨到天亮。彻，彻晓。
⑪ "安得"句：如何能得到千万间宽敞高大的房子。广厦：宽敞的房屋。
⑫ "大庇"句：普遍地庇护天下贫寒的读书人，让他们开颜欢笑。大庇，全部遮盖、掩护起来。庇，遮盖，掩护。寒士，"士"原指士人，即文化人，此处泛指贫寒的士人们。
⑬ 呜呼：感叹词，表示叹息，相当于"唉"。
⑭ 突兀：高耸的样子，此处形容广厦。
⑮ 见：通"现"，出现。
⑯ 亦足：亦，一作"意"。足，值得。

My Cottage Unroofed by Autumn Gales

In the eighth moon the autumn gales furiously howl;

They roll up three layers of straw from my thatched bower.

The straw flies across the river and spreads in shower,

Some hanging knotted on the tops of trees that tower,

Some swirling down and sinking into water foul.

Urchins from southern village know I'm old and weak;

They rob me to my face without a blush on the cheek,

And holding armfuls of straw, into bamboos they sneak.

In vain I call them till my lips are parched and dry;

Again alone, I lean on my cane and sigh.

Shortly the gale subsides and clouds turn dark as ink;

The autumn skies are shrouded and in darkness sink.

My cotton quilt is cold, for years it has been worn;

My restless children kick in sleep and it is torn.

The roof leaks o'er beds, leaving no corner dry;

Without cease the rain falls thick and fast from the sky.

After the troubled times troubled has been my sleep.

Wet through, how can I pass the night so long, so deep!

Could I get mansions covering ten thousand miles,

I'd house all scholars poor and make them beam with smiles.

In wind and rain these mansions would stand like mountains high.

Alas! Should these houses appear before my eye,

Frozen in my unroofed cot, content I'd die.

赠花卿 [1]

锦城 [2] 丝管 [3] 日纷纷 [4]，半入江风半入云。

此曲只应天上 [5] 有，人间能得几回闻 [6]。

---

① 花卿：指成都尹崔光远的部将花敬定。
② 锦城：即锦官城，今成都。
③ 丝管：此处泛指音乐。
④ 纷纷：形容乐曲轻柔悠扬。
⑤ 天上：虚指天宫，实指皇宫。
⑥ 几回闻：本意是听到几回。文中意指人间很少听到。

To General Hua

With songs from day to day the Town of Silk is loud;

They waft with winds across the streams into the cloud.

Such music can be heard but in celestial spheres.

How many times has it been played for human ears?

戏为六绝句（其二）

王杨卢骆当时体^①，轻薄^②为文哂^{shěn}^③未休。

尔曹^④身与名俱灭，不废^⑤江河万古流。

---

① "王杨"句：王杨卢骆，指王勃、杨炯、卢照邻、骆宾王。这四人都是初唐时期著名的诗人，时人称之为"初唐四杰"。其诗风清新、刚健，一扫齐、梁颓靡遗风。当时体，指四杰诗文的体裁和风格在当时自成一体。

② 轻薄：言行轻佻，有玩弄意味。此处指当时守旧文人对"四杰"的攻击。

③ 哂：讥笑。

④ 尔曹：你们这些人。

⑤ 不废：不影响。此处用江河万古流比喻包括四杰在内的优秀诗人的名字和作品将像江河那样万古流传。

A Playful Quatrain

II

Our four great poets write in a creative way;

You shallow critics may make your remarks unfair.

But your bodies and souls will fall into decay

While their fame will last as the rivers flow forever.

闻官军收河南河北

剑外①忽传收蓟北②，初闻涕泪满衣裳。

却看③妻子愁何在，漫卷诗书喜欲狂④。

白日放歌须⑤纵酒，青春⑥作伴⑦好还乡。

即从巴峡穿巫峡，便下襄阳⑧向洛阳⑨。

---

① 剑外：剑门关以南，此处指四川。

② 蓟北：泛指唐代幽州、蓟州一带，今河北北部地区，是安史叛军的根据地。

③ 却看：回头看。

④ "漫卷"句：胡乱地卷起。诗人意指已经迫不及待地去整理行装准备回家乡。

⑤ 须：应当。

⑥ 青春：指春天的景物。作者想象春季还乡，旅途有宜人景色相伴。

⑦ 作伴：与妻儿一同。

⑧ 襄阳：今属湖北。

⑨ 洛阳：今属河南。

Recapture of the Regions North and South of the Yellow River

'Tis said the Northern Gate is recaptured of late;

When the news reach my ears, my gown is wet with tears.

Staring at my wife's face, of grief I find no trace;

Rolling up my verse books, my joy like madness looks.

Though I am white-haired, still I'd sing and drink my fill.

With verdure spring's aglow, 'tis time we homeward go.

We shall sail all the way through Three Gorges in a day.

Going down to Xiangyang, we'll come up to Luoyang.

绝句

两个黄鹂^①鸣翠柳，一行白鹭^②上青天。

窗含西岭^③千秋雪，门泊东吴^④万里船^⑤。

---

① 黄鹂：黄莺。

② 白鹭：体形似鹤而略小一点，颈、腿都较长，全身羽毛纯白。

③ 西岭：西岭雪山。

④ 东吴：泛指长江下游。

⑤ 万里船：不远万里开来的船只。

A Quatrain

Two golden orioles sing amid the willows green;

A flock of white egrets fly into the blue sky.

310

My window frames the snow-crowned western mountain

scene;

My door off says to eastward-going ships "Goodbye"!

旅夜书怀

细草微风岸，危樯①独夜舟。

星垂平野阔②，月涌③大江④流。

名岂文章著⑤，官应老病休。

飘飘⑥何所似，天地一沙鸥。

---

① 危樯：高竖的桅杆。危，高。樯，船上挂风帆的桅杆。

② "星垂"句：星空低垂，原野显得格外辽阔。

③ 月涌：月亮倒映，随水流涌。

④ 大江：指长江。

⑤ "名岂"句：这句连下句，是以"反言以见意"的手法写的。明明是以文章
而著名的，却偏说不是，可见另有抱负，所以这句是自豪语。休官明明是
因论事见弃，却说不是，说什么老且病，所以这句是自解语了。

⑥ 飘飘：飞翔的样子，借沙鸥写人的漂泊，此处有飘零、漂泊的意思。

Mooring at Night

Riverside grass caressed by wind so light,

A lonely mast seems to pierce lonely night.

The boundless plain fringed with stars hanging low,

The moon surges with the river on the flow.

Will fame ever come to a man of letters

Old, ill, retired, no official life betters?

What do I look like, drifting on so free?

A wild gull seeking shelter on the sea.

八阵图 ①

功盖三分国，名成八阵图。

江流石不转 ②，遗恨失吞吴 ③。

---

① 八阵图：由天、地、风、云、龙、虎、鸟、蛇八种阵势组成的一种作战图，
用以操练军队或作战，是诸葛亮的一项军事创造。一种说法认为八阵图遗
址在夔州（今重庆奉节）永安宫前平沙上。

② 石不转：化用《诗经·邶风·柏舟》中的诗句"我心匪石，不可转也"，表
现事物的不易变更。

③ 吞吴：指吞并吴国的计划。

The Stone Fortress

With his exploits history is crowned;

For the stone fortress he's renowned.

The river flows but stones still stand,

Though he'd not taken back lost land.

秋兴八首（其一）

玉露①凋伤枫树林，巫山巫峡②气萧森。

江间波浪兼天涌③，塞上风云接地阴④。

丛菊两开他日泪⑤，孤舟一系故园⑥心。

寒衣处处催刀尺⑦，白帝城高急暮砧⑧。

---

① 玉露：秋天的霜露，因其白，故以玉喻之。

② 巫山巫峡：即指夔州（今奉节）一带的长江和峡谷。

③ 兼天涌：指波浪滔天。

④ "塞上"句：塞上，指巫山。接地阴，风云盖地。接地，一作匝地。

⑤ "丛菊"句：杜甫此前一年秋天在云安，此年秋天在夔州，从离开成都算
　起，已历两秋，故云"两开"。"开"字双关，一谓菊花开，一谓泪眼开。
　他日，往日，指多年来的艰难岁月。

⑥ 故园：此处指长安。

⑦ 催刀尺：指赶裁冬衣。"处处催"，可见家家皆如此。

⑧ 急暮砧：黄昏时急促的捣衣声。砧，捣衣石。

Ode To Autumn

I

The pearl-like dewdrops wither maples in red dye;

The Gorge and Cliffs of Witch exhale dense fog around.

Waves of upsurging river seem to storm the sky;

Dark clouds o'er mountains touch their shadows on the

ground.

Twice full-blown, asters blown off draw tears from the eye;

Once tied up, lonely boat ties up my heart home-bound,

Thinking of winter robes being made far and nigh,

I hear at dusk but nearby washing blocks fast pound.

登高①

风急天高猿啸哀②，渚③清沙白鸟飞回④。

无边落木萧萧下⑤，不尽长江滚滚来。

万里悲秋常作客⑥，百年⑦多病独登台。

艰难苦恨繁霜鬓⑧，潦倒新停浊酒杯⑨。

① 登高：指农历九月九日重阳节登高。
② 猿啸哀：三峡多猿，啼声凄厉哀切。
③ 渚：水中沙洲。
④ 鸟飞回：因风急所以飞鸟盘旋。
⑤ "无边"句：无边，无边无际。落木，落叶。萧萧，落叶声。
⑥ 客：旅居在外的人，这里是诗人自指。
⑦ 百年：指一生。
⑧ "艰难"句：艰难，指长期漂泊在外所经历的艰难困苦。繁霜鬓，指白发增多。
⑨ "潦倒"句：潦倒，失意、衰颓。新停浊酒杯，诗人因肺病而戒酒。

On the Height

The wind so swift, the sky so wide, apes wail and cry;

Water so clear and beach so white, birds wheel and fly.

The boundless forest sheds its leaves shower by shower;

The endless river rolls its waves hour after hour.

A thousand miles from home, I'm grieved at autumn's

plight;

Ill now and then for years, alone I'm on this height.

Living in times so hard, at frosted hair I pine;

Cast down by poverty, I have to give up wine.

江汉[①]

江汉思归客[②]，乾坤一腐儒[③]。

片云天共远，永夜[④]月同孤。

落日[⑤]心犹壮，秋风病欲苏[⑥]。

古来存老马，不必取长途。

---

① 江汉：长江和汉水之间，位于今湖北江陵一带。

② 思归客：杜甫自谓，因为身在江汉，却时刻思归故乡。

③ "乾坤"句：乾坤，天地间。腐儒，迂腐的儒者，此处指不会迎合世俗的、正直的读书人。

④ 永夜：长夜。

⑤ 落日：借指暮年。此时杜甫五十六岁。

⑥ 病欲苏：病快要好了。苏，康复，复苏。

On River Han

On River Han my home thoughts fly.

Bookworm with worldly ways in fright.

The cloud and I share the vast sky;

I'm lonely as the moon all night.

My heart won't sink with sinking sun;

Autumn wind blows illness away.

A jaded horse may not have done,

Though it cannot go a long way.

登岳阳楼

昔闻洞庭水①，今上岳阳楼②。

吴楚东南坼③，乾坤日夜浮④。

亲朋无一字⑤，老病⑥有孤舟。

戎马关山北⑦，凭轩⑧涕泗流。

---

① 洞庭水：即洞庭湖，位于今湖南省，是我国第二大淡水湖。

② 岳阳楼：位于今湖南省岳阳市，下临洞庭湖。

③ "吴楚"句：辽阔的吴楚两地被洞庭湖一水分割。吴楚即春秋时的吴国和楚国，其大致位于今湖南、湖北、江西、安徽、江苏、浙江一带。坼，分割、分裂，此处指划分。

④ "乾坤"句：日月星辰和大地昼夜都漂浮在洞庭湖上。乾坤，天地，此处指日月。

⑤ 无一字：杳无音信。字，指书信。

⑥ 老病：年老多病。杜甫时年五十七岁，患肺病、风痹、右耳聋，他人生最后的三年大部分时间是在船上度过的。这句是杜甫生活的实况。

⑦ "戎马"句：北方边关战事又起。这年秋冬，吐蕃又侵扰，朝廷震动，调兵抗敌。戎马，借指军事、战乱。

⑧ "凭轩"句：倚着楼窗，眼泪禁不住地流下。涕泗，眼泪和鼻涕，偏义复指，即眼泪。

On Yueyang Tower

Long have I heard of Dongting Lake;

Now I'm on Yueyang Tower's height.

Here Eastern and Southern States break;

Here sun and moon float day and night.

No word comes from kinsfolk and friends;

A boat bears my declining years.

War is raging on the northern ends.

O what can I do but shed tears!

江南逢李龟年^①

岐王^②宅里寻常见，崔九^③堂前几度闻。

正是江南^④好风景，落花时节^⑤又逢君。

---

① 李龟年：唐朝开元、天宝年间的著名乐师，擅长唱歌。因受到唐玄宗的喜爱而红极一时。安史之乱后，李龟年流落江南，以卖艺为生。

② 岐王：唐玄宗李隆基的弟弟，名李范，好学爱才，雅善音律。

③ 崔九：即崔涤，在家中排行第九。玄宗时，曾任殿中监，出入禁中，得玄宗宠幸。崔姓在当时是一家大姓，此处借指李龟年原来受赏识。

④ 江南：今湖南省一带。

⑤ 落花时节：暮春。落花的寓意颇多，比如人衰老飘零、社会的凋敝丧乱等。

Coming across a Disfavored Court Musician on the Southern Shore of the Yangtze River

How oft in princely mansions did we meet!

As oft in lordly halls I heard you sing.

Now the Southern scenery is most sweet,

But I meet you again in parting spring.

岑参

CEN SHEN

作者简介

　　岑参（718—770），荆州江陵（今湖北江陵）人或南阳棘阳（今河南南阳）人，唐代诗人，与高适并称"高岑"。

　　五岁读书，九岁属文。天宝三载（744年），进士及第，守选三年后获授右内率府兵曹参军，后两次从军边塞，先任安西节度使高仙芝幕府掌书记，后在天宝末年任安西北庭节度使封常清幕府判官。唐代宗时，曾任嘉州（今四川乐山）刺史，故世称"岑嘉州"。约大历四年（769年）秋冬之际，卒于成都。

　　工诗，长于七言歌行，对边塞风光，军旅生活，以及异域的文化风俗有亲切的感受，现存边塞诗七十余首，尤多佳作。

白雪歌送武判官归京

北风卷地白草折①，胡天八月即飞雪。

忽如一夜春风来，千树万树梨花开。

散入珠帘湿罗幕②，狐裘不暖锦衾薄③。

将军角弓不得控④，都护铁衣冷犹著⑤。

瀚海阑干⑥百丈冰，愁云惨淡⑦万里凝。

---

① 白草折：白草，西北之地所长，牛马所嗜，干枯时呈白色。折，断。

② "散入"句：珠帘，缀有珠子的门帘。罗幕，用绫罗制作的帷幕。

③ "狐裘"句：狐裘，用狐狸皮做的皮袄。锦衾，用锦缎做的被子。

④ 角弓不得控：角弓，用兽角装饰的弓。控，引、拉。

⑤ "都护"句：都护，镇守边疆的长官。唐代设六都护府，各设大都护一人。著，穿。

⑥ 瀚海阑干：瀚海，沙漠。阑干，纵横的样子。

⑦ 惨淡：昏暗的样子。

中军置酒饮归客[8]，胡琴琵琶与羌笛。

纷纷暮雪下辕门[9]，风掣红旗冻不翻[10]。

轮台[11]东门送君去，去时雪满天山路。

山回路转不见君，雪上空留马行处[12]。

---

⑧ "中军"句：中军，古代分兵为左、中、右三军。中军为主帅亲自统率的军队，此处指主帅的营帐。饮归客，招待归客饮酒。归客在此处指即将回京都的武判官。

⑨ 辕门：军营门。古代军队扎营，用车环围，出入处以两车车辕相向竖立，状如门。

⑩ "风掣"句：掣，拉、牵拽。翻，此处指飘扬的意思。

⑪ 轮台：位于今新疆维吾尔自治区乌鲁木齐市西南。

⑫ 马行处：指雪地上马蹄的痕迹。

Song of White Snow in Farewell to Secretary Wu Going Back to the Capital

Snapping the pallid grass, the northern wind whirls low;

In the eighth moon the Tartar sky is filled with snow.

As if the vernal breeze had come back overnight,

Adorning thousands of pear trees with blossoms white.

Flakes enter pearled blinds and wet the silken screen;

No furs of fox can warm us nor brocade quilts green.

The general cannot draw his rigid bow with ease;

E'en the commissioner in coat of mail would freeze.

A thousand feet o'er cracked wilderness ice piles.

And gloomy clouds hang sad and drear for miles and miles.

We drink in headquarters to our guest homeward bound;

With Tartar lutes, pipas and pipes the camps resound.

Snow in huge flakes at dusk falls heavy on camp gate;

The frozen red flag in the wind won't undulate.

At eastern gate of Wheel Tower we bid goodbye

On the snow-covered road to Heaven's Mountain high.

I watch his horse go past a bend and, lost to sight,

His track will soon be buried up by snow in flight.

走马川①行奉送封大夫②出师西征③

君不见走马川，雪海④边，平沙莽莽黄入天⑤。

轮台⑥九月风夜吼，一川碎石大如斗，随风满地石乱走。

匈奴草黄马正肥，金山⑦西见烟尘飞，汉家大将⑧西出师。

---

① 走马川：又名左末河，即今新疆维吾尔自治区车尔成河。
② 封大夫：封常清，唐代将领。天宝十三载（754年）受命为北庭都护、伊西节度、瀚海军使，奏请岑参为节度判官。这年冬，封常清西征播仙部族，岑参写此诗送行。
③ 西征：一作"西行"。
④ 雪海：指西北苦寒之地。
⑤ "平沙"句：莽莽，无边无际。黄入天，形容黄沙弥漫，与天相接。
⑥ 轮台：今新疆维吾尔自治区米泉区境。
⑦ 金山：今新疆维吾尔自治区阿尔泰山。
⑧ 汉家大将：指封常清。

将军金甲夜不脱，半夜军行戈相拨^⑨，风头如刀面如割。
马毛带雪汗气蒸^⑩，五花连钱旋作冰^⑪，幕中草檄^{xí}^⑫砚水凝。
虏骑^⑬闻之应胆慑，料知短兵不敢接^⑭，车师^⑮西门伫献捷。

⑨ 拨：撞击。
⑩ 蒸：蒸发。
⑪ "五花"句：五花，开元天宝年间，社会上最考究马的装饰，常把马的鬃毛剪成花瓣形，剪三瓣的叫三花马，剪五瓣的叫五花马。连钱，指马斑驳的毛色。旋，马上。
⑫ 草檄：起草声讨敌人的檄文。
⑬ 虏骑：指播仙部族的骑兵。
⑭ "料知"句：短兵，指刀、剑类的短武器。接，接战、交战。
⑮ 车师：一作"军师"。车师为唐安西都护府所在地，位于今新疆维吾尔自治区吐鲁番市。

Song of the Running Horse River in Farewell to General Feng on His Western Expedition

Do you not see the Running Horse River flow

Along the sea of snow

And the sand that's yellowed sky and earth high and low?

In the ninth moon at Wheel Tower winds howl at night;

The river fills with boulders fallen from the height;

With howling winds they run riot as if in flight.

When grass turns yellow and plump Hunnish horses neigh,

West of Mount Gold dusts rise, the foe in proud array.

Our general leads his army on his westward way.

He keeps his iron armor on the whole night long,

Spears dang at midnight when his army march along,

Their faces cut by winds that blow so sharp and strong.

Their sweat and snow turn into steam on horse's mane,

Which soon on horse's back turns into ice again;

Ink freezes when challenge's written before campaign.

On hearing this, the foe with fear should palpitate.

Dare they cross swords with our brave men in iron plate?

We'll wait for news of victory at the western gate.

山房春事二首（其二）

梁园^①日暮乱飞鸦，极目^②萧条^③三两家。

庭树不知人去尽，春来还发^④旧时花。

① 梁园：兔园，俗名竹园，西汉梁孝王刘武所建，位于今河南商丘。园中有
百灵山、落猿岩、栖龙岫、雁池、鹤洲、凫渚，宫观相连，奇果佳树，错
杂其间，珍禽异兽，出没其中。
② 极目：尽目而望。
③ 萧条：冷落荒凉。
④ 发：绽放。

Spring in a Deserted Garden

II

What riot do crows run, veiling the setting sun!

As far as eyes can see, there're two houses or three.

The garden trees don't know all men gone but the crow;

In full bloom they appear as when spring came last year.

逢入京使^①

故园^②东望路漫漫^③，双袖龙钟^④泪不干。

马上相逢无纸笔，凭^⑤君传语报平安。

---

① 入京使：回京城的使者。
② 故园：家乡，指长安和自己在长安的家。
③ 漫漫：遥远的样子。
④ 龙钟：涕泪淋漓的样子，此处指沾湿的样子。
⑤ 凭：烦，请。

On Meeting a Messenger Going to the Capital

I look eastward, long, long my homeward road appears.

My old arms tremble and my sleeves are wet with tears.

Meeting you on horseback, with what brush can I write?

I can but ask you to tell my kin I'm all right.

贾至

JIA ZHI

作者简介

贾至（718—772），字幼邻，唐代文学家，贾曾之子。

天宝初，以校书郎、单父县尉，与高适、独孤及等交游。安史乱起，随玄宗奔四川。乾元元年（758年）春，出为汝州刺史，后贬岳州司马，与李白相遇，有诗酬唱。

以文著称，甚受中唐古文作家独孤及、梁肃等推崇。其父贾曾和他都曾为朝廷掌执文笔。玄宗受命册文为贾曾所撰，而传位册文则是贾至手笔。玄宗赞叹"两朝盛典出卿家父子手，可谓继美"。韩愈弟子皇甫湜说："贾常侍之文，如高冠华簪，曳裾鸣玉，立于廊庙，非法不言，可以望为羽仪，资以道义。"指出了贾文典雅华赡的风格特点。也有诗名，其诗风格如其文。

初至巴陵^①与李十二白、裴九^②同泛洞庭湖三首（其二）

枫岸纷纷落叶多，洞庭秋水^③晚来波。

乘兴^④轻舟无近远，白云明月吊湘娥^⑤。

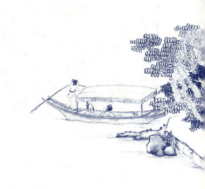

---

① 巴陵：今湖南省岳阳市。

② 李十二白：即李白。裴九，即裴隐。题中的数字是李白和裴隐在家族兄弟中的排行，当时流行这样的称谓。

③ 秋水：秋天的江水、湖水。

④ 乘兴：趁一时高兴，兴会所至。

⑤ 湘娥：即舜帝的妃子娥皇和女英。相传二人投湘水而死，故为湘水之神。

Boating with Li Bai and Pei Di on Lake Dongting

II

Shower by shower fall lakeside maple leaves drear;

Lake Dongting's rippled by autumn breeze towards night.

We sail at will, careless if we've gone far or near,

To mourn o'er Beauties drowned with the moon and clouds

white.

刘方平

LIU
FANGPING

作者简介

刘方平，生卒年不详，洛阳（今河南洛阳）人，匈奴族。

天宝前期曾应进士试，又欲从军，均未如意，从此隐居颍水、汝河之滨，终身未仕。与皇甫冉、元德秀、李颀、严武为诗友，为萧颖士赏识。

工诗，善画山水。其诗多咏物写景之作，尤擅绝句，其诗多写闺情、乡思，善于寓情于景，意蕴无穷。

月夜

更深月色半人家^①，北斗阑干^②南斗^③斜。

今夜偏知^④春气暖，虫声新透^⑤绿窗纱。

---

① "更深"句：更深，古时计算时间，一夜分成五更。更深，夜深了。月色半人家，月光只照亮了人家房屋的一半，另一半隐藏在黑暗里。

② 阑干：此处指横斜的样子。

③ 南斗：位于北斗星以南，形似斗，故称"南斗"，南斗有星六颗。

④ 偏知：才知，表示出乎意料。

⑤ 新透：第一次透过。新，初。

A Moonlit Night

The moon has painted half the room at dead of night;

The slanting Plough and Southern stars shed their dim light.

I can feel in the air the warm breath of new spring.

For through my window screen I hear the crickets sing.

春怨

纱窗日落渐黄昏，金屋①无人见泪痕。

寂寞空庭②春欲③晚，梨花满地不开门④。

① 金屋：原指汉武帝幼时欲金屋藏阿娇事，此处指妃嫔所住的华丽宫殿。
② 空庭：幽寂的庭院。
③ 欲：一作"又"。
④ 不开门：指没人开门。

Loneliness

Out of the window wanes twilight of parting day;

None sees her dry her furtive tears in gilded hall.

In lonely courtyard even spring will pass away;

She won't open the door but lets pear blossoms fall.

司空曙

SIKONG SHU

作者简介

司空曙（720—790），字文初，广平（今河北永年）人，唐代诗人。

大历年间进士。韦皋为剑南节度使，曾召入幕府。累官左拾遗，终水部郎中。为人磊落有奇才，与李约为至交。他是"大历十才子"之一，同时期作家有卢纶、钱起、韩翃等。

其诗多幽凄情调，间写乱后的心情。诗中常有好句，如后世传诵的"乍见翻疑梦，相悲各问年"，像是不很着力，却是常人心中所有。

江村即事 ①

钓罢归来不系船②，江村月落正堪眠③。

纵然一夜风吹去，只在芦花浅水边。

347

---

① 即事：以当前的事物为题材所作之诗。

② 不系船：《庄子》曰"巧者劳而智者忧，无能者无所求，饱食而遨游，泛若不系之舟"，古人以"不系之舟"为无为思想的象征。

③ 正堪眠：正是睡觉的好时候。堪，可以，能够。

Reverie in a Riverside Village

Coming back from fishing, I don't fasten my boat;

The moon sinks o'er riverside village — time to sleep.

What if the breeze at night should set my skiff afloat?

It's still amid the reeds, where water is not deep.

留卢秦卿

知有前期^①在，难分此夜中。

无将^②故人酒，不及石尤风^③。

---

① 前期：指友人定好了再次约会的日期。
② 无将：不要回绝。
③ 石尤风：指能阻止船只航行的顶头逆风。

Farewell to a Friend

Although I know that we shall meet again,

How can we bear to part on such a night?

Do you think wine and friendship can't retain

You here longer than an adverse wind might?

钱起

QIAN QI

作者简介

钱起（722—780），字仲文，吴兴（今浙江湖州）人，唐代诗人。

早年数次赴试落第，唐天宝十载（751年）进士。初为秘书省校书郎、蓝田县尉，后任司勋员外郎、考功郎中、翰林学士等。曾任考功郎中，故世称"钱考功"，与韩翃、李端、卢纶等号称"大历十才子"。

其诗多为赠别应酬，流连光景、粉饰太平之作，与社会现实相距较远。然其诗具有较高的艺术水平，风格清空闲雅、流丽纤秀，尤长于写景，为大历诗风的杰出代表。

归雁①

潇湘何事等闲回②，水碧沙明两岸苔③。

二十五弦④弹夜月，不胜清怨却飞来⑤。

---

① 归雁：指北归的大雁。

② "潇湘"句：潇湘，潇水和湘水在今湖南省永州市芝山区北合流后的统称，位于洞庭湖南面。何事，即何故，什么原因。等闲，无端，轻易，随便。

③ 苔：一种植物，鸟类的食物，雁尤喜食。

④ 二十五弦：指弦乐器瑟。《史记·封禅书》载："或曰：'太帝使素女鼓五十弦瑟，悲，帝禁不止，故破其瑟为二十五弦。'"

⑤ "不胜"句：不胜，忍受不了。清怨，此处指曲调凄清哀怨。却，仍，还。

To the Returning Wild Geese

Why will you stay on South River no more,

With blue water, bright sand and mossy shore?

The moonbeams play on twenty-five sad strings.

Can you not bear the grief the zither brings?

顾况

GU KUANG

作者简介

顾况，生卒年不详，字逋翁，自号华阳真逸（一说华阳真隐），苏州海盐县（今浙江海盐）人。唐代诗人、画家、鉴赏家。

一生官位不高，曾任著作郎，因作诗嘲讽权贵，贬为饶州司户。

工于诗，继承杜甫的现实主义传统，是新乐府诗歌运动的先驱。

宫词五首（其二）

玉楼^①天半起笙歌，风送宫嫔笑语和。

月殿影开闻夜漏^②，水晶帘卷近秋河^③。

---

① 玉楼：华丽的高楼，此处指宫嫔的居所。
② 闻夜漏：指夜深。漏，古代滴水计时的工具。
③ 秋河：指银河。

A Palace Poem

II

From the jade bower songs float halfway up the sky;

The wind carries the palace maids' gay voices high.

The moon is slanting, drips of water-clock are heard;

The screen uprolled, the weaver's seen far from the

cowherd.

张

继

ZHANG JI

作者简介

张继，字懿孙，湖北襄州（今湖北襄阳）人，唐代诗人。

其诗爽朗激越，不事雕琢，比兴幽深，事理双切，对后世颇有影响。最著名的诗是《枫桥夜泊》。

枫桥^①夜泊^②

月落乌啼霜满天，江枫渔火对愁眠。

姑苏^③城外寒山寺^④，夜半钟声^⑤到客船。

---

① 枫桥：位于今江苏省苏州市枫桥镇，原名"封桥"，因张继此诗而改名为"枫桥"。
② 夜泊：夜间把船停靠在岸边。
③ 姑苏：今苏州。苏州市西南有姑苏山，故得名。
④ 寒山寺：位于今苏州，枫桥附近，寺建于南朝梁代，原名妙利普明塔院。相传唐初著名高僧寒山曾在此居住，故而名寒山寺。
⑤ 夜半钟声：当时寺院有半夜敲钟的习惯，多见于唐代诗人的吟咏。

Mooring By Maple Bridge At Night

The crows at moonset cry, streaking the frosty sky ;

Facing dim fishing boats neath maples, sad I lie.

Beyond the city wall, from Temple of Cold Hill

Bells break the ship-borne roamer's dream in midnight still.

韩

HAN HONG 翃

作者简介

韩翃，生卒年不详，字君平，南阳（今河南南阳）人，唐代诗人。与钱起等诗人齐名，时称"大历十才子"。

天宝十三载（754年）考中进士，宝应年间在淄青节度使侯希逸幕府中任从事，后随侯希逸回朝，闲居长安十年。建中年间，因作一首《寒食》而被唐德宗所赏识，晋升不断，最终官至中书舍人。

其诗笔法轻巧，写景别致，在当时传诵很广泛。

寒食

春城①无处不飞花，寒食②东风御柳③斜④^{xiá}。

日暮汉宫⑤传蜡烛⑥，轻烟散入五侯⑦家。

---

① 春城：暮春时的长安城。

② 寒食：古代在清明节前两天的节日，禁火三日，只吃冷食，所以称寒食。

③ 御柳：御苑之柳，即皇城中的柳树。

④ 斜：与花、家押韵。

⑤ 汉宫：此处指唐朝皇宫。

⑥ 传蜡烛：寒食节普天下禁火，但权贵宠臣可得到皇帝恩赐的燃烛。

⑦ 五侯：汉成帝封王皇后的五个兄弟王谭、王商、王立、王根、王逢时为侯，
   受到特别的恩宠。此处泛指天子近幸之臣。

Cold Food Day

Nowhere in vernal town but sweet flowers fly down;

Riverside willow trees slant in the eastern breeze.

At dusk the palace sends privilege candles red

To the five lordly mansions where wreaths of smoke spread.

韦应物

WEI
YINGWU

作者简介

　　韦应物，生卒年不详，字义博，京兆杜陵（今陕西西安）人，唐代山水田园诗派诗人，世称"韦苏州""韦左司""韦江州"。

　　出身京兆韦氏逍遥公房，以门荫入仕，起家右千牛备身，出任栎阳县令，迁比部郎中，加朝散大夫。外放治理滁州、江州刺史，检校左司郎中、苏州刺史等职。

　　其诗风澄澹精致，诗歌内容丰富，风格独特，影响深远，后人每以"王（王维）孟（孟浩然）韦柳（柳宗元）"并称。有《韦江州集》《韦苏州诗集》《韦苏州集》传世。

秋夜寄邱员外^①

怀君属^②秋夜，散步咏凉天。

空山松子落，幽人^③应未眠。

---

① 邱员外：名丹，苏州人，曾任尚书郎，后隐居平山上。一作"邱二十二
员外"。

② 属：正值，适逢，恰好。

③ 幽人：幽居隐逸的人，悠闲的人，此处指邱员外。

To a Hermit on an Autumn Night

Strolling when autumn night is still,

I think of you and softly sing.

As pine cones fall in empty hill,

Hermit, you must be listening.

滁州^① 西涧^②

<ruby>滁<rt>chú</rt></ruby>

独怜^③幽草涧边生，上有黄鹂^④深树鸣。

春潮带雨晚来急，野渡^⑤无人舟自横^⑥。

366

---

① 滁州：今安徽省滁州市。

② 西涧：滁州城西郊的一条小溪，即今天的西涧湖（原滁州城西水库）。

③ 独怜：唯独喜欢，指对幽草的独情。

④ 黄鹂：即黄莺。

⑤ 野渡：荒郊野外无人管理的渡口。

⑥ 自横：指随意漂浮。

On the West Stream at Chuzhou

Alone, I like the riverside where green grass grows

And golden orioles sing amid the leafy trees.

When showers fall at dusk, the river overflows;

A lonely boat athwart the ferry floats at ease.

耿湋

GENG WEI

作者简介

耿湋，字洪源，河东（今山西）人，唐代诗人。

一生久经离乱，所经过的地方比较广，到过辽海，到过西北，时代的纷乱与他个人的遭际使他的诗篇带上感伤色彩。其诗以清淡质朴见长，不深琢削，而风格自胜。

秋日

反照①入闾巷②，忧来与谁语③。

古道无④人行，秋风动禾黍⑤。

---

① 反照：即返照，夕阳的反光。

② 闾巷：里巷，乡里。

③ "忧来"句：一作"愁来谁共语"。

④ 无：一作"少"。

⑤ 禾黍：禾与黍，泛指黍稷稻麦等粮食作物。

A Lonely Autumn Day

Over the lane slants the sun;

I'm grieved but can tell none.

3
7
0

On ancient way none goes;

Over cornfields west wind blows.

卢纶

LU LUN

作者简介

卢纶（739—799），字允言，河中蒲县（今山西永济）人，唐代诗人，"大历十才子"之一。

唐玄宗天宝末年举进士，遇乱不第；唐代宗朝又应举，屡试不第。大历六年（771年）经宰相元载举荐，授阌乡尉；后由宰相王缙荐为集贤学士，秘书省校书郎，升监察御史。出为陕州户曹、河南密县令。之后元载、王缙获罪，遭到牵连。唐德宗朝，复为昭应县令，出任河中元帅浑瑊府判官。

其诗风较为粗犷雄放，军旅边塞诗写得极有生气，为"大历十才子"其他诗人所难及。

塞下曲（四首）①

一

鹫翎②金仆姑③，燕尾④绣蝥^{máo}弧⑤。

独立扬新令⑥，千营共一呼。

二

林暗草惊风⑦，将军夜引弓⑧。

平明⑨寻白羽⑩，没⑪在石棱⑫中。

---

① 塞下曲：古时边塞的一种军歌。
② 鹫翎：鹰的羽毛。鹫，大鹰。翎，羽毛。
③ 金仆姑：箭名，尤指神箭。
④ 燕尾：旗上的飘带。
⑤ 蝥弧：旗名。
⑥ 扬新令：扬旗下达新指令。
⑦ 惊风：突然被风吹动。
⑧ 引弓：拉弓、开弓，这里包含下一步的射箭。
⑨ 平明：天刚亮的时候。
⑩ 白羽：箭杆后部的白色羽毛，这里指箭。
⑪ 没：陷入，这里是钻进的意思。
⑫ 石棱：石头的边角。

三

月黑[13]雁飞高，单于[14]夜遁[15]逃。

欲将[16]轻骑[17]逐[18]，大雪满弓刀。

四

野幕敞[19]琼筵[20]，羌戎贺劳旋。

醉和金甲舞，雷鼓[21]动山川。

---

[13] 月黑：没有月光。

[14] 单于：匈奴的首领。

[15] 遁：逃走。

[16] 将：率领。

[17] 轻骑：轻装快速的骑兵。

[18] 逐：追赶。

[19] 敞：一作"蔽"。

[20] 琼筵：盛宴。

[21] 雷鼓：即擂鼓。

Border Songs

I

His arrow tuft'd with vulture feather,

His pennon shaped like swallowtail.

He gives an order out;

Together a thousand battalions shout, "Hail!"

II

In gloomy woods grass shivers at wind's howl;

The general takes it for a tiger's growl.

He shoots and looks for his arrow next morn

Only to find a rock pierced amid the thorn.

III

Wild geese fly high in moonless night;

The Tartars through the dark take flight.

Our horsemen chase them, armed with bow

And sword covered with heavy snow.

IV

Let sumptuous banquet in the wild be spread!

Let tribesmen give the victors warm welcome!

Let's dance in golden armor, drunk and fed!

Let mountains tremble at thunderous drum!

李益

LI YI

作者简介

李益（746—829），字君虞，陇西狄道（今甘肃临洮）人，后迁河南洛阳，唐代诗人。

大历四年（769年）进士，初任郑县尉，久不得升迁，建中四年（783年）登书判拔萃科。初因仕途失意，后弃官在燕赵一带漫游。后官至幽州营田副使、检校吏部员外郎，迁检校考功郎中，加御史中丞，为右散骑常侍。太和初年，以礼部尚书致仕。

以边塞诗作出名，擅长绝句，尤其是七言绝句。

喜见外弟^①又言别

十年^②离乱^③后，长大^④一相逢。

问姓惊初见，称名忆旧容^⑤。

别来沧海事^⑥，语罢暮天钟^⑦。

明日巴陵^⑧道，秋山又几重。

---

① 外弟：指表弟。古代称呼比自己小的姑姑、舅舅、姨比自己小的的儿子为外弟。

② 十年：指唐代天宝十四载（755年）至宝应二年（763年）之间的安史之乱。
　"十年"是举其成数而言之。

③ 离乱：指诗人与表弟因安史之乱而分离。

④ 长大：指成人。

⑤ 旧容：过去的容貌。

⑥ 沧海事：指变化剧烈、巨大的世事。

⑦ 暮天钟：指傍晚时的钟声。

⑧ 巴陵：地名，位于今湖南省岳阳市。

Meeting and Parting with My Cousin

We parted young for ten long years;

Not till grown up do we meet again.

At first I think a stranger appears;

Your name reminds me of your face then.

We talk of changes night and day

Until we hear the evening bell.

Tomorrow you'll go southward way

Over autumn hills, O, farewell!

宫怨

露湿晴花春殿香，月明歌吹在昭阳①。

似将②海水添宫漏③，共滴长门④一夜长。

---

① 昭阳：汉宫殿名，后泛指后妃所住的宫殿。

② 似将：好似将用。

③ 宫漏：宫中计时器，用铜壶滴漏，故称宫漏。

④ 长门：汉宫名。后人以"长门"指失宠女子居住的寂寥凄清的宫院。

Grief of a Palace Maid

Spring palace fragrant with sweet flowers wet with dew

Is ringing with flute songs when the moon's shining bright.

The water-clock seems filled up with the ocean blue

To make the night appear for me an endless night.

夜上受降城^①闻笛

<small>xiáng</small>

回乐峰^②前沙似雪，受降城外月如霜。

不知何处吹芦管^③，一夜征人尽望乡。

---

① 受降城：位于灵州（今宁夏回族自治区灵武县西南）州治所在地回乐县。
  在唐代，这里是防御突厥、吐蕃的前线。贞观二十年（646年），唐太宗曾
  经亲临灵州接受突厥一部的投降，故称灵州为"受降城"。

② 回乐峰：唐代设有回乐县，灵州治所。一作"回乐烽"，指回乐县附近的烽
  火台。

③ 芦管：题中之"笛"。

On Hearing a Flute at Night Atop the Victor's Wall

Before the beacon tower sand looks white as snow;

Beyond the Victor's Wall like frost cold moonbeams flow.

None knows from where a flute blows a nostalgic song;

All warriors lie awake homesick the whole night long.

江南曲^①

嫁得瞿塘贾^②，朝朝误妾期。

早知潮有信^③，嫁与弄潮儿^④。

---

① 江南曲：古代歌曲名，乐府《相和歌》曲名。这是一首拟乐府，写得很有
  民歌色彩。
② 瞿塘贾：在长江上游一带做买卖的商人。瞿塘，瞿塘峡，长江三峡之一。
  贾，商人。
③ 潮有信：潮水涨落有一定的时间，叫"潮信"。
④ 弄潮儿：潮水涨时戏水的人，或指潮水来时，乘船入江的人。

A Southern Song

Since I became a merchant's wife,

I've in his absence passed my life.

A sailor comes home with the tide;

I should have been a sailor's bride.

戎昱

RONG YU

作者简介

　　戎昱（744—800），荆州（今湖北江陵）人，郡望扶风（今陕西），唐代诗人。

　　少年举进士落第，游名都山川，后中进士。宝应元年（762年），从滑州、洛阳西行，经华阴，遇见王季友，同赋《苦哉行》。大历二年（767年）秋回故乡，在荆南节度使卫伯玉幕府中任从事。后流寓湖南，为潭州刺史崔瓘、桂州刺史李昌巙幕僚。建中三年（782年）居长安，任侍御史。翌年贬为辰州刺史。后又任虔州刺史。晚年在湖南零陵任职，流寓桂州而终。

　　其诗多注重反映现实，语言清丽婉朴，铺陈。描写的手法多样，意境悲气纵横（诗中常有"愁""泪""哭""啼""悲""涕"等字）。

移家^①别湖上亭

好是春风湖上亭，柳条藤蔓系离情。

黄莺久住浑^②相识，欲别频啼^③四五声。

---

① 移家：搬家。

② 浑：全。

③ 频啼：连续鸣叫。

Leaving the Lakeside Pavilion While Moving House

I love the lakeside pavilion in vernal breeze;

My sleeves are twined by twigs of weeping willow trees.

The orioles there nesting seem to know my heart;

They warble "Forget me not" songs before I part.

雍裕之

YONG
YUZHI

作者简介

雍裕之，字与号、生平、生卒年均不详。有诗名，工乐府，极有情致。《新唐书·艺文志》辑有其诗一卷遂传于世。

江边柳

袅袅[①]古堤边，青青一树烟。

若为[②]丝不断，留取系郎船。

---

① 袅袅：形容垂柳随风摆动时的样子。

② 若为：倘若。

To the Riverside Willow

Your long, long branches wave by riverside,

Your green, green leaves like wreaths of smoke afloat.

390

"Make ropes unbreakable of them," she sighed,

"To tie up my beloved ones parting boat!"

韩

愈

HAN YU

作者简介

韩愈（768—824），字退之，河南河阳（今河南孟州）人，自称"郡望昌黎"，世称"韩昌黎""昌黎先生"。唐代文学家、思想家、哲学家、政治家、教育家。

元和十二年（817年）出任宰相裴度的行军司马，参与讨平"淮西之乱"。其后又因谏迎佛骨一事被贬至潮州。晚年官至吏部侍郎，人称"韩吏部"。长庆四年（824年）病逝，追赠礼部尚书，谥号"文"，故称"韩文公"。元丰元年（1078年），追封昌黎伯，并从祀孔庙。

唐代古文运动的倡导者，被后人尊为"唐宋八大家"之首，与柳宗元并称"韩柳"，有"文章巨公"和"百代文宗"之名。后人将其与柳宗元、欧阳修和苏轼合称"千古文章四大家"。他提出的"文道合一""气盛言宜""务去陈言""文从字顺"等散文的写作理论，对后人很有指导意义。

八月十五夜赠张功曹

纤云四卷天无河，清风吹空月舒波^①。

沙平水息声影绝，一杯相属^②君当歌。

君歌声酸辞且苦，不能听终泪如雨。

洞庭连天九疑^③高，蛟龙出没猩鼯^④号。

十生九死到官所，幽居默默如藏逃。

下床畏蛇食畏药^⑤，海气^⑥湿蛰熏腥臊。

昨者州前捶大鼓，嗣皇继圣登夔皋。

赦书一日行万里，罪从大辟皆除死^⑦。

---

① 月舒波：月光四射。
② 属：劝酒。
③ 九疑：山名，位于今湖南省永州市宁远县。
④ 鼯：鼠类的一种，状如小狐，像蝙蝠，有翅能飞，声如人呼。
⑤ 药：指蛊毒。
⑥ 海气：卑湿的空气。
⑦ 大辟皆除死：大辟，死刑。除死，免去死刑。

迁者追回流者还，涤瑕荡垢清朝班。

州家申名使家抑[8]，坎轲只得移荆蛮。

判司卑官不堪说，未免捶楚[9]尘埃间。

同时辈流多上道[10]，天路[11]幽险难追攀。

君歌且休听我歌，我歌今与君殊科[12]。

一年明月今宵多，人生由命非由他。

有酒不饮奈明何。

---

⑧ "州家"句：州家，刺史。申名，将名字报告上去。使家，观察使。抑，压住不报。

⑨ 捶楚：棒杖一类的刑具。

⑩ 上道：指上路回京。

⑪ 天路：指进身于朝廷之途。

⑫ 殊科：不同的意思。此句别本作"我今与君岂殊科"。

To a Disgraced Official on Moon Festival

Fine clouds uprolled, the River of Stars disappears;

Moonbeams flow in waves when wind blows clouds off the

spheres.

No sound nor shade on still water and level sand,

I ask you to drink and sing with wine cup in hand.

But bitter is your voice, melancholy your strain;

Before you end your song, my tears fall down like rain.

"Lake Dongting meets the sky and nine peaks tower high;

Dragons and crocodiles fly; apes and foxes cry.

At a nine-to-one risk of death I reached my post;

As if hidden from woe, in loneliness I'm lost.

I fear poison in food and snakes under my bed;

Putrid air from the lake and musty odor spread.

The county's heavy drumbeats announced yesterday

The new emperor's reign with a brilliant array.

Pardon ran thousands of miles a day out of breath;

The edict e'en commutes the punishment of death.

The exiled are recalled to the imperial town;

Those who prove guiltless may come back to serve the crown.

My name was sent in but I was given no grace,

So I'm only transferred to this primitive place.

My rank is very low and what can I tell you?

When anything goes wrong, punishment is my due.

Most of the exiled are now on their homeward way;

The road to Heaven's full of risks. What can I say?"

Please stop your song and listen to that of my mind!

Do you think my song is of a different kind?

Tonight of all the year is the brightest moonshine.

To propose is human but to dispose divine.

What shall we do if we don't drink when we have wine?

左迁①至蓝关②示侄孙湘

一封朝奏九重天③，夕贬潮州路④八千。

欲为圣明除弊事，肯将衰朽惜残年⑤。

云横秦岭⑥家何在，雪拥蓝关马不前。

知汝⑦远来应有意，好收吾骨瘴江⑧边。

---

① 左迁：降职，贬官，此处指作者被贬到潮州。

② 蓝关：蓝田关，位于今陕西省蓝田县南。

③ 九重天：借指皇帝。

④ 潮州路：指潮阳郡，今广东省汕头市潮阳区。

⑤ "欲为"二句：想替皇帝除去有害的事，哪能因衰老就吝惜残余的生命。
肯，岂肯、怎么能够。将，因为。惜残年，顾惜老年的生命。

⑥ 秦岭：秦岭山脉，位于今蓝田县东南。

⑦ 汝：你，指代韩湘。韩湘，韩愈之侄韩老成的长子，长庆三年进士，任大
理丞。韩湘此时二十七岁，尚未登科及第，远道赶来从韩愈南迁。

⑧ 瘴江：指潮州附近的韩江，是有名的瘴疠之地。

Written for My Grandnephew at the Blue Pass

To the Celestial Court a proposal was made,

And I am banished eight thousand li away.

To undo the misdeeds I would have given aid.

Dare I have spared myself with powers in decay?

The Ridge veiled in barred clouds, where can my home be seen?

The Blue Pass clad in snow, my horse won't forward go.

You have come from afar and I know what you mean:

Not to leave my bones there where miastic waves flow.

步辇图（局部） 〔唐〕阎立本

宫乐图（局部）〔唐〕佚名

千岩万壑图（局部） 【唐】王维

蓬莱飞雪图（局部）　〔唐〕杨升

诗之巅峰，传诵古今

只此唐诗

许渊冲英译唯美唐诗（下）

许渊冲 —————— 编译

读者出版社

目录

CONTENTS

● 张　籍　ZHANG JI

　　002　节妇吟寄东平
　　　　　李司空师道

● 王　建　WANG JIAN

　　005　望夫石
　　007　新嫁娘词三首
　　　　　（其三）

● 张仲素　ZHANG ZHONGSU

　　010　春闺思
　　012　燕子楼诗三首

● 刘禹锡　LIU YUXI

　　016　酬乐天扬州初逢
　　　　　席上见赠
　　019　秋风引
　　021　竹枝词三首
　　025　石头城
　　027　乌衣巷
　　029　和乐天春词
　　031　望洞庭
　　033　饮酒看牡丹
　　035　柳枝词

● 白居易　BAI JUYI

　　038　买花
　　042　上阳白发人
　　047　卖炭翁
　　051　长恨歌
　　066　琵琶行
　　078　花非花
　　080　赋得古原草送别
　　082　惜牡丹花
　　084　燕子楼三首

　　087　大林寺桃花
　　089　问刘十九
　　091　后宫词
　　093　暮江吟
　　095　钱塘湖春行
　　097　白云泉
　　099　病中

● 羊士谔　YANG SHI'E

　　102　登楼

● 柳宗元　LIU ZONGYUAN

　　105　登柳州城楼寄漳汀
　　　　　封连四州刺史
　　107　江雪
　　109　渔翁
　　111　饮酒

● 崔　护　CUI HU

　　115　题都城南庄

● 元　稹　YUAN ZHEN

　　118　遣悲怀三首
　　123　行宫
　　125　菊花
　　127　离思五首（其四）

● 贾　岛　JIA DAO

　　130　剑客
　　132　题兴化寺园亭
　　134　寻隐者不遇

● 李　绅　LI SHEN

　　137　悯农二首

● 薛　涛　XUE TAO

140　春望词四首
144　酬人雨后玩竹
146　寄旧诗与元微之

● 张　祜　ZHANG HU

149　何满子
151　赠内人
153　集灵台二首（其二）
155　题金陵渡

● 李　涉　LI SHE

158　再宿武关

● 崔　郊　CUI JIAO

161　赠婢

● 李　贺　LI HE

164　雁门太守行
166　苏小小墓
168　梦天
170　天上谣
173　浩歌
177　秋来
179　秦王饮酒
183　南园十三首（选五）
188　金铜仙人辞汉歌
　　　并序
192　马诗二十三首
　　　（选四）
196　相和歌辞·神弦曲
198　将进酒
200　官街鼓

● 许　浑　XU HUN

203　咸阳城西楼晚眺
205　塞下曲
207　谢亭送别

● 徐　凝　XU NING

210　忆扬州

● 杜　牧　DU MU

213　过华清宫三首
　　　（其一）
215　将赴吴兴登乐游原
　　　一绝
217　题扬州禅智寺
219　江南春
221　题宣州开元寺水阁
223　登池州九峰楼
　　　寄张祜
225　九日齐山登高
227　齐安郡中偶题二首
　　　（其一）
229　惜春
231　赤壁
233　泊秦淮
235　赠别二首
237　遣怀
239　山行
241　秋夕
243　金谷园
245　清明

● 雍　陶　YONG TAO

248　题情尽桥

● 朱庆馀　ZHU QINGYU

251　宫词
253　近试上张水部

● 温庭筠　WEN TINGYUN

256　过分水岭
258　商山早行

● 李商隐　LI SHANGYIN

261　锦瑟
263　重过圣女祠
265　赠刘司户蕡
267　乐游原
269　北齐二首
271　夜雨寄北
273　风雨
275　寄令狐郎中
277　杜司勋
279　杜工部蜀中离席
281　隋宫二首
284　二月二日
286　筹笔驿
288　无题
290　无题二首（其一）
292　无题二首
296　无题四首（选三）
301　柳
303　碧城三首（其一）
305　齐宫词
307　汉宫词
309　离亭赋得折杨柳
311　宫妓
313　宫辞
315　代赠二首（其一）
317　楚吟

319　板桥晓别
321　银河吹笙
323　春雨
325　晚晴
327　安定城楼
329　天涯
331　日日
333　龙池
335　流莺
337　嫦娥
339　贾生

● 陈　陶　CHEN TAO

342　陇西行四首
　　　（其二）

● 李群玉　LI QUNYU

345　赠人

● 曹　邺　CAO YE

348　官仓鼠

● 赵　嘏　ZHAO GU

351　江楼感旧

● 崔　珏　CUI JUE

354　哭李商隐二首
　　　（其二）

● 罗　隐　LUO YIN

357　赠妓云英
359　自遣
361　鹦鹉
363　雪

● 韦 庄 WEI ZHUANG

　366　忆昔
　368　台城

● 聂夷中 NIE YIZHONG

　371　田家

● 章 碣 ZHANG JIE

　374　焚书坑

● 曹 松 CAO SONG

　377　己亥岁二首（其一）

● 韩 偓 HAN WO

　380　效崔国辅体四首
　　　（其一）

● 杜荀鹤 DU XUNHE

　383　山中寡妇

● 黄 巢 HUANG CHAO

　386　题菊花
　388　菊花

● 王 驾 WANG JIA

　391　社日
　393　雨晴

● 秦韬玉 QIN TAOYU

　396　贫女

● 于武陵 YU WULING

　399　赠卖松人

● 皮日休 PI RIXIU

　402　橡媪叹

● 张 泌 ZHANG BI

　407　寄人

● 代后记　　　　　　409

张籍

ZHANG JI

作者简介

张籍（767—830），字文昌，和州乌江（今安徽和县）人，唐代诗人，新乐府运动的倡导者和参与者。

贞元十五年（799年）登进士第。元和十五年（820年）迁秘书省秘书郎，经韩愈推荐，授国子博士。大和二年（828年），迁国子司业。世称"张水部"或"张司业"。

工诗，尤长乐府古风，与王建齐名，称"张王乐府"。《全唐诗》编诗五卷，有《张司业集》存世。

节妇吟寄东平李司空师道 ①

君知妾 ② 有夫，赠妾双明珠。

感君缠绵意，系在红罗襦 ③。

妾家高楼连苑起 ④，良人执戟 ⑤ 明光 ⑥ 里。

知君用心如日月 ⑦，事 ⑧ 夫誓拟 ⑨ 同生死。

还君明珠双泪垂，恨不 ⑩ 相逢未嫁时。

002

---

① 节妇：能守住节操的妇女，特别是对丈夫忠贞的妻子。吟，一种诗体的名
　称。李司空师道，李师道，时任平卢淄青节度使，拜检校司空、同平章事。
② 妾：古代妇女对自己的谦称，这里是诗人的自喻。
③ 罗襦：罗，丝织品，质薄、手感滑爽而透气。襦，短衣、短袄。
④ 高楼连苑起：耸立的高楼连接着园林。苑，帝王及贵族游玩和打猎的风景
　园林。
⑤ 执戟：指守卫宫殿的门户。戟，古代的一种兵器。
⑥ 明光：本是汉代宫殿名，此处指皇帝的宫殿。
⑦ 如日月：光明磊落的意思。
⑧ 事：服侍、侍奉。
⑨ 拟：打算。
⑩ 恨不：一作"何不"。

Reply of a Chaste Wife

You know I love my husband best,

Yet you send me two bright pearls still.

I hang them within my red silk vest,

So grateful I'm for your good will.

You see my house overlooks the garden and

My husband guards the palace, halberd in hand.

I know your heart as noble as the sun in the skies,

But I have sworn to serve my husband all my life.

With your twin pearls

I send back two tears from my eyes.

Why did we not meet before I was made a wife?

王
建

WANG
JIAN

作者简介

王建（767—835），字仲初，许州颍川（今河南许昌）人，唐代诗人。擅长乐府诗，与张籍齐名，世称"张王乐府"。

中年入仕，历任昭应县丞、太府寺丞、秘书郎、太常寺丞，累迁陕州司马，世称"王司马"。

诗作题材广泛，同情百姓疾苦，生活气息浓厚，思想深刻。语言通俗凝练，富有民歌谣谚色彩。《全唐诗》编诗六卷，有《王建集》存世。

望夫石①

望夫处，江悠悠。

化为石，不回头。

上②头日日风复③雨，

行人归来石应语。

---

① 望夫石：据南朝宋人刘义庆的《幽明录》记载，武昌阳新县北山上有望夫石，其形状像人立。相传有位贞妇，其丈夫从军，她携弱子送行于武昌北山，"立望夫而化为立石"，望夫石因此而得名。

② 上：一作"山"，山上。

③ 复：作"和"，与。

The Woman Waiting for Her Husband

Waiting for him alone

Where the river goes by,

She turns into a stone

Gazing with longing eye.

Atop the hill from day to day come wind and rain;

The stone should speak to see her husband come again.

新嫁娘词三首（其三）

三日入厨下，洗手作羹汤。

未谙①姑②食性，先遣小姑③尝。

---

① 谙：熟悉。

② 姑：婆婆。

③ 小姑：丈夫的妹妹，即小姑子。

A Bride

III

Married three days, I go shy-faced
To cook a soup with hands still fair.
To meet my mother-in-law's taste,
I send to her daughter the first share.

张仲素

ZHANG ZHONGSU

作者简介

张仲素（769—819），字绘之，符离（今安徽宿州）人，唐代诗人。

贞元十四年（798年）进士，又中博学宏词科，为武宁军从事，元和间，任司勋员外郎，又从礼部郎中充任翰林学士，迁中书舍人。

擅长作乐府诗，善写思妇心情，刻画细腻，委婉动人。《全唐诗》存诗一卷，今存《三舍人集》。

春闺思

袅袅^①城边柳，青青陌上^②桑。

提笼忘采叶，昨夜梦渔阳^③。

---

① 袅袅：纤长柔美貌。
② 陌上：路旁。陌，田间的小路。
③ 渔阳：古代郡名，位于今天津蓟州区。因此地处边陲，常有重兵把守，后世遂用以指边境征戍之地。

In Reverie

By city wall wave willows slender

And roadside mulberry leaves tender.

She gathers not, basket in hand,

Still dreaming of the far-off-land.

燕子楼诗三首

一①

楼上残灯伴晓霜，独眠人起合欢床。

相思一夜情多少，地角天涯未是长。

二②

北邙^(máng) 松柏锁愁烟，燕子楼中思悄然。

自埋剑履歌尘散，红袖香销已十年。

三③

适看鸿雁洛阳回，又睹玄禽逼社来。

瑶瑟玉箫无意绪，任从蛛网任从灰。

---

① 该诗写于秋夜，写十多年中经历过的无数不眠之夜中的一夜。
② 该诗抚今追昔，思念张愔，哀怜自己。
③ 该诗写于春日，感节候之变迁，叹青春之消逝。

The Pavilion of Swallows

I

Upstairs the dying lamp flickers with morning frost;

The lonely widow rises from her nuptial bed.

Sleepless the whole night long,

In mournful thoughts she's lost;

The night seems endless as the boundless sky o'erhead,

II

The pines before his grave are shrouded in sad smoke;

In the Swallows' Pavilion pensive she appears.

Her songs are hushed for buried are his sword and cloak;

Her dancing dress has lost its perfume for ten years.

III

She's seen wild geese from her lords grave on backward
way,

And now she sees the swallows come with spring again.

On flute and zither she is in no mood to play;

Buried in spider's webs and dusty they remain.

刘禹锡

LIU
YUXI

作者简介

刘禹锡（772—842），字梦得，唐代文学家、哲学家，有"诗豪"之称。

贞元九年（793年）进士及第，初任太子校书，迁淮南记室参军，后入节度使杜佑幕府，深得杜佑的信任与器重。唐顺宗即位后，参与"永贞革新"。革新失败后，屡遭贬谪。卒于洛阳，追赠户部尚书。

诗文俱佳，涉猎题材广泛，其诗自然流畅、风情俊爽，有空旷开阔的时间感和空间感，有名篇《酬乐天扬州初逢席上见赠》《秋词》《望洞庭》等。

酬乐天扬州初逢席上见赠①

巴山楚水②凄凉地，二十三年弃置身③。

怀旧空吟闻笛赋④，到乡翻似烂柯人⑤。

① 酬：以诗赠答的意思。乐天，指白居易，字乐天。见赠，送给（我）。

② 巴山楚水：指今四川、湖南、湖北一带。刘禹锡被贬后，迁徙于上述边远地区，这里用"巴山楚水"泛指这些地方。

③ 弃置身：指遭受贬谪的诗人自己。弃置，贬谪。置，放置。

④ "怀旧"句：怀旧，怀念故友。闻笛赋，指西晋向秀的《思旧赋》。三国曹魏末年，向秀的朋友嵇康、吕安因不满司马氏篡权而被杀害。后来，向秀经过嵇康、吕安的旧居，听到邻人吹笛，不禁悲从中来，于是作《思旧赋》。刘禹锡借用这个典故怀念已故的王叔文、柳宗元等人。

⑤ "到乡"句：翻似，倒好像。翻，反而。烂柯人，指晋人王质。相传晋人王质上山砍柴，看见两个童子下棋便停下观看。等棋局终了，手中的斧柄（柯）已经朽烂。回到村里，才知道已过了一百年。同代人都已经亡故。刘禹锡借此典故表达世事沧桑、人事全非，暮年返乡恍如隔世的心情，以及遭贬二十三年的感慨。

沉舟⑥侧畔千帆过，病树前头万木春。

今日听君歌一曲⑦，暂凭杯酒长_{zhǎng}精神⑧。

---

⑥ 沉舟：诗人以沉舟自比。下句的"病树"同。

⑦ 歌一曲：指白居易的《醉赠刘二十八使君》。

⑧ 长精神：振作精神。长，增长，振作。

Reply to Bai Juyi Whom I Meet Fop the First Time at a Banquet in Yangzhou

O western mountains and southern streams desolate,

Where I, an exile, lived for twenty years and three!

To mourn for my departed friends I come too late;

In my native land I look like human debris.

Hundreds of sails pass by the side of sunken ship;

Thousands of flowers bloom ahead of injured tree.

Today I hear you chant the praise of comradeship;

I wish this cup of wine might well inspirit me.

秋风引 ①

何处秋风至？萧萧②送雁群。

朝来入庭树，孤客③最先闻。

---

① 引：一种文学或乐曲体裁之一，有序奏之意，即引子、开头。

② 萧萧：形容风吹树木的声音。

③ 孤客：独自一人旅居外地的人，指诗人自己。

The Autumn Breeze

O from where comes the autumn breeze?

It sends wild geese off sad and drear.

At dawn it enters courtyard trees;

The lonely man's the first to hear.

竹枝词^① 三首

一

杨柳青青江水平，闻郎江上唱歌声。

东边日出西边雨，道是^②无晴^③却^④有晴。

二

山桃红花满上头^⑤，蜀江^⑥春水拍山流。

花红易衰似郎意，水流无限似侬^⑦愁。

---

① 竹枝词：巴渝（今四川和重庆）一带的民歌。歌词杂咏当地风物和男女爱
　情，富有浓郁的生活气息，引起一些诗人喜爱。刘禹锡的《竹枝词》现存
　十一首。

② 道是：说是。

③ 晴："情"的同音字，用来暗喻情感的"情"。

④ 却：一作"还"。

⑤ 上头：山头，山顶。

⑥ 蜀江：泛指四川的河流。

⑦ 侬：我。女子自称。

九

山上层层桃李花，云间烟火是人家。

银钏金钗来负水，长刀短笠去烧畲^⑧。

---

⑧ 烧畲：指烧荒种田。

Bamboo Branch Songs

I

Between the green willows the river flows along;

My gallant in a boat is heard to sing a song.

The west is veiled in rain, the east enjoys sunshine,

My gallant is as deep in love as the day is fine.

II

The mountain's red with peach blossoms above;

The shore is washed by spring waves below.

Red blossoms fade fast as my gallant's love;

The river like my sorrow will ever flow.

IX

The mountainside peach and plum trees blossom in tiers;

Smoke rising from the roofs amid clouds disappears.

Silver and gold adorned women draw water and

Men in straw hats with swords till the ash-manured land.

石头城①

山围故国②周遭在，潮打空城寂寞回。

淮水东边旧时月，夜深还过女墙③来。

---

① 石头城：曾是战国时楚国的金陵（今南京清凉山一带）古城。三国时期东
　吴孙权在此地就石壁筑城戍守，故称。

② 故国：即旧都。石头城在六朝时一直是国都。

③ 女墙：指石头城上的矮城。刘师培在《左盦外集·物名溯源续补》中认为
　"女墙"就是指城上的小墙，城垛。

The Town of Stone

The changeless hills round ancient capital still stand;

Waves beating on ruined walls, unheeded, roll away.

The moon which shone by riverside on flourished land

Still shines at dead of night over ruined town today.

乌衣巷①

朱雀桥②边野草花，乌衣巷口夕阳斜。

旧时王谢堂前燕③，飞入寻常百姓家。

---

① 乌衣巷：位于金陵（今南京）城南，因三国时为东吴乌衣营的驻地而得名，东晋时为高门大族聚居的地方。

② 朱雀桥：原是秦淮河上的浮桥，今已不存在。从金陵城去乌衣巷要经过朱雀桥，东晋时桥上曾经建有两只铜雀装饰的重楼，据说是东晋大臣谢安建的。朱雀桥位于金陵城南，此与古代"东苍龙，北玄武，西白虎，南朱雀"的说法相符。

③ "旧时"句：王谢，指东晋的高门大族王家和谢家。当时有种说法："王与马，共天下。"王就是指开国元勋大将军王导所在的琅玡王氏。而陈郡谢氏也是代代都出高官，取得淝水之战胜利的就是谢氏家族的谢安。旧时，晋代。

The Street of Mansions

Beside the Bridge of Birds rank grasses overgrow;

Over the Street of Mansions the setting sun hangs low.

Swallows which skimmed by painted eaves in days gone by,

Are dipping now in homes where humble people occupy.

和乐天春词 ①

新妆宜面②下朱楼③，深锁春光一院愁。

行到中庭数花朵，蜻蜓④飞上玉搔头⑤。

---

① 春词：春怨之词。"春词"为白居易原诗题目。
② 宜面：脂粉和脸色很匀称。一作"粉面"。
③ 朱楼：以红漆装饰的楼房，多指富贵女子的居所。
④ 蜻蜓：暗指头上之香。
⑤ 玉搔头：玉簪，可用来搔头，故称。

A Song of Spring in Reply to Bai Juyi

She comes downstairs in new dress that becomes her face;

When locked up, even spring looks sad in this lonely place.

She counts up flowers in midcourt while passing by;

On her hairpin of jade alights a dragonfly.

望洞庭①

湖光秋月两相和，潭面无风镜未磨②。

遥望洞庭山水翠，白银盘③里一青螺④。

---

① 洞庭湖：湖名，位于今湖南省北部。
② 镜未磨：古人的镜子以铜制作而成。此处是指湖面无风，水平如镜。一说
　　是远望湖中的景物，隐约不清，如同镜面没打磨时照物模糊。
③ 白银盘：形容平静而又清澈的洞庭湖面。
④ 青螺：此处形容洞庭湖中的洞庭山。

Lake Dongting Viewed From Afar

The autumn moon dissolve in soft light of the lake,

Unruffled surface like unpolished mirror bright.

Afar, the isle 'mid clear water without a break

Looks like a spiral shell in a plate silver-white.

饮酒看牡丹 ①

今日花前饮，甘心醉数杯。

但愁花有语，不为老人开。

---

① 饮酒看牡丹：又名《唐郎中宅与诸公同饮酒看牡丹》。

Drinking Before Peonies in Bloom

Today I'll drink with blooms before.

Don't mind if I drink two cups more.

I am afraid lest to be told,

"Our bloom is not for you the old!"

柳枝词

清①江一曲柳千条，二十年前旧板桥。

曾与美人桥上别，恨无消息到今朝②。

---

① 清：一作"春"，两字音韵相同，"清"字更能写出水色澄碧，故"清"字较好。

② 今朝：今日。

The Willows

Thousands of willows see the winding river flow

Beneath the wooden bridge of twenty years ago,

On which my beauty parted with me and went away.

How I regret no news of her comes e'en today!

白居易

BAI JUYI

作者简介

白居易（772—846），字乐天，号香山居士，又号醉吟先生，唐代现实主义诗人，有"诗魔"和"诗王"之称。与元稹共同倡导新乐府运动，世称"元白"，与刘禹锡并称"刘白"。

贞元进士，授秘书省校书郎。元和年间，任左拾遗及左赞善大夫。长庆间任杭州刺史，宝历初任苏州刺史，后官至刑部尚书。

其诗语言通俗，多讽喻，长篇《长恨歌》《琵琶行》深受人们喜爱。

买花

帝城①春欲暮，喧喧车马度。

共道牡丹时，相随买花去。

贵贱无常价，酬直②看花数。

灼灼③百朵红，戋戋^{jiān}五束素④。

上张幄幕⑤庇⑥，旁织笆篱护。

038

---

① 帝城：皇帝居住的城市，指长安。
② 酬直：买花付钱。直，通"值"。
③ 灼灼：形容花鲜艳有光彩的样子。
④ "戋戋"句：戋戋，细小、微小的样子。束，量词，古时帛五匹为一束。
　素，白绸。
⑤ 幄幕：帐篷。一作"帷幄"。
⑥ 庇：庇护。

水洒复泥封^⑦，移来色如故。

家家习为俗，人人迷不悟。

有一田舍翁^⑧，偶来买花处。

低头独长叹，此叹无人喻。

一丛深色花，十户中人赋^⑨。

---

⑦ 泥封：用土培植。

⑧ 田舍翁：农夫。

⑨ 中人赋：即中户、中等人家一年所缴的赋税。唐时按户口征收赋税，户口
分为上户、中户、下户。

Buying Flowers

The capital's in parting spring,

Steeds run and neigh and cab bells ring.

Peonies are at their best hours

And people rush to buy the flowers.

They do not care about the price,

Just count and buy those which seem nice.

For hundred blossoms dazzling red,

Twenty-five rolls of silk they spread.

Sheltered above by curtains wide,

Protected with fences by the side,

Roots sealed with mud, with water sprayed,

Removed, their beauty does not fade.

Accustomed to this way for long,

No family e'er thinks it wrong.

What's the old peasant doing there?

Why should he come to Flower Fair?

Head bowed, he utters sigh on sigh

And nobody understands why.

A bunch of deep-red peonies

Costs taxes of ten families.

上阳① 白发人

上阳人，上阳人，红颜暗老②白发新。

绿衣监使③守宫门，一闭上阳多少春。

玄宗末岁初选入，入时十六今六十。

同时采择④百余人，零落年深残此身⑤。

忆昔吞悲别亲族，扶入车中不教哭。

皆云入内便承恩，脸似芙蓉胸似玉。

未容君王得见面，已被杨妃遥侧目⑥。

妒令潜配上阳宫，一生遂向空房宿。

宿空房，秋夜长，夜长无寐天不明。

耿耿残灯背壁影，萧萧暗雨打窗声。

---

① 上阳：唐代别宫名，位于洛阳皇宫内。
② 红颜暗老：指人的青春容颜在不知不觉中衰老。
③ 绿衣监使：唐代管理宫闱事务的宦官。唐时京都诸苑各设监一人，从六品下；副监一人，从七品下。六、七品官服分别为深、浅绿色。
④ 采择：指选入宫女。
⑤ "零落"句：零落，凋谢，此处指宫女死亡。残，剩余、留下。
⑥ "已被"句：杨妃，指杨贵妃。遥侧目，斜着眼睛看，形容忌恨的样子。

春日迟，日迟独坐天难暮。

宫莺百啭⑦愁厌闻，梁燕双栖老休妒。

莺归燕去长悄然，春往秋来不记年。

唯向深宫望明月，东西四五百回圆。

今日宫中年最老，大家遥赐尚书号⑧。

小头鞋履^{xié}⑨窄衣裳，青黛点眉眉细长。

外人不见见应笑，天宝末年时世妆。

上阳人，苦最多：

少亦苦，老亦苦，少苦老苦两如何？

君不见昔时吕向《美人赋》⑩？

又不见今日上阳白发歌！

043

---

⑦ 百啭：鸟婉转地叫。

⑧ "大家"句：大家，古代宫中侍从对皇帝的称谓。尚书，女尚书，宫中女官
的名称。

⑨ 鞋履：皆是指鞋。

⑩ 吕向《美人赋》：作者自注云："天宝末，有密采艳色者，当时号花鸟使，
吕向献《美人赋》以讽之。"吕向，字子回。

The White-haired Palace Maid

The Shangyang Palace maid,

Her hair grows white, her rosy cheeks grow dark and fade.

The palace gate is guarded by eunuchs in green.

How many springs have passed, immured as she has been!

She was first chosen for the imperial household

At the age of sixteen; now she's sixty years old.

The hundred beauties brought in with her have all gone,

Flickering out through long years, leaving her alone.

She swallowed grief when she left home in days gone by,

Helped into the cab, she was forbidden to cry.

Once in the palace, she'd be favored, it was said;

Her face was fair as lotus, her bosom like jade.

But to the emperor she could never come nigh,

For Lady Yang had cast on her a jealous eye.

She was consigned to Shangyang Palace full of gloom,

To pass her lonely days and nights in a bare room.

In empty chamber long seemed each autumnal night;

Sleepless in bed, it seemed she'd never see daylight.

Dim, dim the lamplight throws her shadow on the walls;

Shower by shower on her window chill rain falls.

Spring days drag slow;

She sits alone to see light won't be dim and low.

She's tired to hear the palace orioles sing and sing,

Too old to envy pairs of swallows on the wing.

Silent, she sees the birds appear and disappear,

And counts nor springs nor autumns coming year by year.

Watching the moon o'er palace again and again,

Four hundred times and more she's seen it wax and wane.

Today the oldest honorable maid of all,

She is entitled Secretary of Palace Hall.

Her gown is tightly fitted, her shoes like pointed prows;

With dark green pencil she draws long, long slender brows.

Seeing her, outsiders would even laugh with tears;

Her old-fashioned dress has been out of date for years.

Oh, Shangyang maid, to suffer is her fate, all told;

She suffered while still young; she suffers now she's old.

Do you not know a satire spread in days gone by?

Today for white-haired Shangyang Palace maid we'll sigh.

卖炭翁^①

卖炭翁，伐薪烧炭南山中。

满面尘灰烟火色，两鬓苍苍^②十指黑。

卖炭得钱何所营？身上衣裳口中食。

可怜身上衣正单，心忧炭贱愿天寒。

夜来城外一尺雪，晓驾炭车辗冰辙^③。

牛困人饥日已高，市南门^④外泥中歇。

翩翩两骑来是谁？黄衣使者白衫儿^⑤。

---

① 卖炭翁：此篇是组诗《新乐府》中的第三十二首，题注云："苦宫市也。"
宫市，指唐代皇宫里需要物品，就向市场上去拿，随便给点钱，而这实际
上就是公开掠夺。唐德宗时，太监专管其事。

② 苍苍：灰白色，形容鬓发斑白。

③ 辗冰辙：轧着结冰的车道行走。辗，同"碾"，轧。辙，车轮滚过地面辗出
的痕迹。

④ 市南门：唐代长安有东、西两个市场，每个市场都有东、南、西、北门。

⑤ "黄衣"句：黄衣使者，指太监，唐代级别较高的太监穿黄衣。白衫儿，太
监手下的爪牙。

手把文书口称敕[6]，回车叱牛牵向北[7]。

一车炭，千余斤，宫使驱将惜不得[8]。

半匹[8]红纱一丈绫，系(xì)[9]向牛头充炭直[10]。

---

⑥“手把”句：口称敕，嘴里说着皇帝的命令。敕，君主的诏命。

⑦ 牵向北：唐代长安市场在城南，皇宫在城北，所以叱牛向北行。

⑧“宫使”句：宫使，即上文所说的黄衣使者。驱将，把牛车赶走。将，语气助词。

⑨ 半匹：唐代四丈为一匹，半匹为二丈。唐代商务交易中，绢帛等丝织品可以代替货币使用。当时钱贵绢贱，半匹纱和一丈绫比一车炭的价值相差很远。这是意指官方用贱价强夺民财。

⑩ 系：绑扎，此处是挂的意思。

⑪ 直：同“值”，即价格。

The Old Charcoal Seller

What does the old man fare?

He cuts the wood in southern hill and fires his ware.

His face is grimed with smoke and streaked with ash and

dust,

His temples grizzled and his fingers all turned black.

The money earned by selling charcoal is not just

Enough for food for his mouth and clothing for his back.

Though his coat is thin, he hopes winter will set in,

For cold weather will keep up the charcoal's good price.

At night a foot of snow falls outside city walls;

At dawn his charcoal cart crushes ruts in the ice.

The sun is high, the ox tired out and hungry he;

Outside the southern gate in snow and slush they rest.

Two riders canter up. Alas! Who can they be?

Two palace heralds in the yellow jackets dressed.

Decree in hand, which is imperial order, one says;

They turn the cart about and at the ox they shout.

A cartload of charcoal a thousand catties weighs;

They drive the cart away.

What dare the old man say?

Ten feet of silk and twenty feet of gauze deep red,

That is the payment they fasten to the ox's head.

长恨歌

汉皇①重色思倾国，御宇②多年求不得。

杨家有女③初长成，养在深闺人未识。

天生丽质难自弃，一朝选在君王侧。

回眸一笑百媚生，六宫粉黛④无颜色。

春寒赐浴华清池⑤，温泉水滑洗凝脂⑥。

侍儿扶起娇无力，始是新承恩泽时。

---

① 汉皇：原指汉武帝刘彻，此处借指唐玄宗李隆基。唐人文学创作常以汉
   称唐。
② 御宇：驾御宇内，指治理天下。
③ 杨家有女：指杨玉环，蒲州永乐（今山西永济）人。自幼由叔父杨玄珪抚
   养，十七岁被册封为玄宗之子寿王李瑁之妃，二十七岁被玄宗册封为贵妃。
   白居易谓"养在深闺人未识"，是有意为帝王避讳的说法。
④ 六宫粉黛：六宫的妃嫔。六宫，此处专指皇后寝宫，后泛指妃嫔居处。粉
   黛，代指美女。
⑤ 华清池：华清宫温泉，位于今陕西临潼。
⑥ 凝脂：指白嫩光泽的肌肤。

云鬓⑦花颜金步摇⑧，芙蓉帐暖度春宵。

春宵苦短⑨日高起，从此君王不早朝。

承欢侍宴无闲暇，春从春游夜专夜⑩。

后宫佳丽三千⑪人，三千宠爱在一身。

金屋⑫妆成娇侍夜，玉楼宴罢醉和春⑬。

姊妹弟兄皆列土，可怜⑭光彩生门户。

遂令天下父母心，不重生男重生女。

骊宫⑮高处入青云，仙乐风飘处处闻。

---

⑦ 云鬓：形容女子鬓发轻盈飘逸、盛美如云。

⑧ 金步摇：一种金制垂珠头钗，行则摇曳生姿。

⑨ 苦短：暗示欢愉无厌，故嫌夜短。

⑩ 夜专夜：一夜连着一夜，整日整夜。

⑪ 佳丽三千：极言美女其多。

⑫ 金屋：用汉武帝"金屋藏娇"典，此处指杨贵妃所居之处。

⑬ 醉和春：指酒与情同醉。

⑭ 可怜：可羡，羡慕。

⑮ 骊宫：指骊山华清宫，位于今陕西临潼。

缓歌慢舞凝丝竹[16]，尽日君王看不足。

渔阳鼙鼓动地来，惊破霓裳羽衣曲。

九重城阙烟尘生[17]，千乘万骑西南行。

翠华[18]摇摇行复止，西出都门百余里，

六军[19]不发无奈何，宛转[20]蛾眉[21]马前死。

花钿委地[22]无人收，翠翘金雀玉搔头[23]，

君王掩面救不得，回看血泪相和流。

黄埃散漫风萧索，云栈萦纡登剑阁[24]。

---

⑯ 凝丝竹：指歌舞紧扣乐声。丝竹，弦乐和管乐的合称。

⑰ "九重"句：九重城阙，指京城长安。烟尘，烽烟尘土，特指战火。

⑱ 翠华：用翠鸟的羽毛装饰的旗帜，皇帝仪仗队用。

⑲ 六军：此指皇帝的扈从军队。

⑳ 宛转：缠绵委屈貌，形容美人临死前哀怨的样子。

㉑ 蛾眉：这里专指杨贵妃。

㉒ 花钿委地：金玉首饰落在地上。花钿，金玉制花形首饰。委地，落地。

㉓ "翠翘"句：首饰名。翠翘，形似翠鸟尾的首饰。金雀，钗名。玉搔头，玉簪。

㉔ "云栈"句：高耸入云的栈道。萦纡，弯曲盘旋。剑阁，位于今四川剑阁，是入蜀的要道。

峨嵋山㉕下少人行，旌旗无光日色薄㉖。

蜀江水碧蜀山青，圣主朝朝暮暮情。

行宫见月伤心色，夜雨闻铃肠断声。

天旋地转㉗回龙驭㉘，到此踌躇不能去，

马嵬坡下泥土中，不见玉颜㉙空死处。

君臣相顾尽沾衣㉚，东望都门㉛信马㉜归。

归来池苑皆依旧，太液芙蓉未央柳；

芙蓉如面柳如眉，对此如何不泪垂？

春风桃李花开日，秋雨梧桐叶落时。

㉕ 峨嵋山：位于今四川峨眉，此泛指蜀山。

㉖ 行宫：皇帝出行时的住所。

㉗ 天旋地转：形容时局大变。一作"天旋日转"。

㉘ 回龙驭：指唐玄宗还京。

㉙ 玉颜：美女，此处指杨贵妃。

㉚ 沾衣：指落泪。

㉛ 都门：长安城门。

㉜ 信马：任马奔走，不加约束。

西宫㉝南内㉞多秋草，落叶满阶红不扫，

梨园弟子㉟白发新，椒房阿监青娥㊱老。

夕殿萤飞思悄然㊲，孤灯挑尽未成眠。

迟迟钟鼓初长夜，耿耿㊳星河㊴欲曙天。

鸳鸯瓦㊵冷霜华㊶重，翡翠衾㊷寒谁与共？

悠悠生死别经年，魂魄不曾来入梦。

临邛道士鸿都客，能以精诚致魂魄。

为感君王辗转思，遂教方士殷勤觅。

排空驭气奔如电，升天入地求之遍。

0
5
5

㉝ 西宫：太极宫。

㉞ 南内：兴庆宫。与太极宫为唐玄宗返京后的两处住所。

㉟ 梨园弟子：由玄宗执教的宫内习艺者。

㊱ 椒房阿监青娥：后妃宫中的女官青春貌美。椒房阿监，后妃宫中的女官。
青娥，年轻的宫女。

㊲ 思悄然：情意萧瑟寂寞。

㊳ 耿耿：微明的样子。

㊴ 河：指银河。

㊵ 鸳鸯瓦：指嵌合成对的瓦片，又称阴阳瓦。

㊶ 霜华：霜花。

㊷ 翡翠衾：指绣有成双翡翠鸟的被子。

上穷碧落[43]下黄泉，两处茫茫皆不见。

忽闻海上有仙山，山在虚无缥缈间。

楼阁玲珑五云起，其中绰约多仙子。

中有一人字太真，雪肤花貌参差是。

金阙西厢叩玉扃^{jiōng}，转教小玉报双成。

闻道汉家天子使，九华帐里梦魂惊。

揽衣推枕起徘徊，珠箔银屏迤逦开。

云鬓半偏新睡觉，花冠不整下堂来。

风吹仙袂飘飖举，犹似霓裳羽衣舞。

玉容寂寞[44]泪阑干，梨花一枝春带雨。

---

[43] 碧落：道家称天界为碧落。

[44] 寂寞：黯淡失神貌。

含情凝睇谢君王，一别音容两渺茫。

昭阳殿里恩爱绝，蓬莱宫中日月长。

回头下望人寰⁴⁵处，不见长安见尘雾。

惟将旧物表深情，钿合金钗寄将去。

钗留一股合一扇，钗擘黄金合分钿。

但教⁴⁶心似金钿坚，天上人间会相见。

临别殷勤⁴⁷重寄词，词中有誓两心知。

七月七日长生殿，夜半无人私语时，

在天愿作比翼鸟，在地愿为连理枝⁴⁸。

天长地久有时尽，此恨绵绵无绝期⁴⁹！

㊺ 人寰：人世间。

㊽ 但教：一作"但令"。

㊼ 殷勤：反复多次。

㊽ 连理枝：两株树木树干相抱。古人常用此比喻情侣相爱，永不分离。

㊾ 绝期：中断的时候。

The Everlasting Regret

The beauty-loving monarch longed year after year

To find a beautiful lady without a peer.

A maiden of the Yangs to womanhood just grown,

In inner chambers bred, to the world was unknown.

Endowed with natural beauty too hard to hide,

She was chosen one day to be the monarch's bride.

Turning her head, she smiled so sweet and full of grace

That she outshone in six palaces the fairest face.

She bathed in glassy water of warm-fountain Pool

Which laved and smoothed her creamy skin when spring

was cool.

Without her maids' support, she was too tired to move,

And this was when she first received the monarch's love.

Flower-like face and cloud-like hair, golden-head dressed,

In lotus-adorned curtain she spent the night blessed.

She slept till the sun rose high for the blessed night was short,

From then on the monarch held no longer morning court.

In revels as in feasts she shared her lord's delight,

His companion on trips and his mistress at night.

In inner palace dwelt three thousand ladies fair;

On her alone was lavished royal love and care.

Her beauty served the night when dressed up

in Golden Bower;

She was drunk with wine and spring at banquet

in Jade Tower.

Her sisters and brothers all received rank and fief,

And honors showered on her household, to the grief

Of fathers and mothers who would rather give birth

To a fair maiden than to any son on earth.

The lofty palace towered high into the cloud;

With divine music borne on the breeze, the air was loud.

Seeing slow dance and hearing fluted or stringed song,

The emperor was never tired the whole day long.

But rebels beat their war drums, making the earth quake

And "Song of Rainbow Skirt and Coat of Feathers" break.

A cloud of dust was raised o'er city walls nine-fold;

Thousands of chariots and horsemen southwestward

rolled.

Imperial flags moved slowly now and halted then,

And thirty miles from Western Gate they stopped again.

Six armies—what could be done—would not march with

speed

Unless fair Lady Yang be killed before the steed.

None would pick up her hairpin fallen on the ground

Nor golden bird nor comb with which her head was

crowned.

The monarch could not save her and hid his face in fear;

Turning his head, he saw her blood mix with his tear.

The yellow dust widespread, the wind blew desolate;

A serpentine plank path led to cloud-capped Sword Gate.

Below the Eyebrow Mountains wayfarers were few;

In fading sunlight royal standards lost their hue,

On Western water blue and Western mountains green,

The monarch's heart was daily gnawed by sorrow keen.

The moon viewed from his tent shed a soul-searing light;

The bells heard in night rain made a heart-rending sound.

Suddenly turned the tide. Returning from his flight,

The monarch could not tear himself away from the

ground

Where' mid the clods beneath the Slope he couldn't forget

The fair-faced Lady Yang who was unfairly slain.

He looked at his courtiers, with tears his robe was wet;

They rode east to the capital but with loose rein.

Come back, he found her pond and garden in old place,

With lotus in the lake and willows by the hall.

Willow leaves like her brows and lotus like her face,

At the sight of all these, how could his tears not fall?

Or when in vernal breeze were peach and plum full-blown

Or when in autumn rain parasol leaves were shed?

In Western as in Southern Court was grass o'ergrown;

With fallen leaves unswept the marble steps turned red,

Actors, although still young, began to have hair grey.

Eunuchs and waiting maids looked old in palace deep.

Fireflies flitting the hall, mutely he pined away;

The lonely lampwick burned out, still he could not sleep.

Slowly beat drums and rang bells, night began to grow long;

Bright shone the Starry Stream, daybreak seemed to come late.

The love bird tiles grew chilly with hoar frost so strong;

His kingfisher quilt was cold, not shared by a mate.

One long, long year the dead with the living was parted;

Her soul came not in dreams to see the broken-hearted,

A taoist sorcerer came to the palace door,

Skilled to summon the spirits from the other shore,

Moved by the monarch's yearning for the departed fair,

He was ordered to seek for her everywhere.

Borne on the air, like flash of lightning flew;

In heaven and on earth he searched through and through.

Up to the azure vault and down to deepest place,

Nor above nor below could he e'er find her trace.

He learned that on the sea were fairy mountains proud,

Which now appeared now disappeared amid the cloud

Of rainbow colors, where rose magnificent bowers

And dwelt so many fairies as graceful as flowers.

Among them was a queen whose name was Ever True;

Her snow-white skin and sweet face might afford a clue.

Knocking at western gate of palace hall, he bade

The fair porter to inform the queen's waiting maid.

When she heard that there came the monarch's embassy,

The queen was startled out of dreams in her canopy.

Pushing aside the pillow, she rose and got dressed,

Passing through silver screen and pearl shade to meet the guest.

Her cloud-like hair awry, not full awake at all,

Her flowery cap slanted, she came into the hall.

The wind blew up her fairy sleeves and made them float

As if she danced still " Rainbow Skirt and Feathered Coat".

Her jade-white face crisscrossed with tears in lonely world

Like a spray of pear blossoms in spring rain impearled.

She bade him thank her lord, lovesick and broken-hearted;

They knew nothing of each other after they parted.

Love and happiness long ended within palace walls;

Days and nights appeared long in the Fairyland halls.

Turning her head and fixing on the earth her gaze,

She found no capital 'mid clouds of dust and haze.

To show her love was deep, she took out keepsakes old

For him to carry back, hairpin and case of gold.

Keeping one side of the case and one wing of the pin;

She sent to her lord the other half of the twin.

"If our two hearts as firm as the gold should remain,

In heaven or on earth some time we'll meet again,"

At parting, she confided to the messenger

A secret vow known only to her lord and her.

On seventh day of seventh moon when none was near,

At midnight in Long life Hall he whispered in her ear:

"On high, we'd be two birds flying wing to wing;

On earth, two trees with branches twined from spring to

spring."

The boundless sky and endless earth may pass away,

But this vow unfulfilled will be regretted for aye.

琵琶行

元和十年，予左迁九江郡司马。明年秋，送客湓浦口，闻舟中夜弹琵琶者，听其音，铮铮然有京都声。问其人，本长安倡女，尝学琵琶于穆、曹二善才，年长色衰，委身为贾人妇。遂命酒，使快弹数曲。曲罢悯然，自叙少小时欢乐事，今漂沦憔悴，转徙于江湖间。予出官二年，恬然自安，感斯人言，是夕始觉有迁谪意。因为长句，歌以赠之，凡六百一十六言。命曰《琵琶行》。

浔阳江^①头夜送客，枫叶荻花^②秋瑟瑟，

主人下马客在船，举酒欲饮无管弦。

醉不成欢惨将别，别时茫茫江浸月。

忽闻水上琵琶声，主人忘归客不发。

---

① 浔阳江：长江流经浔阳城（今江西九江）的一段。
② 荻花：荻是水生植物，似芦苇，秋天开草花色。

寻声暗问弹者谁，琵琶声停欲语迟③。

移船相近邀相见，添酒回灯重开宴，

千呼万唤始出来，犹抱琵琶半遮面。

转轴拨弦三两声，未成曲调先有情，

弦弦掩抑声声思，似诉平生不得志。

低眉信手续续弹，说尽心中无限事。

轻拢慢捻抹复挑④，初为《霓裳》后《六幺》⑤。

大弦嘈嘈如急雨，小弦切切如私语⑥。

嘈嘈切切⑦错杂弹，大珠小珠落玉盘。

---

③ 欲语迟：想回答又有些迟疑。

④ "轻拢"句：弹奏的各种手法。

⑤ 《霓裳》：指《霓裳羽衣曲》，据说是开元时从印度传入的，原名"婆罗门"，经唐明皇润色并改此名。作者还有《霓裳羽衣舞歌》，对此有较详细的描写。《六幺》，琵琶曲名，也作《绿腰》，以乐工进曲录其要点而得名，原名《录要》，是当时流行的曲调。

⑥ "大弦"二句：大弦，指琵琶中最粗的弦。小弦，指最细的弦。

⑦ 嘈嘈切切：嘈嘈，形容低重之音。切切，形容轻细之音。

間关莺语花底滑⑧，幽咽泉流冰下难⑨，

冰泉冷涩弦凝绝，凝绝不通声暂歇。

别有幽愁暗恨生，此时无声胜有声。

银瓶乍破水浆迸，铁骑突出刀枪鸣⑩。

曲终收拨当心画，四弦一声如裂帛⑪；

东船西舫悄无言，唯见江心秋月白。

沉吟放拨插弦中，整顿衣裳起敛容⑫。

自言本是京城女，家在虾蟆陵⑬下住。

⑧ "间关"句：间关，鸟鸣声。滑，形容乐声婉转流畅。
⑨ 冰下难：以泉水流下滩受阻形容乐声艰涩低沉、呜咽断续。一作"冰
   水滩"。
⑩ "银瓶"二句：形容曲调暂歇之后，忽然急促高亢，又进入高潮。
⑪ "曲终"二句：描写演奏结束时，演奏者用拨子对着四弦的中心用力一划，
   琵琶声像猛然撕开布帛时发出的声响。
⑫ "沉吟"二句：沉吟，沉思回味。敛容，整理情绪，从音乐意境中收回心
   来，表现出严肃而又恭敬的神态。
⑬ 虾蟆陵：位于长安城东南曲江附近，是歌女聚居的地方。旧说董仲舒葬此，
   门人经过这里，都下马步行，所以叫下马陵，后人误传为虾蟆陵。"虾"，
   通"蛤"。

十三学得琵琶成，名属教坊第一部^⑭。

曲罢曾教善才伏^⑮，妆成每被秋娘^⑯妒。

五陵年少争缠头^⑰，一曲红绡^⑱不知数。

钿头银篦击节碎^⑲，血色罗裙翻酒污。

今年欢笑复明年，秋月春风等闲度。

弟走从军阿姨死，暮去朝来颜色故，

门前冷落鞍马稀，老大嫁作商人妇。

⑭ "名属"句：教坊，唐高祖时设置的宫内教练歌舞的机构，唐玄宗又设内教坊和左教坊、右教坊。这位弹琵琶的女子当是挂名教坊，临时入宫供奉的。第一部，首席乐队。

⑮ 伏：通"服"，敬佩。

⑯ 秋娘：唐时歌舞伎常用的名字，此处泛指当时貌美艺高的歌伎。

⑰ "五陵"句：五陵年少，指富贵人家子弟。五陵，汉代的长陵、安陵、阳陵、茂陵、平陵，都在长安城北，是汉朝王公贵族的聚居处。争缠头，争先恐后地送缠头。缠头，古代赏赠给歌人舞女的丝织品。

⑱ 红绡：红色的绫缎。绡，精细华美的丝织品。

⑲ "钿头"句：钿，用金玉珠宝等制成的花朵形的首饰。银篦，银制的篦子，也是一种首饰。银篦一作云篦。击节碎，用贵重首饰打拍子，碎了也不可惜。

商人重利轻别离，前月浮梁买茶去[20]。

去来江口守空船，绕船月明江水寒，

夜深忽梦少年事，梦啼妆泪红阑干[21]。

我闻琵琶已叹息，又闻此语重唧唧[22]，

同是天涯沦落人，相逢何必曾相识！

我从去年辞帝京，谪居卧病浔阳城，

浔阳地僻无音乐，终岁不闻丝竹声。

住近湓江地低湿，黄芦苦竹绕宅生。

---

[20] 浮梁：唐天宝间改设的县，治所在今江西景德镇，是个茶叶贸易中心。

[21] "梦啼"句：妆泪，脂粉和眼泪混在一起。阑干，（泪水）纵横。

[22] 重唧唧：重，更加。唧唧，叹息。

其间旦暮闻何物？杜鹃^㉓啼血猿哀鸣。

春江花朝秋月夜，往往取酒还独倾，

岂无山歌与村笛，呕哑嘲哳^㉔难为听。

今夜闻君琵琶语，如听仙乐耳暂明。

莫辞更坐弹一曲，为君翻作^㉕《琵琶行》。

感我此言良久立，却坐^㉖促弦弦转急，

凄凄不似向前声，满座重闻皆掩泣。

座中泣下谁最多？江州司马^㉗青衫湿！

㉓ 杜鹃：又名子规，鸣声凄切。相传古蜀国的一位国君名叫杜宇，又称望帝，
  死后魂化杜鹃，鸣声凄切，常常啼叫得口角流血。
㉔ 呕哑嘲哳：形容乐声杂乱难听。呕哑，拟声词，形容单调的乐声；嘲哳，
  形容声音繁杂，也作啁哳。
㉕ 翻作：按曲填写歌词。
㉖ 却坐：重新坐下。
㉗ 江州司马：诗人自指。

Song of a Pipa Player

One night by riverside I bade a friend goodbye;

In maple leaves and rushes autumn seemed to sigh.

My friend and I dismounted and came into the boat;

We wished to drink but there was no music afloat.

Without flute songs we drank our cups with heavy heart;

The moonbeams blended with water when we were to

part.

Suddenly o'er the stream we heard a pipa sound;

I forgot to go home and the guest stood spell-bound.

We followed where the music led to find the player,

But heard the pipa stop and no music in the air.

We moved our boat towards the one whence came the

strain,

Brought back the lamp, asked for more wine and drank

again.

Repeatedly we called for the fair player till

She came, her face half hidden behind a pipa still.

She turned the pegs and tested twice or thrice each string;

Before a tune was played we heard her feelings sing.

Each string she plucked, each note she struck with pathos strong,

All seemed to say she'd missed her dreams all her life long.

Head bent, she played with unpremeditated art

On and on to pour out her overflowing heart.

She lightly plucked, slowly stroked and twanged loud

The song of Green Waist after that of Rainbow Cloud.

The thick strings loudly thrummed like the pettering rain;

The fine strings softly tinkled in a murmuring strain.

When mingling loud and soft notes were together played,

You heard large and small pearls cascade on plate of jade.

Now you heard orioles warble in flowery land,

Then a sobbing stream run along a beach of sand.

But the stream seemed so cold as to tighten the string;

From tightened strings no more sound could

be heard to sing.

Still we heard hidden grief and vague regret concealed;

Then music expressed far less than silence revealed.

Suddenly we heard water burst a silver jar,

And the clash of spears and sabres come from afar.

She made a central sweep when the music was ending;

The four strings made one sound, as of silk one was

rending.

Silence reigned left and right of the boat, east and west;

We saw but autumn moon white in the river's breast.

She slid the plectrum pensively between the strings,

Smoothed out her dress and rose with a composed mien.

"I spent," she said, "in the capital my early springs,

Where at the foot of Mount of Toads my home had been.

At thirteen I learned on the pipa how to play,

And my name was among the primas of the day.

I won my master's admiration for my skill;

My beauty was envied by songstresses fair still.

The gallant young men vied to shower gifts on me;

One tune played, countless silk rolls were given with glee.

Beating time, I let silver comb and pin drop down,

And spilt-out wine oft stained my blood-red silken gown.

From year to year I laughed my joyous life away

On moonlit autumn night as windy vernal day.

My younger brother left for war, and died my maid;

Days passed, nights came, and my beauty began to fade.

Fewer and fewer were cabs and steeds at my door;

I married a smug merchant when my prime was o'er.

The merchant cared for money much more than for me;

One month ago he went away to purchase tea,

Leaving his lonely wife alone in empty boat;

Shrouded in moonlight, on the cold river I float.

Deep in the night I dreamed of happy bygone years,

And woke to find my rouged face crisscrossed with tears."

Listening to her sad music, I sighed with pain;

Hearing her story, I sighed again and again.

Both of us in misfortune go from shore to shore.

Meeting now, need we have known each other before?

"I was banished from the capital last year

To live degraded and ill in this city here.

The city's too remote to know melodious song,

So I have never heard music all the year long.

I dwell by riverbank on a low and damp ground

In a house with wild reeds and stunted bamboos around.

What is here to be heard from daybreak till nightfall

But gibbon's cry and cuckoo's homeward-going call?

By blooming riverside and under autumn moon

I've often taken wine up and drunk it alone.

Though I have mountain songs and village pipes to hear,

Yet they are crude and strident and grate on the ear.

Listening to you playing on pipa tonight,

With your music divine e'en my hearing seems bright.

Will you sit down and play for us a tune once more?

I'll write for you an ode to the pipa I adore."

Touched by what I said, the player stood for long,

Then sat down, tore at strings and played another song.

So sad, so drear, so different, it moved us deep;

Those who heard it hid their face and began to weep.

Of all the company at table who wept most?

It was none other than the exiled blue-robed host.

花非花①

花非花，雾非雾。

夜半来，天明去。

来如②春梦几多时③？

去似朝云无觅处④。

---

① 花非花：《花非花》成为词牌始于此诗。
② 来如：来时，来的时候。
③ 几多时：没有多少时间。
④ "去似"句：去了以后，如早晨飘散的云彩，无处寻觅。朝云，此处借用楚
   襄王梦巫山神女之典故。

A Flower in the Haze

In bloom, she's not a flower;

Hazy, she's not a haze.

She comes at midnight hour;

She goes with starry rays.

She comes like vernal dreams that cannot stay;

She goes like morning clouds that melt away.

赋得^①古原^②草送别

离离^③原上草，一岁一枯荣。

野火烧不尽，春风吹又生。

远芳^④侵古道，晴翠^⑤接荒城。

又送王孙^⑥去，萋萋^⑦满别情。

---

① 赋得：借古人句或成语命题作诗，照例要在题目上加"赋得"二字。"赋得
体"多见于学习作诗、文人聚会、科举考试等场合的诗文中。

② 古原：古原野。一说是乐游原，位于陕西西安。

③ 离离：青草茂盛的样子。

④ 远芳：形容春草的芳香播散得很远。

⑤ 晴翠：阳光下翠绿的野草。

⑥ 王孙：本指贵族子弟，后来成为对他人的尊称，此处指即将远游的友人。

⑦ 萋萋：形容草木茂盛的样子。

Grass on the Ancient Plain in Farewell to a Friend

Wild grasses spread over ancient plain;

With spring and fall they come and go.

Fire tries to burn them up in vain;

They rise again when spring winds blow.

Their fragrance overruns the way;

Their green invades the ruined town.

To see my friend going away;

My sorrow grows like grass overgrown.

惜牡丹花

惆怅^①阶前红牡丹，晚来唯有两枝残^②。

明朝风起应吹尽，夜惜衰红^③把火^④看。

---

① 惆怅：伤感，愁闷，失意。

② 残：凋谢。

③ 衰红：凋谢的牡丹花。衰，枯萎，凋谢。红，此处指牡丹花。

④ 把火：手持火把。

The Last Look at the Peonies at Night

I'm saddened by the courtyard peonies brilliant red,

At dusk only two of them are left on their bed.

I am afraid they can't survive the morning blast,

By lantern light I take a look at the long, long last.

燕子楼三首

一

满窗明月满帘霜，被冷灯残拂卧床①。

燕子楼中霜月夜，秋来只为一人长。

二

钿晕罗衫色似烟，几回欲著即潸然。

自从不舞霓裳曲，叠在空②箱十一年。

三

今春有客洛阳回，曾到尚书墓上来。

见说白杨堪作柱，争教红粉③不成灰？

① 拂卧床：此处暗示盼盼侍妾的身份，也表明其生活的变化。
② 空：形容精神上的空虚。
③ 红粉：此处指盼盼的红颜。

The Pavilion of Swallows

I

Her room is drowned in moonlight and the screen in frost;

The quilt grows cold with dying lamp, she makes the bed.

The moonlit night in which Swallows' Pavilion's lost,

Since autumn came, lengthens for one who mourns the dead.

II

Her silken dress with golden flowers fades like smoke;

She tries to put it on, but soon she melts in tears.

Since she no longer danced to the air

of "Rainbow Cloak",

It has been stored up in the chest for ten long years.

III

Some friends coming back from ancient capital say

They've visited the grave of her dear lord again.

The graveyard poplar white grows high as pillar gray.

How can her rosy face still beautiful remain?

大林寺①桃花

人间②四月芳菲③尽，山寺桃花始盛开。

长恨④春归无觅处，不知转入此中来⑤。

---

① 大林寺：位于今庐山香炉峰上。庐山有三个大林寺，这里的大林寺是上大
   林寺，是晋代僧昙诜创建。
② 人间：此处指平原的村落。
③ 芳菲：花草繁茂、芳香。
④ 长恨：常常惋惜。
⑤ "不知"句：不知，岂料，想不到。转，反。此中，指深山的寺庙里。

Peach Blossoms in the Temple of Great Forest

All flowers in late spring have fallen far and wide,

But peach blossoms are full-blown on the mountainside.

I oft regret spring's gone without leaving its trace;

I do not know it's come up to adorn this place.

问刘十九 ①

绿蚁新醅酒 ②，红泥小火炉。

晚来天欲雪，能饮一杯无 ③ ？

---

① 刘十九：白居易留下的作品中，提到刘十九的不多，仅两首，但提到刘二十八（刘禹锡）的就很多了。刘十九乃刘禹锡的堂兄刘禹铜，系洛阳一富商，与白居易常有应酬。

② "绿蚁"句：酒是新酿的酒。新酿酒未滤清时，酒面浮起酒渣，其色微绿，形泡沫，细如蚁，故称绿蚁。

③ 无：表示疑问的语气词，相当于吗。

An Invitation

My new brew gives green glow;

My red clay stove flames up.

At dusk it threatens snow,

Won't you come for a cup?

后宫词

泪湿罗巾梦不成，夜深前殿按歌声[1]。

红颜[2]未老恩[3]先断，斜倚熏笼[4]坐到明。

---

[1] 按歌声：依照歌声的韵律打拍子。

[2] 红颜：此处指宫女。

[3] 恩：指君恩。

[4] 熏笼：覆罩香炉的竹笼。香炉用来熏衣被，为宫中之物。

The Deserted

Her handkerchief soaked with tears, she cannot fall asleep,

But overhears band music waft when night is deep.

Her rosy face outlasts the favor of the king;

She leans on her perfumed bed till morning birds sing.

暮江吟①

一道残阳②铺水中，半江瑟瑟③半江红。

可怜④九月初三夜，露似真珠⑤月似弓⑥。

---

① 暮江吟：黄昏时分在江边所作的诗。吟，诗歌的一种形式。
② 残阳：快落山的太阳的光，也指晚霞。
③ 瑟瑟：本指碧色珍宝，此处指碧绿色。
④ 可怜：可爱。
⑤ 真珠：即珍珠。
⑥ 月似弓：上弦月，指农历九月初三这日，月弯如弓。

Sunset and Moonrise on the River

The departing sunbeams pave a way on the river;

Half of its waves turn red and the other half shiver.

How I love the third night of the ninth moon aglow!

The dewdrops look like pearls, the crescent like a bow.

钱塘湖^①春行

孤山^②寺北贾亭^③西，水面初平云脚^④低。

几处早莺争暖树^⑤，谁家新燕^⑥啄春泥。

乱花渐欲迷人眼，浅草才能没马蹄。

最爱湖东行不足^⑦，绿杨阴里白沙堤^⑧。

① 钱塘湖：杭州西湖。
② 孤山：独立于西湖里湖与外湖之间的一座小山。
③ 贾亭：贾公亭。西湖名胜之一，唐朝贾全所筑。
④ 云脚：白云重重叠叠，同湖面上的波澜连成一片，看上去浮云很低，故云。
⑤ 暖树：向阳的树木。
⑥ 新燕：指春燕，可以理解为刚从南方飞回来的燕子。
⑦ 行不足：游赏不尽。足，满足。
⑧ 白沙堤：白堤，位于孤山东北面。

On Qiantang Lake in Spring

096

West of Jia Pavilion and north of Lonely Hill,

Water brims level with the bank and clouds hang low.

Disputing for sunny trees, early orioles trill;

Pecking vernal mud in, young swallows come and go.

A riot of blooms begin to dazzle the eye;

Amid short grass the horse hoofs can barely be seen.

I love best the east of the lake under the sky,

The bank paved with white sand is shaded by willows

green.

白云泉

天平山^①上白云泉^②，云自无心水自闲^③。

何必奔冲山下去，更添波浪^④向人间！

---

① 天平山：位于苏州城西二十里左右，因为山势高峻，峭拔入云，故又称白
云山。此山宋代时被赐给范仲淹及其后人，所以又称为赐山。天平山有三
绝，分别为怪石、清泉、红枫。白云亭和白云泉就在此山上。

② 白云泉：位于天平山上，被称为"吴中第一水"。上天平山的路有三段，称
为"三白而云"，下白云处有白云亭，亭侧就是白云泉。泉水清冽而晶莹，
据说用白云泉水泡沏的茶水，香味四溢，远近闻名。

③ 闲：从容自得。

④ 波浪：水中浪花，此处喻指令人困扰的事情。

White Cloud Fountain

Behold the White Cloud Fountain on the Sky-blue

Mountain!

White clouds enjoy pleasure while water enjoys leisure.

Why should the torrent dash down from the mountain high

And overflow the human world with waves far and nigh?

病中

交亲不要苦相忧，亦拟时时强出游。

但有心情何用脚，陆乘肩舆^①水乘舟。

---

① 肩舆：指轿子。

Illness

My bosom friends need not worry too much for me;

Somehow I'll take a walk if from illness I'm free.

When I want to go far, I need not use my feet;

Sedan by land and boat on water are as fleet.

羊士谔

YANG SHI'E

作者简介

羊士谔（762—820），泰山（今山东泰安）人。

贞元元年（785年）登进士第，授常州义兴尉。累至宣歙巡官，顺宗朝时，为王叔文所恶，贬汀州宁化尉。元和初，擢为监察御史，掌制诰。后因与窦群、吕温等诬论宰执被贬，后出为资州刺史。元和十四年（820年），擢为户部郎中。

工诗，妙造梁《选》，作皆典重。著集有《墨池编》《晁公武群斋读书志》。

登楼

槐柳萧疏绕郡城，夜添山雨作江声。

秋风南陌无车马，独上高楼故国情。

Mounting the Tower

Sparse scholar-trees and willows gird the city walls;

Rain's streamed downhill since last night as a river bawls.

When autumn gale blows, nor horse nor cart are in sight.

How can I not be homesick alone on the height!

柳宗元

LIU ZONGYUAN

作者简介

柳宗元（773—819），字子厚，汉族，祖籍河东郡（今山西运城）人，世称"柳河东""河东先生"。因官终柳州刺史，又称"柳柳州"。唐代文学家、哲学家、散文家、思想家。

贞元九年（793年）登进士第。贞元十四年（798年），登博学宏词科，授集贤正字，调蓝田尉。贞元十九年（803年），入为监察御史里行。永贞元年（805年），擢礼部员外郎，参与革新。唐宪宗即位，贬邵州刺史，再被加贬永州司马。元和十年（815年）召还，但终未被重用，只复出为柳州刺史。

其诗多抒写抑郁悲愤、思乡怀友之情，语言朴实自然。《全唐诗》编诗四卷，有《柳河东集》存世。

登柳州城楼寄漳汀封连四州刺史 ①

城上高楼接大荒②，海天愁思③正茫茫。

惊风乱飐^{zhǎn}芙蓉水④，密雨斜侵薜荔⑤墙。

岭树重遮千里目，江流曲似九回肠⑥。

共来百越文身地⑦，犹自⑧音书滞一乡。

---

① 登柳州城楼寄漳汀封连四州刺史：柳州，今属广西。漳，漳州，汀，汀洲，皆属今福建。封，封州；连，连州，皆属今广东。《旧唐书·宪宗纪》："乙酉（元和十年）三月，以虔州司马韩泰为漳州（今福建漳州）刺史，永州司马柳宗元为柳州（今广西柳州）刺史，饶州司马韩晔为汀州（今福建长汀县）刺史，朗州司马刘禹锡为播州刺史，台州司马陈谏为封州（今广东封开县）刺史。御史中丞裴度以禹锡母老，请移近处，乃改授州（今广东连州）刺史。"

② 接大荒：连接边远地区。接，一说目接、看到。大荒，泛指荒僻的边远地区。

③ 海天愁思：如海如天的愁思。

④ "惊风"句：惊风，急风、狂风。乱飐，吹动。芙蓉，指荷花。

⑤ 薜荔：一种蔓生植物，也称木莲。

⑥ 九回肠：愁肠九转，形容愁绪缠结难解。

⑦ "共来"句：共来，指和韩泰、韩晔、陈谏、刘禹锡四人同时被贬边远地区。百越，泛指五岭以南的少数民族。文身，身上文刺花绣，古代有些民族有此习俗。

⑧ 犹自：仍然是。

To Four Friends in Exile

From the high tower I see the wilderness looms;

My sad thoughts mingle with the boundless sea and sky.

A sudden gale disturbs the pool with lotus blooms;

A slanting rain attacks the wall where vines climb high.

Dense trees on mountain ridge shut out the distant view;

The river meanders like tortuous bowels long.

Coming among barbarians together with you,

I've not received your message brought by wild geese's song.

江雪

千山鸟飞绝①，万径②人踪灭。

孤舟蓑笠③翁，独钓寒江雪。

① 绝：无，没有。

② 万径：虚指，指千万条路。

③ 蓑笠：蓑衣和斗笠。笠，用竹篾编成的帽子。

Fishing in Snow

From hill to hill no bird in flight;

From path to path no man in sight.

A lonely fisherman afloat

Is fishing snow in lonely boat.

渔翁

渔翁夜傍西岩①宿，晓汲清湘燃楚竹。

烟销②日出不见人，欸乃③一声山水绿。

回看天际下中流④，岩上无心云相逐。

---

① 傍西岩：靠近西山。傍，靠近。西岩，当指永州境内的西山，可参见诗人的《始得西山宴游记》。

② 销：消散。一作"消"。

③ 欸乃：象声词，一说指桨声，一说是人长呼之声。

④ 下中流：由中流而下。

A Fisherman

Under western cliff a fisherman passed the night;

At dawn he makes bamboo fire to boil water clean.

Mist clears off at sunrise but there's no man in sight;

Only the fisherman's song turns hill and rill green.

He goes down mid-stream and turns to look on the sky.

What does he see but clouds freely wafting on high?

饮酒

今夕少愉乐，起坐开清尊。

举觞酹^{lèi}先酒^①，为我驱忧烦。

须臾^②心自殊，顿觉天地喧。

连山变幽晦^③，绿水函^④晏温^⑤。

---

① "举觞"句：酹先酒，祭奠第一个发明酒的人。酹，以酒洒地，表示祭奠或立誓。先酒，指第一个发明酿酒的人。相传杜康是我国酿酒的创始人。

② 须臾：一会儿。

③ 幽晦：昏暗不明。

④ 函：包含。

⑤ 晏温：晴天的暖气。

蔼蔼南郭门⑥，树木一何⑦繁。

清阴⑧可自庇，竟夕⑨闻佳言。

尽醉无复辞，偃卧⑩有芳荪⑪。

彼哉晋楚富⑫，此道⑬未必存。

⑥ "蔼蔼"句：蔼蔼，茂盛的样子。南郭门，指永州外城的南门。郭，外城。

⑦ 一何：一，助词，用以加强语气。何，多么。

⑧ 清阴：此处指草木。

⑨ 竟夕：整夜。

⑩ 偃卧：仰卧。

⑪ 芳荪：指草地。

⑫ 晋楚富：此处指一方富豪。

⑬ 此道：指饮酒之乐。

Drinking

I fill my cup with drink divine;

It is another boring day.

First let me drink to Lord of Wine,

Who helps to drive the blues away.

One draught and different I feel;

At once the world revives anew.

See what the hidden hills reveal!

The river takes on warming hue.

Exuberant at southern gate,

Leafy trees look like paradise.

With shade their roots are saturate;

All night you hear silent advice.

Drink your fill and gargle your mouth!

Drunk, you may lie on fragrant grass.

O rich revelers north and south!

What have you in your cups, alas!

崔

护

CUI HU

作者简介

崔护（772—846），字殷功，博陵（今河北定州）人，唐代诗人。

贞元十二年（796年），进士及第。大和三年（829年）为京兆尹，同年为御史大夫、岭南节度使。

其诗诗风精练婉丽，语极清新。《全唐诗》存诗六首，皆是佳作，尤以《题都城南庄》流传最广，脍炙人口，有目共赏。

题都^①城南庄

去年今日此门中，人面^②桃花相映红。

人面不知何处去，桃花依旧笑^③春风。

---

① 都：国都，指唐时的京城长安。

② 人面：姑娘的脸。第三句中的"人面"指代姑娘。

③ 笑：形容桃花盛开的样子。

Written in a Village South of the Capital

In this house on this day last year a pink face vied

In beauty with the pink peach blossom side by side.

I do not know today where the pink face has gone;

In vernal breeze still smile pink peach blossoms

full blown.

元積

YUAN ZHEN

作者简介

　　元稹（779—831），字微之，别字威明，洛阳（今河南）人。唐代大臣、文学家。

　　贞元九年（793年）明经及第，授左拾遗，进入河中幕府，擢校书郎，迁监察御史。长庆二年（822年）由工部侍郎拜相，后出任同州刺史，入为尚书右丞。大和四年（830年）出任武昌军节度使。大和五年（831年）去世，追赠尚书右仆射。

　　与白居易同科及第，结为终生诗友，同倡新乐府运动，共创"元和体"，世称"元白"。其乐府诗创作受到张籍、王建的影响，"新题乐府"缘于李绅。有《元氏长庆集》传世。

遣悲怀三首

一

谢公^①最小偏怜女，自嫁黔娄百事乖^②。

顾我无衣搜荩箧^③，泥^④他沽酒拔金钗。

野蔬充膳甘长藿^⑤，落叶添薪仰古槐。

今日俸钱过十万，与君营奠复营斋。

① 谢公：东晋宰相谢安，他最偏爱侄女谢道韫。
② "自嫁"句：黔娄，战国时齐国的贫士，此处自喻。意指其妻韦丛以名门闺秀屈身下嫁。百事乖，什么事都不顺遂。
③ 荩箧：用竹或草编的箱子。
④ 泥：软缠，央求。
⑤ 藿：豆叶，嫩时可食。

二

昔日戏言身后意⑥，今朝都到眼前来。

衣裳已施行看尽⑦，针线犹存未忍开。

尚想旧情怜婢仆，也曾因梦送钱财。

诚知此恨⑧人人有，贫贱夫妻百事哀。

---

⑥ 身后意：指死后的设想。

⑦ 行看尽：眼看就要完了。

⑧ 此恨：指夫妻死别之情。

三

闲坐悲君[9]亦自悲，百年[10]都是几多时。

邓攸无子寻知命[11]，潘岳悼亡[12]犹费词。

同穴窅^{yǎo}冥何所望[13]，他生[14]缘会更难期。

唯将终夜长开眼[15]，报答平生[16]未展眉[17]。

⑨ 君：指韦氏，诗人的妻子。

⑩ 百年：指一生。

⑪ "邓攸"句：邓攸，字伯道，西晋时人，曾任河东太守，在战乱中舍弃自己的儿子而保全侄子，后来终生无子，当时人有"天道无知，使伯道无儿"之叹。知命，认识到是命中注定的。

⑫ 潘岳悼亡：西晋诗人潘岳写了很悲痛的悼亡诗，但死去的妻子也不会知道。此处是诗人自指。

⑬ "同穴"句：同穴，指夫妻合葬。窅冥，深远幽暗的样子。何所望，意思是死后合葬的悲哀之情难以相通。

⑭ "他生"句：他生，来生。缘会，姻缘遇合。期，期待。

⑮ "唯将"句：唯将，只将。长开眼，指彻夜不眠。

⑯ 平生：指韦氏生前。

⑰ 未展眉：指韦氏生前一直过着清苦的生活，很少欢悦。

To My Deceased Wife

I

Youngest daughter of your family, loved the best,

Unluckily you married into my poor household.

To patch my clothes you would search your dowry chest;

Coaxed to buy me wine you'd pledge a hairpin of gold.

For fuel you'd burn dry leaves from old locust tree;

For meals we were glad to eat but wild herbs and rice.

More than a hundred thousand coins are now paid me,

But I can bring you only temple sacrifice.

II

"What if one of us should die?" we said for fun one day;

But now it has come true and passed before my eyes.

I can't bear to see your clothes and give them away;

I seal your embroidery lest it should draw my sighs.

Remembering your kindness, I'm kind to our maids;

Dreaming of your bounty, I give bounties as before.

I know there is no mortal but returns to the shades,

But a poor couple like us have more to deplore.

III

Sitting idle, I grieve for myself as for you;

How many days are left for my declining years?

Another childless man fared better than I do;

Another widower lavished vain verse and tears.

Could I await a better fate than our same tomb?

Could you be born again and again be my wife?

With eyes unclosed all night long I'll lie in the gloom

To repay you for your unknit brows in your life.

行宫

寥落^①古行宫^②，宫花^③寂寞红。

白头宫女^④在，闲坐说玄宗^⑤。

---

① 寥落：寂寞冷落。
② 行宫：皇帝在京城之外的宫殿，这里指当时皇帝的行宫上阳宫（位于今洛阳市）。
③ 宫花：行宫里的花。
④ 白头宫女：据白居易《上阳白发人》，天宝末年一些宫女被"潜配"到上阳宫，在这冷宫里一待就四十多年，成了白发老人。
⑤ 说玄宗：谈论唐玄宗。

At an old Palace

Deserted now imperial bowers,

For whom still redden palace flowers?

A white-haired chambermaid at leisure

Tells of the late emperor s pleasure.

菊花

秋丛绕舍似陶家^①，遍绕篱边日渐斜^②。

不是花中偏爱菊，此花开尽更^③无花。

---

① 陶家：这里指陶渊明家。陶渊明，东晋诗人，隐居名士。后人常常将陶渊明与菊花联系在一起，表现一种隐士的高洁。

② 日渐斜：太阳渐渐落山。斜，倾斜。

③ 更：再。

Chrysanthemums

Around the cottage like Tao's autumn flowers grow;

Along the hedge I stroll until the sun slants low.

Not that I favor partially the chrysanthemum,

But it is the last flower after which none will bloom.

离思五首（其四）

曾经沧海①难为水，除却②巫山不是云。

取次③花丛懒回顾，半缘④修道半缘君。

---

① "曾经"句：曾经，曾经到临。沧海，大海。难为，这里指不足为顾、不值得一观的意思。

② "除却"句：相形之下，除了巫山，别处的云便不称其为云。此句与前句均暗喻自己之前的一段恋情。

③ 取次：任意，随便。

④ 半缘：此指"一半是因为……"。

Thinking of My Dear Departed

IV

No water's wide enough when you have crossed the sea;

No cloud is beautiful but that which crowns the peak.

I pass by flowers which fail to attract poor me

Half for your sake and half for Taoism I seek.

贾岛

JIA DAO

作者简介

贾岛（779—843），字阆仙，一作浪仙，河北道幽州范阳（今河北涿州）人。自号"碣石山人"。唐代诗人，人称"诗奴"。

早年出家为僧，法号无本。据说洛阳曾有令禁止和尚午后外出，贾岛作诗发牢骚，被韩愈发现才华，并成为"苦吟诗人"。后受教于韩愈，还俗参加科举，但累举不中第。唐文宗时被排挤，贬做遂州长江县（今遂宁市大英县）主簿，故称"贾长江"。唐武宗会昌年初，由普州司仓参军改任司户，未任病逝。

其诗多写荒凉枯寂之境，长于五律，重词句锤炼。与孟郊齐名，后人以"郊寒岛瘦"喻其诗之风格。有《长江集》传世。

剑客 ①

十年磨一剑，霜刃 ② 未曾试。

今日把示君 ③，谁有不平事？

---

① 剑客：指行侠仗义之人。

② 霜刃：形容剑锋寒光闪闪，十分锋利。

③ 把示君：拿来给你看。

A Swordsman

I've sharpened my sword for ten years;

I do not know if it will pierce.

I show its blade to you today.

O who has any grievance? Say!

题兴化寺园亭①

破却②千家作一池，不栽桃李种蔷薇。

蔷薇花落秋风起，荆棘满亭君始知③。

132

My Lord's Garden

A thousand homes shattered, a garden is laid out;

Roses grow everywhere, but no fruit-bearing trees.

When the autumn wind blows and roses fall about,

Can you sit in the thorn-choked pavilion with ease?

寻隐者不遇①

松下问童子，言②师采药去。

只在此山中，云深③不知处④。

1
3
4

---

① 寻隐者不遇：寻，寻访。隐者，隐士，隐居在山林中的人，指不肯做官而隐居在山野之间的人，一般指的是贤士。

② 言：回答，说。

③ 云深：指山上的云雾。

④ 处：行踪，所在。

For an Abent Recluse

I ask your lad beneath a pine.

"My master has gone for herbs fine.

He stays deep in the mountain proud,

I know not where, veiled by the cloud."

李绅

LI SHEN

作者简介

李绅（772—846），字公垂，唐代诗人。

青年时目睹农民终日劳作而不得温饱，以同情和愤慨的心情，写出《悯农二首》，流传甚广，千古传诵，被誉为"悯农诗人"。

与元稹、白居易交游甚密，为新乐府运动的倡导者和参与者。有《乐府新题》二十首，已佚。

悯①农二首

一

春种一粒粟②，秋收万颗子。

四海无闲田③，农夫犹④饿死。

137

二

锄禾⑤日当午⑥，汗滴禾下土。

谁知盘中餐⑦，粒粒皆辛苦！

---

① 悯：怜悯，此处有同情的意思。
② 粟：泛指谷类。
③ "四海"句：四海，指全国。闲田，没有耕种的田。
④ 犹：仍然。
⑤ 禾：禾苗，这里泛指谷类植物。
⑥ 日当午：指中午。
⑦ 餐：饭菜。

The Peasants

I

Each seed when sown in spring

Will make autumn yields high.

What will fertile fields bring?

Of hunger peasants die.

II

At noon they weed with hoes;

Their sweat drips on the soil.

Each bowl of rice, who knows?

Is the fruit of hard toil.

薛

涛

XUE TAO

作者简介

薛涛（768—832），字洪度，长安（今陕西西安）人，唐代女诗人。

辩慧工诗、多才多艺，与元稹、白居易、杜牧、刘禹锡等人竞相酬唱，诗名大振。称号"文妖"，中唐李肇记载："乐妓而工诗者，涛亦文之妖也。"

与卓文君、花蕊夫人、黄娥并称蜀中四大才女，与鱼玄机、李冶、刘采春并称唐代四大女诗人，流传诗作九十余首，收于《锦江集》。

春望词四首

一

花开不同赏，花落不同悲。

欲问①相思处，花开花落时。

二

揽草②结同心③，将以遗知音。

春愁正断绝，春鸟复哀吟。

---

① 欲问：想要问。

② 揽草：采草。

③ 结同心：同心结。古代用它作为男女相爱的象征。

三

风花日将老，佳期犹渺渺④。

不结同心人，空结同心草。

四

那堪花满枝，翻作⑤两相思。

玉箸⑥垂朝镜，春风知不知。

Spring View

I

Blooming flowers not together enjoyed,

At their fall we're not together annoyed.

Don't ask me why I'm lovesick, sad and drear

To see flowers appear and disappear!

II

I braid two blades of grass into one heart

And send it to my lover far apart.

I've just got rid of my old vernal sorrow.

Who knows birds sing again a mournful morrow!

III

Like bloom in wind I'm growing old;

Our happy date can't be foretold.

When our hearts are not one, alas!

What's the use of love-knot in grass?

IV

How can I bear a lovesick heart

From blooming flowers kept apart?

Does spring wind know my face appears

Before the mirror wet with tears?

酬人雨后玩竹^①

南天春雨时，那鉴雪霜姿。

众类亦云茂，虚心宁自持。

多留晋贤醉^②，早伴舜妃悲^③。

晚岁君能赏，苍苍劲节奇。

---

① 这是一首酬人之作，有人雨后赏竹，写了一首诗送给诗人，诗人应照原作
写了这首酬答诗。

② "多留"句：诗人借用典故——晋代山涛、王戎等七位高士在竹林中饮酒赋
诗，世人将他们称为"竹林七贤"。

③ "早伴"句：舜南巡死于苍梧，他的两位妃子在竹林哭泣，泪洒竹竿，那竹
便被称为湘妃竹，也叫斑竹。

To the Bamboo after Rain

When spring rain falls on southern roof

Who remembers you are cold-proof?

From the lush plants you stand apart;

Alone you keep your modest heart.

The drunken sages are your compeers;

Your stems are stained with royal tears.

We know your worth in winter cold;

E'er green and strong, you won't grow old.

寄旧诗与 ① 元微之 ②

诗篇调态人皆有，细腻风光我独知。

月夜咏花怜暗澹 ③，雨朝题柳为敧垂。

长教碧玉藏深处，总向红笺 ④ 写自随。

老大不能收拾得，与君开似教男儿。

---

① 与：赠予、给予。

② 元微之：元稹，字微之。

③ 暗澹：形容花柳的可爱之姿，和后一句的"敧垂"是一样的意思。

④ 红笺：指的是薛涛独创的风靡一时、名传千古的深红色薛涛笺。

Sending old Poems to Yuan Zhen

Each poet or poetess has his style or her own;

I know mine is subtle and delicate alone.

I sing of moonlit flowers in melancholy strain;

I write of weeping willows shedding tears in rain.

Like hidden emerald I'm ever kept apart;

On my self-made rosy leaf I pour out my heart.

Growing too old to sort my poems one by one,

I send you these old ones you may show to your son.

张

ZHANG HU 祜

作者简介

张祜（785—849），字承吉，清河（今河北）人，唐代诗人。

家世显赫，被人称作张公子，有"海内名士"之誉。早年曾寓居姑苏。长庆中，令狐楚表荐之，不报。辟诸侯府，为元稹排挤，遂至淮南寓居，爱丹阳曲阿地，隐居以终。

"故国三千里，深宫二十年"，张祜以诗得名，《全唐诗》收录其三百四十九首诗歌。

何满子 ^①

故国^②三千里，深宫二十年。

一声何满子，双泪落君^③前。

---

① 何满子：曲名。又题作《宫词》。一般宫怨诗多写宫女失宠或不得幸之苦，
  而此诗却一反其俗，写在君王面前挥泪埋怨，还一个被夺去幸福与自由的
  女性的本来面目，这是此诗独到之处。
② 故国：指故乡。
③ 君：此处指唐武宗。

The Swan Song

Homesick a thousand miles away,

Shut in deep palace twenty years,

Singing the dying swan's sweet lay,

O how can she hold back her tears!

赠内人 ①

禁门②宫树月痕过，媚眼惟看宿鹭③窠。

斜拔玉钗灯影畔，剔开红焰④救飞蛾。

---

① 内人：指宫女。因皇宫又称大内，故称宫女为内人。
② 禁门：宫门。
③ 宿鹭：栖息的鹭。
④ 红焰：指灯芯。

A Palace Maid

The moon cast shadows of a tree on palace door;

Her longing eyes saw a nest of birds and no more.

Drawing her jade hairpin near a candle she came

To save a moth by brushing aside the red flame.

集灵台二首（其二）

虢国夫人^①承主恩，平明^②骑马入宫门。

却嫌脂粉污颜色，淡扫蛾眉朝至尊。

---

① 虢国夫人：杨贵妃三姐的封号。
② 平明：天刚亮的时候。

Long-Life Terrace

The Duchess of Guo State had won imperial grace;

At dawn she rode through palace gates with dignity.

Disdainful of the paint which might have marred her face,

With lightly touched-up brows she met His Majesty.

题金陵渡

金陵津渡小山楼①，一宿行人自可愁②。

潮落夜江斜月③里，两三星火④是瓜洲⑤。

---

① "金陵"句：金陵渡，渡口名，位于今江苏省镇江市一带。津，渡口。小山
　楼，渡口附近小楼，诗人住宿之处。

② "一宿"句：宿，过夜。行人，旅客，指诗人自己。可，当。

③ 斜月：下半夜偏西的月亮。

④ 星火：形容远处三三两两像星星一样闪烁的火光。

⑤ 瓜州：在长江北岸，今江苏省扬州市邗江区，与镇江市隔江相对，向来是
　长江南北水运的交通要道。

At Jinling Ferry Head

In little hut at ferry head where people part,

A lonely traveler can't but feel sad at heart.

The moon slants o'er the ebbing river in the gloom,

And on the islet two or three weak flickers loom.

李涉

LI SHE

作者简介

　　李涉，生卒年不详，自号清溪子，洛阳（今河南）人，唐代诗人。

　　早岁客梁园，逢兵乱，避地南方，与弟李渤同隐庐山香炉峰下。后出山作幕僚。宪宗时，曾任太子通事舍人。不久，贬为峡州（今湖北宜昌）司仓参军，在峡州蹭蹬十年，遇赦放还，复归洛阳，隐于少室。文宗大和中，任国子博士，世称"李博士"。著有《李涉诗》一卷。

再宿武关①

远别秦城②万里游，乱山高下出商州③。

关门④不锁寒溪水，一夜潺湲⑤送客愁。

---

① 武关：位于今陕西省商洛市，与函谷关、萧关、大散关并称"秦之四塞"。
② 秦城：此处指京都长安。
③ "乱山"句：乱山，指商州一带的商山。商州，指商州城，位于今陕西省商洛市。
④ 关门：指武关的大门。
⑤ 潺湲：水缓慢流动的样子。潺，水缓流的样子。湲，水流声。

Lodging Again at the Southern Pass

Leaving the capital with a long way to go,

I stay at Southern Pass where hills rise high and low.

The city gate cannot lock in the cold brook's song;

It murmurs about my parting grief all night long.

崔郊

CUI JIAO

作者简介

崔郊，生卒年、字与号均不详，唐元和间秀才，《全唐诗》收录其诗一首。

赠婢

公子王孙逐后尘^①，绿珠^②垂泪滴罗巾^③。

侯门一入深如海，从此萧郎^④是路人。

① "公子"句：公子王孙，古代贵族、官僚、王公贵族的子弟。后尘，指人过
  处扬起来的尘土，喻公子王孙争相追求的情景。
② 绿珠：西晋富豪石崇的宠妾，貌美可人，这里喻指被人夺走的婢女。
③ 罗巾：丝制手巾。
④ 萧郎：原指梁武帝萧衍，南朝梁的建立者，风流多才，很有名气。后成为
  诗词中习用语，泛指女子所爱恋的男子。此处是作者自谓。

To the Maid of My Aunt

Even sons of prince and lord try to find thy trace;

Thy scarf is wet with pearl-like tears dropped from thy

face.

The mansion where thou enter is deep as the sea;

Thy master from now on is a stranger to thee.

李贺

LI HE

作者简介

李贺（790—817），字长吉，陇西成纪（今甘肃秦安）人，居于福昌（今河南宜阳）昌谷。

元和五年（810年）举河南府乡贡进士，然以父讳晋肃，不得应进士举。为奉礼郎，郁郁不得志，以病辞归。

长于乐府，句锻字炼，色彩瑰丽。《全唐诗》编诗五卷，有《昌谷集》《李贺歌诗编》存世。

雁门太守行

黑云压城城欲摧①，甲光向日金鳞开②。

角③声满天秋色里，塞上燕脂凝夜紫④。

半卷红旗临易水⑤，霜重鼓寒声不起⑥。

报君黄金台⑦上意，提携玉龙⑧为君死。

---

① "黑云"句：形容敌军兵临城下的紧张气氛和危急形势。黑云，厚厚的乌云，此处指攻城敌军的气势。摧，毁坏。

② "甲光"句：甲光，铠甲迎着太阳闪出的光。甲，铠甲、战衣。金鳞，形容铠甲闪耀如金色鱼鳞。

③ 角：古代军中一种吹奏乐器，也是号角，多用兽角制成。

④ "塞上"句：夜色中塞上泥土有如胭脂凝成，浓艳得近似紫色。燕脂：即胭脂，此处指暮色中塞上泥土犹如胭脂凝成。据说长城附近多半是紫色泥土。"塞上"一作"塞土"。

⑤ 易水：河名，大清河上游支流，源出今河北省保定市易县。

⑥ "霜重"句：霜重鼓寒，天寒霜降，战鼓声沉闷而不响亮。声不起，形容鼓声低沉；不高扬。

⑦ 黄金台：位于今河北省保定市易县东南。相传战国燕昭王所筑，置千金于台上，以招揽贤士。

⑧ 玉龙：一种珍贵的宝剑，此处代指剑。

Defense of the Wild Geese Gate

Dark clouds threaten the town, its walls risk to be worn;

Defenders' sunlit armour glitters like scales bright.

The sky in autumn hue is loud with blowing horn;

The rouge-congealed frontier dissolves in purple night.

Our half-unfurled red flags come to shivering stream;

Laden with heavy frost, cold drumbeats can't rise high.

We'd do our best to realize our lord's golden dream,

Jade-dragon sword in hand, we're not afraid to die.

苏小小墓

幽兰露^①，如啼眼。

无物结同心，烟花^②不堪剪。

草如茵^③，松如盖^④。

风为裳，水为佩。

油壁车^⑤，夕^⑥相待。

冷翠烛^⑦，劳^⑧光彩。

西陵^⑨下，风吹雨。

---

① 幽兰露：兰花上凝结着露珠。

② 烟花：此处指墓地中艳丽的花。

③ 茵：指垫子。

④ 盖：车盖，即车上遮阳防雨的伞盖。

⑤ 油壁车：妇人所乘的车，车身以油漆饰。

⑥ 夕：一作"久"。

⑦ 冷翠烛：即磷火，俗称鬼火，有光无焰，所以说"冷翠烛"。

⑧ 劳：不辞劳苦的意思。

⑨ 西陵：位于今杭州西泠桥一带。

Tomb of Su, Young Beauty

On lonely orchid dew

Looks like tear in your eye.

Whose heart is one with you?

Flowers in mist would cry.

Carpet-like grass would sing

Canopy-like pine trees.

Ripples as pendants ring;

Your robe wafts in the breeze.

Your cab of painted sheen

Waits long for happy night.

Your chilly candle green

Kindles flames and sheds light

On your west tomb in vain,

For wind has changed to rain.

梦天 ①

老兔寒蟾泣天色 ②，云楼半开壁斜白 ③。

玉轮轧露湿团光 ④，鸾佩 ⑤ 相逢桂香陌。

黄尘清水三山 ⑥ 下，更变千年如走马。

遥望齐州 ⑦ 九点烟，一泓 ⑧ 海水杯中泻。

---

① 梦天：梦游天上。

② "老兔"句：在一个幽冷的月夜，阴云四合，空中飘洒下阵阵寒雨，就像兔和蟾在哭泣。老兔寒蟾，传说中住在月宫里的动物。

③ "云楼"句：云层变幻，月光斜穿过云隙，把云层映照得像海市蜃楼一样。

④ "玉轮"句：月亮带着光晕，像被露水打湿了似的。

⑤ 鸾佩：雕刻着鸾凤的玉佩，此代指仙女。此句是诗人想象自己在月宫中桂花飘香的路上遇到了仙女。

⑥ 三山：指东海上的三座神山。

⑦ 齐州：即中州，指中国。此处指的是在月宫中俯瞰中国。

⑧ 泓：量词，指一道或一片水。

Dreaming of the Sky

The lunar toad's and rabbit's tears wash the cold sky;

Half-open bowers in the cloud shed slanting ray.

Jade wheels roll over dew and moisten light on high;

The Beauty of the Moon comes down her laurel way.

Dust turns to water pure as in a fairy star;

A thousand years have changed like horses on the run.

I see nine wreaths of smoke rise from the land afar,

And the sea pours into a cup under the sun.

天上谣

天河夜转漂回星，银浦流云学水声^①。

玉宫桂树花未落，仙妾采香垂佩缨^②。

秦妃^③卷帘北窗晓，窗前植^④桐青凤小^⑤；

---

① "银浦"句：银浦，天河。学水声，行云像发出声音的流水一样。

② 缨：系玉佩的丝带。

③ 秦妃：指秦穆公的女儿弄玉，此处借指仙女。《列仙传》载，弄女嫁给仙人
萧史，随凤升天。

④ 植：倚。

⑤ 青凤小：即小青凤，为了押韵，此处倒置。

王子吹笙鹅管长⑥，呼龙耕烟⑦种瑶草。

粉霞红绶藕丝裙⑧，青洲步拾兰苕春⑨。

东指羲和⑩能走马，海尘新生石山下。

⑥ "王子"句：王子即王子乔，周灵王太子，名晋，传说擅长吹笙，此处代指
　 仙子。鹅管，形状像鹅毛的笙管。
⑦ 耕烟：在云烟中耕耘。
⑧ "粉霞"句：粉霞即粉红色的衣衫。绶，丝带。藕丝裙，纯白色的裙子。藕
　 丝，纯白色。
⑨ "青洲"句：青洲，即清邱，南海中草木茂密的仙洲。步拾，边走边采集。
　 兰苕，兰草的茎，此处泛指香花香草。
⑩ 羲和：神话中给太阳驾车的神。

Song of Heaven

Stars float on Heavenly River turning at night;

Clouds over silver shores mimic the rippling song.

Laurel flowers have not fallen from Lunar Height;

Fairies gather fragrance with pendants hanging long.

The princess rolls up screens to welcome dawning day;

The blue phoenix is overshadowed by the plane tree.

An immortal blows the painted flute in his way

And calls dragons to plough mist and plant herb with glee.

In rainbow dress and lotus skirt with ribbon red,

Fairies gather spring orchids in Azure Isle.

Pointing to the charioteer of the Sun God ahead,

They find sea dust form stony mountain in a while.

浩歌

南风吹山作平地，帝遣天吴①移海水。

王母桃花千遍红，彭祖巫咸几回死②？

青毛骢^{cōng}马参差钱③，娇春杨柳含缃烟④。

筝人劝我金屈卮^{zhī}⑤，神血未凝身问谁⑥？

不须浪饮丁都护⑦，世上英雄本无主。

① 天吴：指水神。

② "彭祖"句：彭祖，即传说中颛顼之玄孙钱铿，生于夏代，尧封其于彭地，到殷末时已有七百六十七岁（一说八百余岁）。巫咸，一作巫戊，商王太戊的大臣。相传他发明鼓，发明用筮占卜，又会占星，是神仙人物。

③ "青毛"句：青毛骢马，名马。参差钱，指马身上的斑纹参差不齐。

④ 含缃烟：形容杨柳嫩黄。缃，浅黄色的绢。缃，一作细。

⑤ "筝人"句：筝人，弹筝的女子。屈卮，一种有把的酒盏。

⑥ "神血"句：酒醉时飘飘然，似乎形神分离了，不知自己是谁。神血未凝，即精神和血肉不能长期凝聚，它是生命短促的婉曲说法。身问谁，"身向谁"的意思。

⑦ 丁都护：刘宋高祖时的勇士丁旿，官拜都护。

买丝绣作平原君⑧，有酒唯浇赵州土。

漏⑨催水咽玉蟾蜍，卫娘发薄不胜梳⑩。

羞见秋眉换新绿⑪，二十男儿那刺促⑫？

174

⑧ 平原君：赵胜，战国时赵国贵族，惠文王之弟，善养士，门下有食客数千人，任赵相。赵孝成王七年，秦军围赵都邯郸，平原君指挥抗秦，坚守三年，后楚、魏联合，击败秦军。

⑨ 漏：古代的计时器。玉蟾蜍，漏上面玉制的装饰。可能诗人写的这种漏壶就是蟾蜍形状的，水从其口中滴出。

⑩ "卫娘"句：卫娘即汉武帝的皇后卫子夫。传说她发多而美，深得汉武帝的宠爱。此处"卫娘"代指妙龄女子，或即侑酒歌女。发薄不胜梳，意指卫娘年老色衰，头发稀疏了。

⑪ "羞见"句：秋眉，稀疏变黄的眉毛。换新绿，画眉。唐人用青黑的黛色画眉，因与浓绿色相近，故唐人诗中常称黛色为绿色。

⑫ 刺促：烦恼。

A Full Song

The southern wind blows down hills and flat land
appears;

The God of Water moves the sea from east to west.

The peach divine has turned red many thousand years;

The oldest man and witch are dead and lie in rest.

I ride a piebald horse dappled in color fine;

Willows exhale light wreaths of smoke in charming
spring.

The lute-player offers a golden cup of wine.

Before my blood and spirit fuse, what can I sing?

Don't drink and sing in praise of the governor old!

A hero may not meet a connoisseur in his life.

I would like to buy silk and embroider in gold

The image of the lord who had won all in strife.

As water drips from the clock, time passes away,

Thin would become the hair of the beautiful queen.

How could a twenty-year-old man not fight his way,

When he sees autumn eyebrows change into new green?

秋来

桐风惊心壮士苦①，衰灯络纬②啼寒素。

谁看青简一编书③，不遣花虫粉空蠹（dù）④？

思牵今夜肠应直，雨冷香魂吊书客⑤。

秋坟鬼唱鲍家诗⑥，恨血千年土中碧⑦。

---

① "桐风"句：桐风，吹过梧桐叶的秋风。壮士，诗人自称。
② 衰灯络纬：衰灯，暗淡的灯光。络纬，虫名，俗称纺织娘，因秋天季节转凉而哀鸣，其声似纺线。
③ 一编书：指诗人的一部诗集。
④ "不遣"句：此句意思是竹简书久无人读，蠹虫就在其中生长。不遣，不让。花虫，蛀蚀器物、书籍的虫子。蠹，蛀蚀。
⑤ "雨冷"句：香魂吊书客，指前代诗人的魂魄来慰问诗人。书客，诗人自指。
⑥ 鲍家诗：指南朝宋鲍照的诗。鲍照曾写过诗文《行路难》抒发怀才不遇之情。
⑦ "恨血"句：《庄子》曰："苌弘死于蜀，藏其血，三年化为碧。"碧血千年难消。

Autumn Comes

The wind blows down plane leaves and moves my heart
to rue;

Spinners weaving cold silk weep by flickering light.

Who will read the deep words inscribed on the bamboo

And keep worms boring powderly holes out of sight?

Such nocturnal thoughts would stretch my intestine
straight,

But sweet phantoms cold tears would rain down for
their peer.

Ghosts would come out of tombs to mourn the poet's
fate;

Blood would turn earth to emerald from year to year.

秦王^①饮酒

秦王骑虎游八极^②，剑光照空天自碧。

羲和敲日玻璃声^③，劫灰飞尽^④古今平。

龙头泻酒邀酒星^⑤，金槽琵琶夜 枨 枨^{chéng} ^⑥。

洞庭雨脚来吹笙，酒酣喝月使倒行。

179

---

① 秦王：有几种说法。一说指秦始皇，但篇中并未涉及秦代故事。一说指唐
太宗李世民，他做皇帝前是秦王。一说指唐德宗李适，他做太子时被封为
雍王，雍州属秦地，故又称秦王，曾以天下兵马元帅的身份平定史朝义，
又以关内元帅之职镇守咸阳，防御吐蕃。

② 八极：四面八方，此处指天下各地。

③ "羲和"句：羲和，传说中为驭日女神。敲日，鞭打着太阳。玻璃声，发出
敲打玻璃的声音。

④ 劫灰飞尽：指灾难结束。

⑤ 酒星：传说中主管饮宴的星君。

⑥ "金槽"句：金槽，用金装饰琵琶上端架弦的地方。枨枨，形容琵琶声。

銀云栉栉瑶殿明⑦，宫门掌事⑧报一更。

花楼玉凤声娇狞⑨，海绡红文⑩香浅清，

　　黄鹅跌舞千年觥⑪。

仙人烛树⑫蜡烟轻，清琴⑬醉眼泪泓泓⑭。

---

⑦ "银云"句：银云，月光照耀下的云彩。栉栉，形容云朵排列整齐的样子。
　 瑶殿，华美的宫殿。

⑧ 宫门掌事：掌管宫里杂事的人。

⑨ "花楼"句：玉凤，歌女。娇狞，形容歌声娇柔而有穿透力。"狞"字大约
　 是当时的一种赞语，含有不同寻常之类的意思。

⑩ 海绡红文：用海绡纱做的红色花纹的舞衣。海绡，鲛绡纱。

⑪ "黄鹅"句：黄鹅，即黄娥，歌姬舞女。跌舞，献酒时的舞蹈动作。觥，一
　 种酒器。

⑫ 仙人烛树：指高大的烛台。

⑬ 清琴：青琴，传说中的神女。此处借指宫女。

⑭ 泪泓泓：眼泪汪汪。

The Drinking Song of the King of Qin

The King of Qin rode the tiger to eight Poles high:

His sword shone in the air and brightened the blue sky.

His driver struck the sun with a glass-breaking sound;

All were reduced to ashes on the battleground.

Stars were invited to drink wine poured from dragon's head;

The golden pipa played at night would grieve the dead.

The rain treading on Dongting Lake would blow the lute;

The King ordered the moon to go back to its root.

Silver cloud on cloud made the crystal palace bright;

The gate-keeper announced it was still early night.

The phoenix in the tower sang her bewitching song;

Clear fragrance of ladies' silken dress wafted long.

The dancers drank to his health of a thousand years.

From the candles on the fairy trees rose smoke light.

From the lutist's drunken eyes streamed down copious

tears.

南园^①十三首（选五）

其一

花枝草蔓眼中开，小白长红越女腮^②。

可怜日暮嫣^③香落，嫁与东风不用媒。

其五

男儿何不带吴钩^④，收取关山五十州。

请君暂上凌烟阁^⑤，若个书生万户侯？

---

① 南园：园名，位于福昌昌谷（今河南省宜阳县三乡镇）。

② "小白"句：小白长红，指花有小有大，颜色各种各样。越女，此处泛指美女。

③ 嫣香：娇艳芳香，指花。

④ 吴钩：吴地出产的弯形的刀，此处指宝刀。一作"横刀"。

⑤ 凌烟阁：唐太宗为表彰功臣而建的殿阁，绘有秦琼等二十四人的像。

其六

寻章摘句老雕虫^⑥，晓月当帘挂玉弓。

不见年年辽海上，文章何处哭秋风^⑦？

其七

长卿^⑧牢落悲空合，曼倩^⑨诙谐取自容。

见买^⑩若耶溪^⑪水剑，明朝归去事猿公^⑫。

⑥ "寻章"句：寻章摘句，指创作时谋篇琢句。老雕虫，老死于雕虫的生活之中。

⑦ 哭秋风：悲秋。

⑧ 长卿：汉代辞赋家司马相如的字。

⑨ 曼倩：汉代滑稽家东方朔的字。东方朔持论诙谐。

⑩ 见买：拟买。

⑪ 若耶溪：位于越州，即欧冶子铸剑之所。

⑫ 猿公：指剑术高明的隐者。越王勾践曾请一位善剑法的女子到王都去，女子途中遇到一位自称袁公的老翁，二人以竹竿比剑术，后来老翁飞上树梢，化作白猿。

其八

春水初生乳燕飞，黄蜂小尾扑花归。

窗含远色通书幌[13]，鱼拥香钩近石矶。

---

⑥ 书幌：书斋之幔帏也。

My Southern Garden

I

Blooming branches and creepers spread before the eye;

Rosy flowers with maiden's cheeks in beauty vie.

At sunset fallen fragrant petals cannot please,

But wed without a go-between to vernal breeze.

V

Why does a man not join the army sword in hand,

And pass mountains and streams to occupy the land?

If you should go up the tower scraping the sky,

You'd find no scholar could become a general high.

VI

Should I waste time to find the best words in best order

Until the waning moon looks like a jade bow?

Do you not see the war raging on northern border?

How can a poet grieve to hear autumn wind blow?

VII

The unemployed talent lived in an empty room;

The humorist made fun to lighten the deep gloom.

I'd like to buy and sharpen a sword by the stream,

And learn from Master Ape how to fulfill my dream.

VIII

Spring water rises when young swallows learn to fly;

Bees come back when they've gathered honey from the

flowers.

The window screens enframe scenes far-off and near-by;

A scented hook attracts the fish where a lock towers.

金铜仙人^① 辞汉歌并序

魏明帝青龙元年^②八月，诏宫官牵车西取汉孝武捧露盘仙人，欲立置前殿。宫官既拆盘，仙人临载乃潸然泪下^③，唐诸王孙李长吉遂作《金铜仙人辞汉歌》。

茂陵刘郎秋风客^④，夜闻马嘶晓无迹^⑤。

① 金铜仙人：《三辅黄图》记载，汉武帝时建造了神明台，上面有承露盘，金铜仙人"舒掌捧铜盘玉杯"接"云表之露"，用露水调匀玉屑，汉武帝认为吃下这露水所和的玉屑即可成仙。

② 魏明帝青龙元年：魏明帝，即曹叡，曹操之孙。青龙元年（233年），青龙元年与历史不符，据《三国志·魏书·明帝纪》记载，在青龙五年三月改元为景初元年（237年），迁徙长安铜人承露盘即在这一年。

③ 潸然泪下：《汉晋春秋》记载魏明帝迁徙铜人时，拆承露盘的声音响彻数十里，金铜仙人也落下了眼泪，所以被留在了霸城。其实是因为铜人太重，难以运到洛阳。

④ "茂陵"句：茂陵，汉武帝刘彻的陵墓，位于今陕西省兴平市。秋风客，这里是指悲秋的人。汉武帝曾写有《秋风辞》，其中有名句"欢乐极兮哀情多，少壮几时兮奈老何"。

⑤ "夜闻"句：传说汉武帝的魂魄出入汉宫，有人曾在夜中听到他坐骑的嘶鸣声。

画栏桂树悬秋香，三十六宫土花⑥碧。

魏官牵车指千里，东关酸风⑦射眸子。

空将汉月⑧出宫门，忆君清泪如铅水。

衰兰送客咸阳道⑨，天若有情天亦老。

携盘独出月荒凉，渭城已远波声小。

---

⑥ 土花：此处指青苔。
⑦ 东关酸风：东关，从长安到魏的国都洛阳要经过长安东门，所以称为东关。酸风，令人心酸落泪之风。
⑧ 汉月：指承露盘。以月比喻玉盘。
⑨ "衰兰"句：衰兰，秋兰已老，故称衰兰。客，指铜人。咸阳，秦都城名，汉改为渭城县，离长安不远，此处代指长安。咸阳道，此指长安城外的道路。

The Bronze Statue Leaving Han Palace

In the eighth month of the year 237 the emperor of Wei sent
A eunuch to bring from the west the bronze statue holding
A moon-shaped plate to catch the immortal dew, erected by
Emperor Wu of the Han Dynasty and to place it in the front
Court at Luoyang. Dismantled, the bronze shed tears before

The emperor was gone just like his autumn breeze;
At night his steed would neigh, at dawn no trace was seen.
By painted rails fragrance still wafts over laurel trees,
His thirty palaces overgrown with mosses green.
Wei eunuch drove a dray to go a long, long way;
In Eastern Pass the sour wind stung the bronze's eyes.
Only the moon of yore saw him leave palace door;
Thinking of his dear lord, he shed tears and heaved sighs.

Withered orchid would say, "Farewell and go your way."

Heaven would have grown old if it could feel as man.

He went with moon-shaped plate beneath the moon

desolate;

The waves unheard, far from the town the horses ran.

马诗二十三首（选四）

一

龙①脊贴连钱②，银蹄白踏烟。

无人织锦韂③^{chàn}，谁为铸金鞭④。

四

此马非凡马，房星⑤本是星。

向前敲瘦骨⑥，犹自带铜声⑦。

---

① 龙：此处指健壮的骏马。

② 连钱：形容毛色斑点状如连接的铜钱。

③ 韂：也叫障泥，垂覆在马腹两侧以遮挡泥土的布帘。

④ 金鞭：以金为饰物的马鞭。

⑤ "房星"句：房星，星名，二十八宿之一。本是星，一作"是本星"，一作"本是精"。古人认为地下非凡的人或物与天上的星宿相应，称马对应的星宿为房星，故言。

⑥ 瘦骨：清瘦的骨头。

⑦ 铜声：铜器发出的声音，这里指马骨的坚劲。

五

大漠沙如雪，燕山⑧月似钩。

何当⑨金络脑⑩，快走踏清秋。

二十三

武帝⑪爱神仙，烧金⑫得紫烟。

厩中皆肉马⑬，不解上青天。

---

⑧ 燕山：此指燕然山，是西北产良马之地。此处借指边塞。

⑨ 何当：何时将要。

⑩ 金络脑：用黄金装饰的马笼头。此处指贵重的辔头、鞍具等。

⑪ 武帝：即汉武帝刘彻。汉武帝"尤敬鬼神之祀""好神仙之道"。据《汉书·武帝纪》载，武帝喜爱西域汗血马，使将军李广利伐大宛，得马甚众。

⑫ 烧金：烧炼金石药物以制丹，信者认为服之可以长生不老。

⑬ 肉马：痴肥的马、凡庸的马。

Horse Poems (Four Selections)

I

A string of coins on the horse's back, noble and proud,

His hoofs silver-white as though born to trot in cloud.

But where are whip of gold and saddle cloth of brocade?

The cloth is not yet woven and whip not yet made.

IV

This is no ordinary steed

But an incarnate star indeed.

When I tap his bony frame, what's found?

I seem to hear metallic sound.

V

The desert sand looks white as snow;

The crescent moon hangs like a bow.

When would the steed in golden gear

Gallop all night through autumn clear?

XXIII

"I'll have elixir." Emperor Wu says,

And heaps of gold go up in purple haze.

All steeds in royal stable, ah, must die,

For none of them can run up to the sky.

相和歌辞·神弦曲①

西山日没东山昏，旋风吹马马踏云②。

画弦素管声浅繁，花裙_{cuì cài}綷縩步秋尘③，

　桂叶刷风桂坠子，青狸哭血寒狐死。

古壁彩虬金帖尾，雨工骑入秋潭水④。

百年老_{xiāo}鸮成木魅⑤，笑声碧火巢中起。

---

① 神弦曲：乐府古题，属清商曲辞。
② "西山"两句：写黄昏时神降临的景象。
③ "画弦"两句：写女巫起舞迎神。
④ "古壁"两句：古壁上画的彩虹也成了精灵，作孽害人，因此也被神驱赶到潭水中去了。彩虬，彩绘之龙。雨工，雨师，行雨之神。骑入秋潭水，一作"夜骑入潭水"。
⑤ "百年"句：百年老鸮也有变成精怪者，则驱逐并焚其巢穴。鸮，似斑鸠，古人将其视为祸鸟。

Song of the Holy Strings

East hills are darkened when on west hills sinks the sun;

The whirlwind blows clouds away on which horses run.

The painted lute and pipe play music high and low;

The witch in rustling flowered skirt comes in sunset glow.

Laurel leaves and seeds are blown down by autumn breath;

Blue racoons weep over the fox frozen to death.

Dragons with golden tails are painted on the wall,

But God of Rain drives them to autumn waterfall.

The hundred-year-old owl transformed into a pest

Bursts in laughter to see green flames rise from its nest.

将进酒

琉璃钟^①，琥珀浓，小槽^②酒滴真珠红。

烹龙炮凤^③玉脂泣，罗帏绣幕围香风。

吹龙笛，击鼍鼓^④；皓齿歌，细腰舞。

况是青春日将暮，桃花乱落如红雨，

劝君终日酩酊醉，酒不到刘伶^⑤坟上土。

① 琉璃钟：形容酒杯之名贵。
② 小槽：古时制酒器中的一个部件，酒由此缓缓流出。此处指酿酒。
③ 烹龙炮凤：指厨肴珍异。
④ 鼍鼓：用鼍皮制成的鼓。鼍，即扬子鳄，产于长江中下游，亦称鼍龙，俗
  称猪婆龙。
⑤ 刘伶：魏晋时期的文坛领袖、"竹林七贤"之一。他酷好饮酒，自诩为"天
  生刘伶，以酒为名"。其每每外出饮酒，必带一小童背铁锹相随，告之曰：
  "死便埋我。"旷世骇俗，无出其右。

Drinking Song

A glazed cup fall of amber wine,

The stroug drink drops like red pearls fine.

The dragon boiled and phoenix roasted would weep;

The fragrant breeze blows into broidered curtains deep.

The dragon flute is played;

Beaten the drams covered with alligator's skin

The songstress sings with teeth as bright as jade,

And dancers dance with waist as slender as hairpin.

The prime of your life like the sun on the decline,

Peach blossoms fall pell-mell like rain of petals pink.

So I advise you to get drank with wine.

When buried in the gave, what could you take to drink?

官街鼓①

晓声隆隆催转日，暮声隆隆呼月出。

汉城黄柳映新帘②，柏陵③飞燕埋香骨。

碓④碎千年日长白，孝武秦王听不得。

从君翠发芦花色，独共南山守中国。

几回天上葬神仙，漏声⑤相将无断绝。

---

① 官街鼓：长安城大街上的鼓，用以报时和戒夜。
② "汉城"句：此句暗示改朝换代，新帝登基，什物更换。汉城，指唐都城长安。黄柳，刚发嫩芽的春柳。
③ 柏陵：帝王陵墓。帝王陵地常植松柏，故称。
④ 碓：敲击，此处有消磨之意。
⑤ 漏声：铜壶滴漏的声音。滴漏是古代计时的漏器，用铜壶盛水滴漏来计时刻。

Official Drums

At dawn official drumbeats hasten the sunrise;

At dusk the booming drums call the moon to the skies.

When yellow willows pat forth new buds in the town,

In tomb is buried the favorite of the crown.

The drums have boomed a thousand years, still shines the sun,

But ancient emperors of Qin and Han have down.

Your hair once black may turn white as reed flowers stand,

The drums witn southen hills will ever guard our land.

Even immortals were buried in the sky,

The drumbeats and the warer-clock will never die.

许浑

XU HUN

作者简介

许浑（791—858），字用晦（一作仲晦），润州丹阳（今江苏丹阳）人，晚唐最具影响力的诗人之一。

文宗大和六年（832年）进士及第。大中年间入为监察御史，因病乞归，后复出仕，任润州司马。历虞部员外郎，转睦、郢二州刺史。晚年归润州丁卯桥村舍闲居，自编诗集，曰《丁卯集》。

一生不作古诗，专攻律体，题材以怀古、田园诗为佳，以偶对整密、诗律纯熟为特色。其诗中多描写水、雨之景，后人拟之与"诗圣"杜甫齐名，并以"许浑千首湿，杜甫一生愁"评价之。

咸阳城西楼晚眺

一上高城万里愁，蒹葭杨柳似汀洲。

溪云初起日沉阁①，山雨欲来风满楼。

鸟下绿芜秦苑夕，蝉鸣黄叶汉宫秋②。

行人莫问当年③事，故国东来渭水流。

---

① "溪云"句：作者自注，"南近磻溪，西对慈福寺阁"。

② "鸟下"二句：夕照下，飞鸟下落至长着绿草的秦苑中，秋蝉也在长着黄叶的汉宫中鸣叫着。

③ 当年：一作"前朝"。

Gazing a far in the Evening from the West Tower of Xianyang

On city wall I see grief spread for miles and miles

O'er reeds and willow trees as planted on flats and isles.

The sun beneath the cloud sinks o'er waterside bower;

The wind before the storm fills the mountainside tower.

In the wasted Qin garden only birds fly still;

'Mid yellow leaves in Han palace cicadas shrill.

O wayfarer, don't ask about the days gone by!

Coming from east, I hear only the river sigh.

塞下曲

夜战桑干北①，秦兵半不归。

朝来有乡信，犹自寄寒衣②。

---

① 桑干北：桑干河北岸。桑干河，永定河的上游，发源于山西，流经华北
平原。
② "犹自"句：犹自，仍然。寒衣，御寒的衣服。

Frontier Song

In snow our men did fight;

Half of them died at night.

But letters came next day:

Winter clothes on the way.

谢亭送别

劳歌^①一曲解行舟，红叶青山水急流^②。

日暮酒醒人已远，满天风雨下西楼^③。

---

① 劳歌：本指在劳劳亭送客时唱的歌，此处泛指送别歌。劳劳亭，位于今南京市南。

② 水急流：暗指行舟远去，与日暮酒醒、满天风雨共同渲染无限别意。

③ 西楼：送别的谢亭。诗词中的南浦、西楼等，皆指送别之所。

Parting at Riverside Tower

After the farewell song your boat departs by day

On rapid stream between green mountains and red

leaves.

When I'm sober from wine at dusk, you're far away;

When I go down, a sky full of wind and rain grieves.

徐凝

XU NING

作者简介

徐凝，生卒年、字与号均不详，唐代诗人。明人杨基《眉庵集》卷五"长短句体"赋诗云："李白雄豪妙绝诗，同与徐凝传不朽。"

工诗，其诗朴实无华，意境高远。《全唐诗》编诗一卷。

忆扬州

萧娘^①脸薄难胜泪，桃叶^②眉长易觉愁。

天下三分明月夜，二分无赖^③是扬州。

---

① 萧娘：女子的代称。

② 桃叶：代指女子。

③ 无赖：蛮不讲理，或顽皮可爱之意。"无赖"二字写出扬州无限风姿。

To One in Yangzhou

Your bashful face could hardly bear the weight of tears;

Your long, long brows would easily feel sorrow nears.

Of all the moonlit nights on earth when people part,

Two-thirds shed sad light on Yangzhou with broken

heart.

杜牧

DU MU

作者简介

杜牧（803—853），字牧之，京兆万年（今陕西西安）人，杜佑之孙。唐代诗人、文学家。以别于杜甫，称其为"小杜"。

历任弘文馆校书郎、淮南节度使掌书记、监察御史、宣州团练判官、左补阙、史馆编撰、司勋员外郎以及黄、池、睦、湖等州刺史。晚年长居樊川别业，世称杜樊川。

工诗，尤擅七言近体，清丽俊爽，自成一家，与李商隐齐名，亦称"李杜"。其甥裴延翰集其诗文为《樊川文集》二十卷，今存。

过华清宫①三首（其一）

长安回望绣成堆②，山顶千门次第开。
一骑红尘③妃子笑，无人知是荔枝来。

---

① 华清宫：位于今陕西省西安市临潼骊山之上，原称温泉宫，天宝六年改名为华清宫，唐明皇与杨贵妃常来此游乐。
② 绣成堆：指花草林木和建筑物像一堆堆锦绣。骊山左侧有西绣岭，右侧有东绣岭。唐玄宗时，岭上广植树木花卉，远远望去，犹如锦绣。
③ 红尘：飞扬的尘土。

The Spring Palace

I

Viewed from afar, the hill's paved with brocade in piles;

The palace doors on hilltops opened one by one.

A steed which raised red dust won the fair mistress'

smiles.

How many steeds which brought her fruit died on the

run!

将赴吴兴登乐游原一绝 [①]

清时有味是无能 [②]，闲爱孤云静爱僧。

欲把一麾 [③] 江海去，乐游原上望昭陵 [④]。

[①] 吴兴：即今浙江湖州。乐游原，位于长安城（今西安）南，地势高敞，可以眺望全城，是当时的游览胜地。

[②] "清时"句：意指当清平无所作为之时，自己所以有此闲情。

[③] 麾：旌旗。

[④] 昭陵：指唐太宗的陵墓。

Writen at Pleasure Seeking Plain Before Leaving for the Southern Seaside town

Useless when unemployed under a peaceful reign,

I love a lonely cloud and a monk's tranquillity.

With flags and banners I'd leave for the seaside plain,

How could I leave the great tomb of His Majesty!

题扬州禅智寺 ①

雨过一蝉噪，飘萧 ② 松桂秋。

青苔满阶砌 ③，白鸟故迟留 ④。

暮霭生深树，斜阳下小楼。

谁知竹西路 ⑤，歌吹 ⑥ 是扬州。

---

① 禅智寺：又称上方寺、竹西寺。其地势居高临下，风景绝佳，是扬州胜景之一。史载原是隋炀帝之所，后建为寺。
② 飘萧：飘摇萧瑟。
③ 阶砌：台阶。
④ "白鸟"句：白鸟，通常指白色羽毛的鸟，如鹤、鹭一类。迟留，徘徊不愿离去。
⑤ 竹西路：指禅智寺前官河北岸的道路。竹西，位于扬州甘泉之北。后人在此筑亭，名竹西亭，或称歌吹亭。
⑥ 歌吹：歌声和音乐声。吹，指吹奏乐器。此处用典，出自鲍照《芜城赋》："车挂轊，人驾肩。廛闱扑地，歌吹沸天。"

The West Bamboo Temple at Yangzhou

A cicada's loud after rain;

Pine trees of sad autumn complain.

Green moss spreads o'er steps at the gate;

White birds intend to linger late.

Out of deep woods evening mist grows;

Down the tower the setting sun goes.

From West Bamboo Road further down,

You'll hear songs of Riverside Town.

江南春

千里莺啼绿映红，水村山郭酒旗^①风。

南朝^②四百八十寺，多少楼台^③烟雨中。

---

① 酒旗：古时民间称"酒望子"，是酒家的标志。
② 南朝：指宋、齐、梁、陈四朝，南朝皇帝大多信佛。
③ 楼台：原指楼阁亭台，此处指寺院建筑。

Spring on the Southern Rivershore

Orioles sing for miles amid red blooms and green trees;

By hills and rills wine shop streamers wave in the breeze.

Four hundred eighty splendid temples still remain

Of Southern Dynasties in the mist and the rain.

题宣州开元寺①水阁

阁下宛溪②，夹溪居人。

六朝③文物草连空，天澹云闲④今古同。

鸟去鸟来山色里，人歌人哭水声中。

深秋帘幕千家雨，落日楼台一笛风。

惆怅无因见范蠡⑤，参差烟树五湖⑥东。

---

① 宣州开元寺：宣州，今安徽省宣城。开元诗，始建于东晋，初名永安寺，
   后改为景德寺，唐开元二十六年（738年）又改为开元寺。
② 宛溪：位于安徽宣城，又名东溪。
③ 六朝：指三国时的吴、东晋和南朝的宋、齐、梁、陈。
④ 天澹云闲：一作"天淡云闲"。此处用以形容六朝遗迹的祥和宁静。澹，宁
   静。闲，闲适。
⑤ 范蠡：春秋时期越国的大夫，辅佐越王勾践灭吴，事成后泛舟而去，归隐
   五湖。
⑥ 五湖：太湖及周围的四个湖泊，合称为五湖。这里泛指太湖一带。

Ruined Splendor

Rank grasses grow,

Six dynasties' splendors no more;

The sky is lightly blue and clouds free as of yore.

Birds come and go into the gloom of wooded hills,

And songs and wails alike merge in murmuring rills.

Like countless window curtains falls late autumn rain;

High towers steeped in sunset, wind and flute's refrain.

O how I miss the lakeside sage of bygone days!

I see but ancient trees loom rugged in the haze.

登池州九峰楼 ① 寄张祜

百感中②来不自由，角声孤起夕阳楼。

碧山终日思无尽，芳草③何年恨即④休？

睫在眼前长不见⑤，道非身外更何求。

谁人得似⑥张公子⑦，千首诗轻⑧万户侯。

---

① 九峰楼：位于今安徽池州贵池东南的九华门上。一作"九华楼"。

② 中：指内心。一作"衷"。

③ 芳草：意指贤者。

④ 即：一作"始"。

⑤ "睫在"句：此句批评白居易评价不公，发现不了近在眼前的人才。长，一作"犹"。

⑥ 得似：比得上。

⑦ 张公子：指张祜。

⑧ 轻：轻视、蔑视的意思。

Written for Zhang Hu at Nine Peak Tower

How could I be free from my upsurging regret

To hear the lonely horn rise at Tower of Sunset!

Green mountains extend far as my longing for you.

When may I see the outspread fragrant grass anew?

The eye can't see the eyelash though it is nearby.

What need you seek when you find the way low and

high?

No one is higher than your poetical mind;

A thousand verses leave ten thousand lords behind.

九日齐山登高

江涵秋影雁初飞，与客携壶上翠微^①，

尘世难逢开口笑，菊花须插满头归。

但将酩酊酬佳节，不用登临^②恨落晖。

古往今来只如此，牛山^③何必独沾衣。

---

① 翠微：此处代指山。
② 登临：登山临水或登高临下，泛指游山览水。
③ 牛山：位于今山东淄博。

On Mountain-Climbing Day

Autumn's dissolved in waves when wild geese

backward fly;

Wine cup in hand, we climb Emerald Mountain high.

It is not easy to laugh with mouth open wide;

Back, with chrysanthemums we should be beautified.

Let us drink our fill to enjoy our holiday;

Do not regret with setting sun time passed away!

Life is full of ups and downs now as long ago.

Why should we shed vain tears for the past weal and woe?

齐安^①郡中偶题二首（其一）

两竿^②落日溪桥上，半缕轻烟柳影中。

多少绿荷相倚^③恨，一时回首背西风。

① 齐安：今湖北省黄冈市黄州一带。

② 两竿：此处形容落日有两根竹竿高。

③ 相倚：指荷叶繁多，紧紧依偎在一起。

On My Way to Lakeside Town

Halfway over creek side bridge the sun's going to set;

Half a wreath of light smoke wafts amid willow trees.

How lotus leaves lean on each other with regret?

All at once they turn back against the western breeze.

惜春

春半年已除，其余强为有^①。

即此醉残花，便同尝腊酒。

怅望送春杯，殷勤扫花帚。

谁为驻东流，年年长在手^②。

---

① "春半"二句：除，去。春天过了一般，一年算是过去了，其余的时间只能勉强打发了。
② "谁为"二句：谁能使时间停止不前，让它年年都握在我手中不消逝啊？东流，东流水，比喻不断消逝的时间。

Spring Abides Not

Spring days half gone to the years end amount;

For all the other seasons do not count.

I drink to flowers loath to say adieu

And feel e'en wine would taste like winter brew.

I am distressed after the parting cup;

The broom will sweep all fallen petals up.

From year to year thus life will pass away.

O who can stop it on its eastward way!

赤壁^①

折戟^②沉沙铁未销^③，自将磨洗认前朝^④。

东风不与周郎便，铜雀春深锁二乔。

---

① 赤壁：赤壁山，位于今湖北省黄冈市黄州。
② 戟：古代兵器。长杆的一端装有青铜或铁制成的枪尖，旁边附有月牙形锋刃。
③ 未销：一作"半销"。销，销蚀，腐蚀。
④ 前朝：指三国时期，东吴破曹。

The Red Cliff

We dig out broken halberds buried in the sand

And wash and rub these relics of an ancient war.

Had the east wind refused General Zhou a helping hand,

His foe'd have locked his fair wife on Northern shore.

泊秦淮 ①

烟笼寒水月笼沙，夜泊秦淮近酒家。

商女②不知亡国恨，隔江犹唱后庭花③。

① 秦淮：即秦淮河，经南京流入长江。相传为秦始皇南巡会稽时开凿，用以疏通淮水，故有此称。

② 商女：以卖唱为生的歌女。

③ 后庭花：歌曲《玉树后庭花》的简称。南朝陈皇帝陈叔宝溺于声色，作此曲与后宫美女寻欢作乐，终致亡国，所以后世称此曲为"亡国之音"。

Moored on River Qinhuai

Cold water and sand bars veiled in misty moonlight,

I moor on River Qinhuai near wineshops at night.

The songstress knows not the grief of the captive king,

By riverside she sings his song of Parting Spring.

赠别二首

一

娉娉袅袅[①]十三余，豆蔻[②]梢头二月初。

春风十里扬州路，卷上珠帘[③]总不如。

二

多情却似总无情[④]，唯觉樽前笑不成。

蜡烛有心还惜别，替人垂泪到天明。

---

① 娉娉袅袅：此处指女子娇弱、美好的姿态。袅，柔弱。
② 豆蔻：多年生草本植物，外形像芭蕉，叶子细长，开花淡黄，有香气。后
  人称女子十三四岁的年纪为豆蔻年华。
③ 珠帘：缀以珍珠的帘子。
④ "多情"句：多情者满腔情绪，一时无法表达，只能无言相对，如此反倒像
  彼此无情。

At Parting

I

Not yet fourteen, she's fair and slender

Like early budding flower tender.

Though Yangzhou Road's beyond compare,

Pearly screen uprolled, none's so fair.

II

Deep, deep our love, too deep to show;

Deep, deep we drink, silent we grow.

The candle grieves to see us part,

It melts in tears with burnt-out heart.

遣怀

落魄①江湖载酒行,楚腰纤细掌中轻②。

十年③一觉扬州梦,赢得青楼④薄幸名。

---

① 落魄:指仕宦潦倒不得意,漂泊江湖。魄,一作"拓"。楚腰,指细腰美女。

② 掌中轻:汉成帝皇后赵飞燕"体轻,能为掌上舞"(《飞燕外传》)。

③ 十年:一作三年。

④ 青楼:旧指精美华丽的楼房,也指妓院。

A Confession

I roved the rivers, indulged in pleasure and wine

With slender Southern girls who'd dance on palms

of mine.

Having dreamed happy dreams ten years, I woke a rover

Who earned in mansions green the name of fickle lover.

山行

远上寒山^①石径斜^{xiá}^②，白云深^③处有人家。

停车坐^④爱枫林晚^⑤，霜叶红于二月花。

---

① 寒山：深秋季节的山。

② 斜：倾斜。

③ 深：云雾缭绕的深处。一作"生"，指在白云生成之处。

④ 坐：因为。

⑤ 枫林晚：傍晚时的枫树林。

Going up the hill

A slanting stony path leads far to the cold hill;

Where fleecy clouds are born, there appear cots and
bowers.

I stop my cab at maple woods to gaze my fill;

Frost-bitten leaves look redder than early spring flowers.

秋夕①

银烛②秋光冷画屏，轻罗小扇③扑流萤。

天阶④夜色凉如水，坐看⑤牵牛织女星。

---

① 秋夕：秋天的夜晚。
② 银烛：色银而精美的蜡烛。银，一作"红"。
③ 轻罗小扇：轻巧的丝质团扇。
④ 天阶：露天的石阶。天，一作"瑶"。
⑤ 坐看：坐着朝天看。坐，一作"卧"。

An Autumn Night

Autumn has chilled the painted screen in candlelight;

A palace maid uses a fan to catch fireflies.

The steps seem steeped in water when cold grows

the night;

She sits to watch two stars in love meet in the skies.

金谷园①

繁华事散逐香尘②，流水无情草自春。

日暮东风怨啼鸟，落花犹似坠楼人③。

---

① 金谷园：晋代石崇的豪华宅第，位于今河南洛阳。
② 香尘：石崇为了让家中的舞女练习舞步，以沉香屑铺象牙床上，行于上而无迹者赐以珍珠。
③ 坠楼人：指石崇爱姬绿珠。绿珠在石崇遭人陷害被捕时，跳楼自殉。

The Golden Valley Garden in Ruins

244

Past splendors are dispersed and blend with fragrant dust;

Unfeelingly rivers run and grass grows in spring.

At dusk the flowers fall in the eastern wind just

Like Green Pearl tumbling down and birds mournfully

sing.

清明①

清明时节雨纷纷，路上行人欲断魂②。

借问③酒家何处有，牧童遥指杏花村。

---

① 清明：二十四节气之一，在阳历四月五日前后。此时民间有扫墓、踏青、
插柳等活动，宫中以当天为秋千节。
② 断魂：神情凄迷，烦闷不乐，指伤心的样子。
③ 借问：请问。

The Mourning Day

A drizzling rain falls like tears on the Mourning Day;

The mourner's heart is going to break on his way.

Where can a wine shop be found to drown his sad hours?

A cowherd points to a cot amid apricot flowers.

雍陶

YONG TAO

作者简介

雍陶，字国钧，成都（今四川）人，晚唐诗人。

文宗大和八年（834年）进士，曾任侍御史。大中六年（852年），授国子毛诗博士。大中八年（854年），出任简州（今四川简阳市）刺史，世称雍简州。

其诗多旅游题咏、送别寄赠之作，擅长律诗和七绝。

题情尽桥

从来^①只有情难尽^②，何事名为情尽桥。

自此改名为折柳^③，任他离恨一条条。

---

① 从来：向来。

② 尽：完。

③ 折柳：表示挽留之意。折柳送别是古代习俗，取"柳"谐音"留"。

The Bridge of Love's End

Why should this bridge be called Love's End,

Since love without an end will last?

Plant willow trees for parting friend;

Your longing for him will stand fast.

朱庆馀

ZHU QINGYU

作者简介

朱庆馀，生卒年不详，名可久，字庆馀，以字行，越州（今浙江绍兴）人，唐代诗人。

宝历二年（826年）进士，官至秘书省校书郎。

诗学张籍，近体尤工，诗意清新，描写细致。内容则多写个人日常生活。《全唐诗》存其诗两卷。

宫词

寂寂①花时②闭院门，美人相并立琼轩③。

含情欲说宫中事，鹦鹉前头不敢言。

---

① 寂寂：寂静无声的样子。

② 花时：百花盛开的时节，常指春日。

③ 琼轩：廊台的美称。轩，长廊。

Within the Palace

The palace gate is closed, even flowers feel lonely;

Fair maidens side by side in shade of arbour stand.

They will complain of their lonesome palace life,

Only afraid the parrot might tell a tale secondhand.

近试上张水部^①

洞房昨夜停红烛^②，待晓堂前拜舅姑^③。

妆罢低声问夫婿，画眉深浅入时无^④。

---

① 张水部：张籍。水部，水部司，官署名，隋朝始置，为工部所属四司之一，
　张籍时任水部员外郎。
② 停红烛：让红烛通宵点着。停，留置。
③ 舅姑：公婆。
④ "画眉"句：深浅即浓淡。入时无，是否时髦，此处借喻文章是否合适。

To an Examiner on the Eve of Examination

Last night red candles burned bright in the bridal room;

At dawn the bride will bow to new parents with the

groom.

She whispers to him after touching up her face:

"Have I painted my brows with fashionable grace?"

温庭筠

WEN TINGYUN

作者简介

　　温庭筠，本名岐，字飞卿，太原祁县（今山西祁县）人。唐代诗人、词人。

　　文思敏捷，每入试，押官韵，八叉手而成八韵，故有"温八叉"之称。然恃才不羁，又好讥刺权贵，多犯忌讳，又不受羁束，纵酒放浪。因得罪权贵，屡试不第，一生坎坷，终身潦倒。

　　其诗辞藻华丽，秾艳精致，内容多写闺情。现存诗七十余首，《商山早行》中的"鸡声茅店月，人迹板桥霜"千古流传。

过分水岭 ①

溪水无情似有情，入山三日得同行。

岭头 ② 便是分头处，惜别潺湲 ③ 一夜声。

---

① 分水岭：一般指两个流域分界的山。此处指今陕西省汉中市略阳的嶓冢山，
它是汉水和嘉陵江的分水岭。

② 岭头：山头。

③ 潺湲：河水缓缓流动的样子，此处指的是溪水流动的声音。

At the Watershed

The heartless stream appears to have a heart;

Three days among the hills we go along.

At watershed on mountain crest we part;

All the night long it sings a farewell song.

商山早行

晨起动征铎①，客行悲故乡。

鸡声茅店月，人迹板桥霜。

槲②叶落山路，枳③花明驿墙④。

因思杜陵⑤梦，凫⑥雁满回塘⑦。

---

① 动征铎：震动出行的铃铛。征铎，车行时悬挂在马颈上的铃铛。
② 槲：一种落叶乔木。
③ 枳：也叫"臭橘"，一种落叶灌木。
④ 驿墙：驿站的墙壁。驿，古时候递送公文的人或来往官员暂住、换马的
    处所。
⑤ 杜陵：位于长安城南，因汉宣帝陵墓在此而得名。这里指长安。作者此时
    从长安赴襄阳投友，途经商山。
⑥ 凫：野鸭。
⑦ 回塘：岸边弯曲的湖塘。此处是指"杜陵梦"的梦境。

Early Departure on Mount Shang

At dawn I rise, with ringing bells my cab goes,

But grieved in thoughts of my home, I feel lost.

As the moon sets over thatched inn, the cock crows;

Footprints are left on wood bridge paved with frost.

The mountain path is covered with oak leaves,

The post-house bright with blooming orange trees.

The dream of my homeland last night still grieves,

A pool of mallards playing with wild geese.

李商隐

LI
SHANGYIN

作者简介

李商隐（813—858），字义山，号玉溪生，怀州河内（今河南沁阳）人。唐代著名诗人，和杜牧合称"小李杜"。

开成二年（837年）进士及第，起家秘书省校书郎，迁弘农县尉，成为泾原节度使王茂元（岳父）幕僚。卷入"牛李党争"的政治旋涡，备受排挤，一生困顿不得志。

其诗构思新奇，风格秾丽，爱情诗和无题诗写得缠绵悱恻，优美动人，广为传诵。但部分诗歌（以《锦瑟》为代表）过于隐晦迷离，难于索解，至有"诗家总爱西昆好，独恨无人作郑笺"之说。

锦瑟

锦瑟①无端②五十弦，一弦一柱思华年③。

庄生晓梦迷蝴蝶④，望帝春心托杜鹃⑤。

沧海月明珠有泪⑥，蓝田日暖玉生烟⑦。

此情可待⑧成追忆，只是当时已惘然。

---

① 锦瑟：一般说法，古瑟是五十条弦，后来有二十五弦或十七弦等不同的瑟。《周礼·乐器图》："雅瑟二十三弦，颂瑟二十五弦，饰以宝玉者曰宝瑟，绘文如锦者曰锦瑟。"

② 无端：没来由，无缘无故。此隐隐有悲伤之感，乃全诗之情感基调。

③ "一弦"句：柱，用以架弦的小木柱，也叫"码子"。"思"字应变读去声，律诗中不许有一连三个平声的出现。

④ "庄生"句：《庄子·齐物论》："庄周梦为蝴蝶，栩栩然蝴蝶也；自喻适志与！不知周也。俄然觉，则蘧蘧然周也。不知周之梦为蝴蝶与？蝴蝶之梦为周与？"李商隐引庄周梦蝶之典，以言人生如梦、往事如烟之意。

⑤ "望帝"句：望帝，古代蜀国的君主，名杜宇，传说他死后化为杜鹃鸟，悲啼不已。春心，伤春之心。

⑥ "沧海"句：相传珍珠是由南海鲛人的眼泪化成，古人还认为海里的蚌珠随月亮盈亏而有圆缺变化，此处糅合了以上的典故。

⑦ "蓝田"句：蓝田，即蓝田山，位于今陕西蓝田县，为有名的产玉之地。日暖玉生烟，相传宝玉埋在地下，在阳光的照耀下，良玉上空会出现烟云。

⑧ 可待：岂待，何待。

The Sad Zither

Why should the sad zither have fifty strings?

Each string, each strain evokes but vanished springs:

Dim morning dream to be a butterfly;

Amorous heart poured out in cuckoo's cry.

In moonlit pearls see tears in mermaid's eyes;

From sunburnt jade in blue field let smoke rise.

Such feeling cannot be recalled again;

It seemed lost even when it was felt then.

重过圣女祠

白石岩扉^①碧藓滋，上清沦谪得归迟^②。

一春梦雨^③常飘瓦，尽日灵风不满旗^④。

萼绿华^⑤来无定所，杜兰香^⑥去未移时。

玉郎会此通仙籍^⑦，忆向天阶问紫芝^⑧。

---

① 白石岩扉：指圣女祠的门。岩扉，岩洞的门。
② "上清"句：上清，道教传说中仙家的最高天界。沦谪得归迟，谓神仙被贬谪到人间，迟迟未归。此句喻自己蹉跎于下多年。沦，一作"论"。
③ 梦雨：迷蒙细雨。
④ "尽日"句：尽日，终日，整天。不满旗，谓灵风轻微，不能把旗全部吹展。
⑤ 萼绿华：传说中女仙名。
⑥ 杜兰香：传说中的仙女。典出晋人曹毗所作《杜兰香传》。据传她是后汉时人，三岁时被渔父收养于湘江边，长至十余岁，有青童灵人自空而降，携之而去。
⑦ "玉郎"句：玉郎，道家所称天上掌管神仙名册的仙官。诗文引用玉郎，或自喻，或喻柳仲郢，时柳奉调将为吏部侍郎，执掌官吏铨选。通仙籍，古称登第入仕为通籍，通仙籍即取得登仙界的资格。
⑧ "忆向"句：忆，此言想往、期望。天阶，天宫的殿阶。问，求取。紫芝，一种真菌，古人以之为瑞草，道教称之为仙草，此喻指朝中之官职。

Passing Again the Temple of a Goddess

Over your door of white rock I see green moss grow;

You're banished from the paradise where you can't go.

The dreaming vernal rains with your tiles often play;

The wonder-working wind won't swell your flag all day.

There is no place to shelter fair Emerald Flower,

And Fragrant Orchid won't stay here more than an hour.

The Registrar of Jade knows you come from on high.

Let miraculous herb bring you back to the sky!

赠刘司户蕡①

江风扬浪动云根②，重碇危樯白日昏③。

已断燕鸿初起势，更惊骚客后归魂④。

汉廷急诏谁先入⑤，楚路高歌自欲翻⑥。

万里相逢欢复泣，凤巢西隔九重门⑦。

---

① 蕡：刘蕡，字去华，幽州昌平（今北京）人，宝历二年（826）进士。

② 云根：指江边的山石。

③ "重碇"句：由于江风所致，山石摇动，江船危系于石上，景色也是天昏地暗。碇，系船的石墩。危樯，即危船。

④ "更惊"句：江风蔽日的景象惊动了刘蕡迟迟不归的魂灵。骚客，指刘蕡。后归，迟归。刘蕡被贬长达七年之久，所以言此。

⑤ 汉廷急诏：指汉代朝廷曾急诏征贾谊回长安，并拜他为梁怀王太傅，作者以此喻指不知何时朝廷能召回刘蕡。

⑥ "楚路"句：楚路高歌，以屈原比刘蕡，屈原放逐乃赋《离骚》，故为"楚路高歌"。高歌，形容诗情悲壮。翻，以旧曲制作新词。

⑦ "凤巢"句：此句意谓贤者皆被放逐远离朝廷。凤巢，比喻贤臣在朝。传说黄帝时，凤凰栖于东园，或巢于阿阁。西隔，当时诗人在荆楚之地，长安位于荆楚西北，所以谓西隔。九重门，指皇帝居住的地方。

For an Exiled Friend

Waves surge when blows the wind, clouds rooted in

rocks shiver,

The mast and anchor tremble on the darkened river.

How could the northern swan fly up with broken wings?

How could the exiled poet find his Southern springs?

Who would answer the summons of the royal court?

A poet would sing freely the days long or short.

Happy to meet so far from homeland, we shed tears.

When could the phoenix fly to nine celestial spheres!

乐游原

向晚①意不适②，驱车登古原。

夕阳无限好，只是近黄昏。

---

① 向晚：傍晚。
② 意不适：情绪不好。

On the Plain of Imperial Tombs

At dusk my heart is filled with gloom;

I drive my cab to ancient tombs.

The setting sun seems so sublime,

But it is near its dying time.

北齐二首

一

一笑相倾国便亡①，何劳荆棘始堪伤②。

小怜③玉体横陈夜，已报周师入晋阳④。

二

巧笑⑤知堪敌万几⑥，倾城最在著戎衣。

晋阳已陷休回顾，更请君王猎一围⑦。

---

① "一笑"句：意指君主一旦为美色所迷，便种下亡国祸根。倾，倾倒、倾心。
② "何劳"句：晋时索靖有先识远量，预见天下将乱，曾指着洛阳宫门的铜驼道："会见汝在荆棘中耳！"
③ 小怜：冯淑妃，北齐后主高纬之宠妃。
④ "已报"句：《北齐书》载：武平七年，北周在晋州大败齐师，次年北周军队攻入晋阳（今山西太原）。此时与小怜进御时间相距甚远，此句意为色荒之祸。
⑤ 巧笑：甜美的笑。
⑥ 万几：万机，指君王政务纷杂。
⑦ "晋阳"二句：《北史·后妃传》载："周师取平阳，帝猎于三堆。晋州告急，帝将还。淑妃请更杀一围，从之。"所陷者系晋州平阳，而非晋阳，作者一时误记。

The Downfall
of Kingdom Qi

I

The king loved less his kingdom than his beauty's smiles.

Could his palace not be buried in briars for miles?

His favored lady lay in bed on full display,

While the foe entered his capital in array.

II

How could a beauty's smile overshadow state affair?

The king was charmed by his lady in hunting dress.

Of his capital in danger he did not care;

He would go hunting one more round nevertheless.

夜雨寄北 ①

君问归期未有期，巴山②夜雨涨秋池。

何当③共剪西窗烛，却话④巴山夜雨时。

---

① 夜雨寄北：写寄给北方的人。诗人的亲友在长安，所以说"寄北"。一作"夜雨寄内"。

② 巴山：大巴山的简称，此处指巴蜀一带。

③ 何当：何时。

④ 却话：再说，回头说。

Written on a Rainy Night to My Wife in the North

You ask me when I can return, but I don't know;

It rains in western hills and autumn pools overflow.

When can we trim by window side the candlelight

And talk about the western hills in rainy night?

风雨

凄凉宝剑篇②，羁泊欲穷年③。

黄叶④仍风雨，青楼⑤自管弦。

新知遭薄俗⑥，旧好隔良缘。

心断新丰酒，销愁斗几千⑦。

---

① 这首诗取第三句诗中"风雨"二字为题，实为无题。

② 宝剑篇：又名"古剑篇"，为唐初郭震所作诗篇名。《新唐书·郭震传》载，武则天召他谈话，索其诗文，郭即呈上《宝剑篇》，中有句云："非直结交游侠子，亦曾亲近英雄人。何言中路遭捐弃，零落漂沦古狱边。虽复尘埋无所用，犹能夜夜气冲天。"武则天看后大加称赏，立即重用。

③ 穷年：终生。

④ 黄叶：诗人自喻。

⑤ 青楼：青色的高楼，此处泛指精美的楼房，即富贵人家。

⑥ 遭薄俗：遇到轻薄的世俗。

⑦ "心断"二句：心断，意绝。新丰，地名，位于今陕西临潼，古时以产美酒闻名。《新唐书·马周传》载，马周不得意时，宿新丰旅店，店主人对他很冷淡，马周便要了一斗八升酒独酌。几千，指酒价，美酒价格昂贵。

Wind and Rain

As an unused sword I'm as drear.

Oh, when will end my roaming year?

Yellow leaves fall in winds and rains;

Green mansions play strings and sing strains.

My new friends are left in the cold;

Can I often meet my peers old?

How I long for nectar divine

To drown my lonely grief in wind!

寄令狐郎中

嵩①云秦树久离居，双鲤②迢迢一纸书。

休问梁园③旧宾客，茂陵④秋雨病相如。

---

① 嵩：嵩山，位于今河南。

② 双鲤：指书信。

③ 梁园：梁孝王根据自然景色，在梁地大兴土木，修建了一个很大的花园，
名东苑、菟园，后人称梁园。

④ 茂陵：位于今陕西，以汉武帝陵墓而得名。

For a Friend

We're severed long by northern cloud and western trees;

Your letter's sent to quench my thirst from far away.

Don't ask about your friend in lonely garden, please!

Just read the poet sick with rainy autumn day!

杜司勋 ①

高楼风雨感斯文 ②，短翼差池 ③ 不及群。

刻意伤春复伤别 ④，人间唯有杜司勋。

---

① 杜司勋：即杜牧，曾于唐宣宗大中二年（848）三月入朝为司勋员外郎、史馆修撰，故称杜司勋。

② "高楼"句：风雨，语出《诗经·郑风·风雨》："风雨如晦，鸡鸣不已。"此借意以怀杜牧，并以风雨迷茫之景象征时局之昏暗。斯文，此文，指他当时正在吟诵的杜牧诗作，即第三句所谓"刻意伤春复伤别"之作。

③ 差池：参差，指燕飞时尾羽参差不齐。语出《诗经·邶风·燕燕》："燕燕于飞，差池其羽。"此处自谦才短，不能奋飞远举。

④ "刻意"句：刻意，此处指别有寄托。伤春，因春天到来而引起忧伤、苦闷。伤别，因离别而悲伤。

For Du Mu

Your verse exhales spring wind and rain in tower high,

Left far behind with my short swallow wings, I sigh.

At parting spring and parting with friends old and new,

Who in the world is drowned in deeper grief than you?

杜工部蜀中离席 ①

人生何处不离群 ②，世路干戈惜暂分，

雪岭 ③ 未归天外使 ④，松州 ⑤ 犹驻殿前军 ⑥。

座中醉客延醒客 ⑦，江上晴云杂雨云 ⑧。

美酒成都堪送老 ⑨，当炉仍是卓文君 ⑩。

---

① 杜工部：杜甫。因杜甫被授有检校工部员外郎官衔，因此称其杜工部。此处表明是模仿杜诗风格，因而以"蜀中离席"为题。

② 离群：分别。

③ 雪岭：即大雪山，一名蓬婆山。

④ 天外使：往来唐朝的吐蕃使者。

⑤ 松州：唐设松州都督府，属剑南道，治下辖地颇广，治所位于今四川省阿坝藏族羌族自治州内。因西邻吐蕃国，是唐朝西南边塞，故有军队驻守。

⑥ 殿前军：本指禁卫军，此借指戍守西南边陲的唐朝军队。

⑦ 延醒客：延，请，劝。醒客，指诗人自己。

⑧ 晴云杂雨云：明亮的晴云夹杂着雨云，此处喻指边境军事的形势变幻不定。

⑨ 送老：度过晚年。

⑩ "当炉"句：当炉，面对酒炉，指卖酒者。卓文君，汉代才女，姿色娇美，精通音律，善弹琴，因与司马相如相爱而被逐出家门，而后卓文君在临邛当炉卖酒。此处借卓文君喻卖酒的女子。

Would Du Fu not Leave the Farewell Feast?

Could we have no meeting and parting in our life?

But parting would bring grief in time of war and strife.

The peace envoy has not come back from the frontiers;

Our forts are guarded still by royal cavaliers.

The drunken in the feast talk to the sober loud,

While on the river float fleecy cloud and dark cloud.

Won't good wine intoxicate you all your life long,

If accompanied by a beauty's sweeter song?

隋宫^① 二首

一

紫泉^②宫殿锁烟霞，欲取芜城作帝家。

玉玺不缘归日角，锦帆应是到天涯^③。

于今腐草无萤火^④，终古垂杨有暮鸦^⑤。

地下若逢陈后主，岂宜重问后庭花。

---

① 隋宫：隋炀帝杨广所建的行宫。
② 紫泉：即紫渊，因唐高祖名李渊，为避讳而改。
③ "玉玺"二句：如果不是李渊夺取了隋朝的政权，杨广的船大概会开到天边去了吧。玉玺，皇帝的玉印。
④ "于今"句：此句采用夸张的手法，意为炀帝已把萤火虫捕捉完了。
⑤ "终古"句：意为隋亡后，隋堤上只有杨柳依旧，暮鸦哀鸣。

二

乘兴南游不戒严^①，九重谁省谏书函^②。

春风举国裁宫锦，半作障泥^③半作帆。

---

① "乘兴"句：意谓炀帝骄横无忌，毫无戒备。《晋书·舆服志》："凡车驾亲戎，中外戒严。"

② "九重"句：《隋书·炀帝纪》载，隋炀帝巡游，大臣上表劝谏者皆斩之，遂无人敢谏。九重，指皇帝居住的深宫。省，明察、懂得。谏书函，给皇帝的谏书。

③ 障泥：马鞯，垫在马鞍的下面，两边下垂至马镫，用以挡泥土。

The Sui Palace

I

The Palace of Purple Spring lost in rainbow cloud

Might be replaced by new one in riverside town.

Were the emperor not overthrown by the crowd,

His royal ship might sail to new sky's end unknown.

But now no fireflies overspread the withered grass;

Only dark crows perch on his weeping willow trees.

If he met underground his captive king, alas!

Could the sweet song of their palace flowers still please?

II

The pleasure-seeking monarch toured the South at will.

Who dare alert him in the ninth celestial sphere?

People were forced to weave brocade through the mill,

But half was used as mudguard and half as sail too dear.

二月二日 ①

二月二日江上行，东风日暖闻吹笙。

花须柳眼各无赖②，紫蝶黄蜂俱有情。

万里忆归元亮井③，三年从事亚夫营④。

新滩莫悟游人⑤意，更作风檐雨夜声⑥。

---

① 二月二日：蜀地风俗，二月二日为踏青节。

② "花须"句：花须，花蕊，因花蕊细长如须，所以称为花须。柳眼，柳叶的嫩芽，因嫩芽如人睡眼方展，所以称为柳眼。无赖，本指人多诈狡狯，此处形容花柳都在任意地生长，从而撩起游人的羁愁。

③ 元亮井：此处指故里。

④ 亚夫营：这里借指柳仲郢的军幕。亚夫，即周亚夫，汉代的将军。他曾屯兵在细柳（今陕西咸阳）防御匈奴，以军纪严明著称，后人称为亚夫营、细柳营或柳营。

⑤ 游人：诗人自指。

⑥ 风檐雨夜声：夜间檐前风吹雨打的声音，此处用来形容江边浪潮声的凄切。

The Second Day of the Second Moon

On second day of second moon I sail on stream,

The vernal wind brings warmth and I hear flutist sing.

Red flowers have no heart and green willows no dream,

But purple butterflies and golden bees love spring.

How can I live from my homeland so far apart?

In willow camp I've done my duty for three years.

The rippling stream can't understand a roamer's heart;

The night rain dripping from old roof assails my ears.

筹笔驿 ①

猿鸟犹疑畏简书，风云常为护储胥 ②。

徒令上将 ③挥神笔，终见降王走传车 ④。

管乐有才原不忝 ⑤，关张无命欲何如？

他年 ⑥锦里经祠庙，梁父吟成恨有余。

① 筹笔驿：旧址位于今四川广元。诸葛亮曾驻军于此。
② "猿鸟"二句：诸葛亮治军以严明称，至今连猿鸟还在惊畏他的简书。疑，惊。简书，指军令。储胥，军用的篱栅。
③ 上将：犹主帅，指诸葛亮。
④ "终见"句：降王，指后主刘禅。走传车，魏元帝景元四年（263年），邓艾伐蜀，后主出降，全家东迁洛阳，出降时经过筹笔驿。传车，古代驿站的专用车辆。后主是皇帝，这时坐的却是传车，隐含讽刺意。
⑤ "管乐"句：管，管仲，春秋时期齐相，曾佐齐桓公成就霸业。乐，乐毅，战国时人，燕国名将，曾大败强齐。原不忝，真不愧。诸葛亮隐居南阳时，每自比管仲、乐毅。
⑥ 他年：往年。

The Premier's Military Station

Monkeys and birds have not forgot the Premier's order;

Still wind and cloud would screen and shield his ancient

border.

In vain had he made prodigeous strategic plan;

At last the captive king was gone in prison van.

He had the talent of wise marshals in their prime.

What could he do with generals lost before their time?

When people visit his temple in later days,

Their regret would outlast the song sung in his praise.

无题

  相见时难别亦难，东风无力百花残。

  春蚕到死丝^①方尽，蜡炬成灰泪^②始干。

  晓镜但愁云鬓改，夜吟应觉月光寒。

  蓬山^③此去无多路，青鸟^④殷勤为探看。

---

① 丝：与"思"谐音，含相思之意。
② 泪：烛泪，喻人的眼泪。
③ 蓬山：蓬莱山，传说中的三仙山之一。
④ 青鸟：《汉武故事》载，西王母下见汉武帝，有青鸟先到殿前报信，此句指
 托青鸟代主人探望对方。

To One Unnamed

It's difficult for us to meet and hard to part;

The east wind is too weak to revive flowers dead.

Spring silkworm till its death spins silk from love-sick

heart;

A Candle but when burned out has no tears to shed.

At dawn I'm grieved to think your mirrored hair turns

grey;

At night you would feel cold while I croon by moonlight.

To the three fairy hills it is not a long way.

Would the blue birds oft fly to see you on the height!

无题二首（其一）

昨夜星辰昨夜风，画楼西畔桂堂东①。

身无彩凤双飞翼，心有灵犀②一点通。

隔座送钩③春酒暖，分曹④射覆⑤蜡灯红。

嗟余听鼓⑥应官⑦去，走马兰台类转蓬⑧。

---

① 画楼：指富贵人家的屋舍。桂堂意同。

② 灵犀：犀角中心的髓质像一条白线贯通上下，借喻双方心灵的感应和暗通。

③ 送钩：也称藏钩。古代腊日的一种游戏，分二曹以较胜负，把钩互相传送后，藏于一人手中，让人猜。

④ 分曹：分组。

⑤ 射覆：在覆器下放着东西令人猜。分曹、射覆未必是实指，只是借喻宴会时的热闹。

⑥ 鼓：指更鼓。

⑦ 应官：犹上班。

⑧ "走马"句：从字面看，指诗人参加宴会后，随即骑马到兰台，类似蓬草之飞转，实则隐含自伤飘零意。兰台，秘书省，掌管图书秘籍。李商隐曾任秘书省正字。

Untitled Poems

I

As last night twinkle stars, as last night blows the breeze,

West of the painted bower, east of Cassia Hall.

Having no wings, I can't fly to you as I please;

Our hearts at one, your ears can hear my inner call.

Maybe you're playing hook in palm and drinking wine

Or guessing what the cup hides under candle red.

Alas! I hear the drum call me to duties mine;

Like rootless weed to Orchid Hall I ride ahead.

无题二首

一

凤尾香罗^①薄几重，碧文圆顶^②夜深缝。

扇裁^③月魄羞难掩，车走雷声语未通。

曾是寂寥金烬暗，断无消息石榴红。

斑骓^④只系垂杨岸，何处西南任好风。

---

① 凤尾香罗：凤纹罗。罗，绫的一种。
② 顶：指帐顶。
③ 扇裁：指以团扇掩面。
④ 斑骓：此处用典，典出自《神弦歌·明下童曲》，意指与日思夜想的意中人相距并不远，也许此刻他的马匹正系在垂柳岸边呢，只是咫尺天涯，无缘相见罢了。骓：毛色青白相杂的马。

二

重帏深下莫愁堂，卧后清宵细细长。

神女⑤生涯原是梦，小姑居处本无郎。

风波不信菱枝弱⑥，月露谁教桂叶香。

直道相思了无益，未妨惆怅是清狂⑦。

---

⑤ 神女：即宋玉《神女赋》中的巫山神女。

⑥ "风波"句：意谓菱枝虽弱质，却不相信会任凭风波欺负。

⑦ "直道"二句：意谓即使相思全无好处，但这种惆怅之心，也好算是痴情
了。直道，即使，就说。了，完全。清狂，痴情。

Untitled Poems

I

On manifold silk canopy with phoenix tail
She stitches green patterns in the deep of night.
Shy looked her face the moon-shaped fan could
hardly veil;
Gone was his rolling cab, speechless, soon lost to sight.
The lonely candle sheds its dim light to deplore;
Red pomegranates see her wait for news with zest.
His dappled horse is tethered to the willow shore.
When can she enjoy the good wind from the southwest?

II

The grief laden curtains hang deep in her Griefless Hall,
Awake from sleeps, she finds the sleepless night grow long.
A happy life in love is a dream beyond call;
A lonely virgin deprived of amorous song.

Against the wind and waves can't stand her cresses frail.

Will the moon shed dew to make her laurel leaves sweet?

Although she knows her lovesickness of no avail,

How can a passionate poor heart no longer beat?

无题四首（选三）

一

来是空言去绝踪，月斜楼上五更钟。

梦为远别啼难唤，书被催成墨未浓。

蜡照^①半笼金翡翠^②，麝熏^③微度绣芙蓉^④。

刘郎^⑤已恨蓬山^⑥远，更隔蓬山一万重。

---

① 蜡照：烛光。
② 半笼金翡翠：半笼，半映，指烛光隐约，不能全照床上被褥。金翡翠，指镶有翡翠鸟图案的金色屏风。
③ 麝熏：本指香獐，这里指麝香的香气。
④ 绣芙蓉：指绣有芙蓉花图案的帷帐。
⑤ 刘郎：指刘晨。据说汉末刘晨、阮肇上天台采药，山中迷路，遇二仙女，结成一段奇缘，返回家乡时人间已过了七世，后以"刘"指情郎。
⑥ 蓬山：海中三仙山之一蓬莱山，此处指仙境。

二

飒飒东风细雨来，芙蓉塘外有轻雷。

金蟾⑦啮锁烧香入，玉虎牵丝⑧汲井回。

贾氏窥帘韩掾少⑨，宓妃⑩留枕魏王才。

春心⑪莫共花争发，一寸相思一寸灰。

---

⑦ 金蟾：金蛤蟆，此处指锁上的装饰。

⑧ 玉虎：用玉石作装饰的井上辘轳，形如虎状。丝，指井索。

⑨ "贾氏"句：贾氏，西晋贾充的次女。她在门帘后窥见韩寿，爱悦他年少俊
美，两人私通。贾氏以皇帝赐贾充的异香赠寿，被贾充发觉，遂以女嫁给
韩寿。韩掾，指韩寿。韩曾为贾充的掾属。

⑩ 宓妃：传说伏羲之女名宓妃（洛神），溺死于洛水上。这里借指三国时曹丕
的皇后甄氏。魏王，指曹植。

⑪ 春心：指相思之情。

四

何处哀筝随急管[12]，樱花永巷垂杨岸。

东家老女嫁不售[13]，白日当天三月半。

溧阳公主[14]年十四，清明暖后同墙看[15]。

归来展转到五更，梁间燕子闻长叹。

---

[12] 哀筝随急管：哀筝，高亢清亮的筝声。急管，急促的管乐。

[13] "东家"句：东家老女，宋玉《登徒子好色赋》："臣里之美者，莫若臣东家之子。"此处意指这位老女是容华美艳的姑娘。嫁不售，嫁不出去。

[14] 溧阳公主：梁简文帝的女儿，此处泛指贵家女子。

[15] 同墙看：意指东家老女也随俗游春，同在看花。

Untitled Poems

I

You said you'd come but you have gone and left no trace;

I hear in the moonlit tower the fifth watch bell.

In dream my cry could not call you back from distant

place;

In haste with ink unthickened I cannot write well.

The candlelight illuminates half our broidered bed;

The smell of musk still faintly sweetens lotus screen.

Beyond my reach the far-off fairy mountains spread;

But you're still farther off than fairy mountains green.

II

The rustling eastern wind came with a drizzle light,

And thunder faintly rolled beyond the lotus pool.

When doors were locked and incense burned,

I came at night,

And went at dawn when windlass pulled up water cool.

You peeped at me first from behind a curtained bower;

I'm left at last but with the pillow of a dame.

Let my desire not bloom and vie with vernal flower!

For inch by inch my heart is consumed by the flame.

IV

From where come happy song and lyric full of gloom?

From willowy shore and long lane where cherries bloom.

The eastern villager's poor beauty is not wed,

Though like the sun of late spring shining overhead.

The rich and noble princess is only fourteen;

Suitors on mourning day break walls and willow screen.

How could the old maid not toss in bed deep in night?

Even swallows on the beam would sigh for her plight.

柳^①

曾逐东风^②拂舞筵，乐游春苑^③断肠天。

如何肯到清秋日，已带斜阳又带蝉。

① 柳：指曲江柳。长安城南曲江盛产柳树，而且与乐游苑相邻，是京城士女游览之所。

② 东风：这里指春天之风。古人把四方与四季相对应：春对东，夏对南，秋对西，冬对北。

③ 乐游春苑：即乐游苑，又称乐游原。位于今西安城南大雁塔东北的高地，本来是汉宣帝时的乐游庙。乐游苑是长安城最高处，登苑可眺望全城，每到三月三（上巳）、九月九（重阳），京城士女多到此登赏，诗人也著有众多吟咏乐游苑的诗篇，李商隐就有一首《登乐游原》。

To the Willow Tree

Having caressed the dancers in the vernal breeze,

You're ravished amid the merry-making trees.

How can you wait until clear autumn days are done

To shrill like poor cicadas in the setting sun?

碧城三首（其一）

碧城十二曲阑干①，犀辟尘埃玉辟寒②。

阆苑③有书多附鹤④，女床⑤无树不栖鸾。

星沉海底当窗见⑥，雨过河源⑦隔座看。

若是晓珠⑧明又定，一生长对水晶盘⑨。

---

① "碧城"句：碧城，道教传为元始天尊之所居，后引申指仙人、道隐、女冠居处。十二，意为极多。阑干，栏杆。
② "犀辟"句：犀辟尘埃，指女冠华贵高雅，头上插着犀角簪，一尘不染。犀，指犀角。辟，辟除。玉辟寒，传说玉性温润，可以辟寒。
③ 阆苑：神仙居处，此处借指道观。
④ 附鹤：仙道以鹤传书，称鹤信。
⑤ 女床：山名。
⑥ "星沉"句：星沉海底，即星没，谓天将晓。"当窗见"与下句的"隔座看"皆形容碧城之高峻。
⑦ 雨：兼取"云雨"之意。雨过河源，隐喻欢会既毕。
⑧ 晓珠：晨露。
⑨ 水晶盘：水晶制成的圆盘，此处指圆月。

Green Rainbow Cloud

I

Twelve balustrades wind in the town of rainbow cloud,

Where rhino and jade keep dust and cold air away.

The crane would send the fairy's love to phoenix proud,

There is no tree by the wall where lovebirds stay.

Stars seen before the window sink deep into the night,

And bring showers for thirsting flowers by the stream.

If the pearl of the morning should be ever bright,

How could the fairy face the crystal moon in dream?

齐宫词

永寿①兵来夜不扃②，金莲③无复印中庭。

梁台④歌管三更罢，犹自风摇九子铃⑤。

---

① 永寿：殿名。南齐废帝萧宝卷宠爱潘妃，修建永寿、玉寿、神仙等宫殿，
四壁皆用黄金涂饰。
② 扃：关闭宫门。中兴元年（501），雍州刺史萧衍（后来的梁武帝）率兵攻
入南齐京城建康（今江苏南京），齐的叛臣王珍国等作内应，夜开宫门入
殿。时齐废帝正在含德殿作乐，兵入斩之。
③ 金莲：齐废帝凿金为莲花贴地，令潘妃行其上，曰："此步步生莲花也。"
此处意指齐亡后，宫殿荒凉，再也不见潘妃妙曼的舞姿了。
④ 梁台：萧梁宫禁之地，位于今南京玄武湖畔。台，晋、宋间称朝廷禁省
为台。
⑤ 九子铃：挂在宫殿寺庙檐前作装饰用的铃，用金、玉等材料制成。

Song of the ancient Palace

When the foe came at night, unguarded was palace door;

In mid-court golden lotus blooms left trace no more.

At midnight the new emperor did not stop singing;

The ancient palace bells in the breeze still kept ringing.

汉宫词

青雀^①西飞竟未回，君王长在集灵台^②。

侍臣最有相如渴^③，不赐金茎露^④一杯。

---

① 青雀：指青鸟，即西王母之神鸟。
② "君王"句：君王，明指汉武帝，暗喻唐武宗。集灵台，汉时台名，此处意指汉事。
③ "侍臣"句：侍臣，侍奉帝王的廷臣。相如渴，相如即司马相如，司马相如患有消渴疾，后人即借此作患消渴病。
④ 金茎露：传说将此露和玉屑服之，可得仙道。

The Han Palace

The blue bird did not bring elixir from the sky;

In vain the monarch waited in his tower high.

His talented poet thirsty for drink divine

Was never given a drop of immortal wine.

离亭赋得折杨柳[①]

一

暂凭樽酒送无憀[②]，莫损愁眉与细腰[③]。

人世死前唯有别，春风争拟[④]惜长条。

二

含烟惹雾[⑤]每依依[⑥]，万绪千条拂落晖。

为报行人休尽折，半留相送半迎归。

---

① 离亭赋得折杨柳：离亭，离别的释亭，即驿站，是离别处。赋得折杨柳，
赋诗来咏折柳送别。

② 送无憀：送，遣散。无憀，无聊，无所依赖，指愁苦。

③ 愁眉与细腰：柳叶比眉，柳枝的柔软比腰，有双关意。

④ 争拟：怎拟，即不拟，意指为了惜别，不想爱惜柳条。

⑤ 含烟惹雾：烟雾中的茂密的柳条。

⑥ 依依：恋恋不舍。

Breaking Willow Twigs at Parting

I

What can I do but pour wine for your broken heart?

Don't aggravate your eyebrows and waist slender!

Before our death there's nothing sadder than to part.

Why should the vernal breeze save willow branches

tender?

II

Willow leaves drink smoke and mist, unwilling to leave,

And thousands of branches caress the setting sun.

Don't break all the twigs,

O lover, lest it should grieve.

Your friend on his return to see all trees stripped and done.

宫妓①

珠箔轻明拂玉墀，披香新殿斗腰支。

不须看尽鱼龙戏②，终遣君王怒偃师③。

① 宫妓：指宫廷教坊中的歌舞伎。唐时，京城长安设有左右教坊，左多善歌，
右多工舞。诗中所写的宫妓，当指教坊中的女乐。

② 鱼龙戏：指古代百戏中由人装扮成动物进行各种奇幻的表演，是一种变幻
莫测、炫人眼目的表演。

③ "终遣"句：此句意在告诫那些在君王面前卖弄机巧、溜须拍马的人是不会
有好下场的。

Palace Dancers

The crystal screens caressed the royal steps of jade;

The dancers vied to show slender waist in brocade.

Although the fish and dragon play might please the Sire,

The musician risked to be killed at his ire.

宫辞

君恩如水^①向东流，得宠忧移^②失宠愁。

莫向尊前奏花落^③，凉风^④只在殿西头。

宫辞

君恩如水[①]向东流，得宠忧移[②]失宠愁。

莫向尊前奏花落[③]，凉风[④]只在殿西头。

宫辞

君恩如水[①]向东流，得宠忧移[②]失宠愁。

莫向尊前奏花落[③]，凉风[④]只在殿西头。

313

---

① 君恩如水：君王的恩泽就像流水般漂移不定。

② 忧移：害怕转移，这里指害怕君王的恩宠转移到别人身上。

③ 花落：指的是《梅花落》，汉乐府《横吹曲》中的笛曲名。

④ 凉风：喻指被冷落，和上一句结合起来，暗示女子色衰被弃的可悲命运。

A Palace Poem

Imperial favor flows like eastward running stream:

When won, it brings fear for loss; when lost, it brings woe.

Don't sing before winecups the Fallen Blossom's Dream,

For from Western Palace the cold wind will soon blow.

代赠二首（其一）

楼上黄昏欲望休，玉梯横绝月如钩。

芭蕉不展丁香结^①，同向春风各自愁^②。

---

① "芭蕉"句：芭蕉不展，芭蕉的蕉心没有展开。丁香结，本指丁香之花蕾丛
生如结，此处用以象征固结不解之愁绪。

② "同向"句：意指芭蕉和丁香一同对着黄昏清冷的春风。诗以芭蕉喻情人，
以丁香喻女子自己，意指同是春风吹拂，而二人异地同心，都在为不得与
对方相会而愁苦。此处既是思妇眼前实景的真实描绘，同时又是借物写人。

Lovesickness

At dusk she will not gaze afar in tower high;

The hook-like moon shines on untrodden stairs nearby.

Banana leaves uprolled and lilacs in a knot;

Reveal their lovesickness the vernal breeze knows not.

楚吟

山^①上离宫^②宫上楼，楼前宫畔暮江流。

楚天长短^③黄昏雨，宋玉^④无愁亦自愁。

---

① 山：指巫山。
② 离宫：巫山西北的楚宫。即宋玉在《高唐赋并序》中所写的与楚襄王一同游览的地方。
③ 长短：无论长短，即总之、横竖。
④ 宋玉：战国楚辞赋家，其在《九辩》中有"余萎约而悲愁"，诗人此处以宋玉自况，感慨身世之悲。李商隐此处以宋玉自比，亦有感叹怀才不遇之意。

The Southern King's Tryst with the Mountain Goddess

Uphill the palace stands, above the halls a bower.

The stream before the halls carries twilight away.

The evening sky brings fresh showers for thirsting flower.

How could the griefless poet without sorrow stay?

板桥^①晓别

回望高城落晓河^②，长亭窗户压微波^③。

水仙欲上鲤鱼^④去，一夜芙蓉红泪多^⑤。

---

① 板桥：指开封城西的板桥。

② 晓河：此处指银河。

③ 微波：指银河之波，也指长亭下的水波。

④ 鲤鱼：典故出自《列仙传》，赵国人琴高会神仙术，曾乘赤鲤来，留月余，复入水去。

⑤ 红泪：典故出自《拾遗记》，魏文帝美人薛灵芸离别父母登车上路，用玉之唾壶承泪，壶呈红色，及至京师，壶中泪凝如血。

Parting at Morning on the Wooden Bridge

The Milky Way fades over the high city wall;

The parting pavilion overlooks the rippling stream.

The fairy riding a carp goes up the waterfall,

Leaving the lotus bloom shed red tears in her dream.

银河吹笙[①]

怅望银河吹玉笙，楼寒院冷接平明[②]。

重衾[③]幽梦他年断，别树羁雌[④]昨夜惊。

月榭[⑤]故香因雨发，风帘残烛隔霜清。

不须浪作缑山意[⑥]，湘瑟[⑦]秦箫[⑧]自有情。

---

① 玉笙：用玉做的笙，或以玉为装饰的笙。

② 平明：拂晓。

③ 重衾：两层衾被，借以喻男女欢会。

④ 羁雌：失偶之雌鸟。

⑤ 月榭：观月之台榭。榭，台上的屋子。

⑥ "不须"句：浪，随意、轻率。缑山意，指入道修仙。缑山，即缑氏山，位于今河南省洛阳市偃师区。

⑦ 湘瑟：湘灵鼓瑟，即湘水神女鼓瑟传情。

⑧ 秦箫：传说秦穆公时，有一个名叫箫只（亦作萧史）的人长于箫，箫声能引来白鹤、孔雀，甚至凤凰。穆公的女儿弄玉爱上了箫只，穆公便把女儿嫁给了他。穆公为他们修建凤台。箫只夫妇居台上数年不下，后分乘龙凤，双双飞去。

Playing on Flute in Sight of the Silver River

Gazing on Milky Way, on flute of jade I play

In bower and courtyard cold near the break of day.

Gone are sweet dreams in heavy quilt of bygone year;

A lonely bird on lonely tree shivers with fear.

Fragrance of moonlit bower spreads out with the rain;

Flickering candle flame and frost sing the refrain.

Why should you go on crane divine to Heaven high?

The music played by fairies would bring you to the sky.

春雨

怅卧新春白袷衣①，白门②寥落意多违。

红楼③隔雨相望冷，珠箔④飘灯独自归。

远路应悲春晼晚⑤，残宵犹得梦依稀。

玉珰⑥缄札何由达，万里云罗⑦一雁飞。

---

① 白袷衣：即白夹衣，唐人以白衫为闲居便服。
② 白门：指今南京。
③ 红楼：华美的楼房，多指女子的住处。
④ 珠箔：珠帘，此处比喻春雨细密。
⑤ 晼晚：夕阳西下的光景，此处还蕴含年复一年、人老珠黄之意。
⑥ 玉珰：玉制的耳饰。
⑦ 云罗：螺纹般的云。

Spring Rain

Gloomy in early spring, I lie still clad in white;

How much I miss our rendezvous now in sad plight!

Your rosy bower chills my heart when viewed in rain;

Back when dim lamplight is screened, lonely I remain.

Far on your way, you should be grieved when spring
is late;

Deep in the night, I but dimly dream of my mate.

How could I send my love letter with two jade rings?

Could miles of clouds be pierced by a swan on the
wings?

晚晴

深居俯夹城，春去夏犹清。

天意怜幽草①，人间重晚晴。

并添高阁迥②，微注③小窗明。

越鸟④巢干后，归飞体更轻。

---

① 幽草：幽暗地方的小草。

② 迥：高远。

③ 微注：因晚景斜晖，光线显得微弱柔和，故曰。

④ 越鸟：南方的鸟。

A Sunny Evening after Rain

I look down on town wall from my retreat;

With spring just gone, summer weather is clear.

It's Heaven's will to pity green grass sweet;

In human world sunny evening's held dear.

I can see afar from my tower high;

The parting rays make my small window bright.

The Southern birds find their nest again dry;

When they fly back, they feel their bodies light.

安定^①城楼

迢递^②高城百尺楼，绿杨枝外尽汀洲。

贾生^③年少虚垂泪，王粲^④春来更远游。

永忆江湖归白发，欲回天地入扁舟。

不知腐鼠成滋味，猜意鹓雏^⑤竟未休。

① 安定：唐代泾原节度使府所在地，位于今甘肃省泾川县北。唐文宗大和九年（835年），李商隐的岳父王茂元任泾原节度使，李商隐于唐文宗开成三年（838年）在其幕府中任掌书记，诗当写于此时。

② 迢递：遥远连绵，此处指楼高且绵延。

③ 贾生：指西汉贾谊。贾谊年少即颇通诸子百家之书，文帝召其为博士。贾谊认为"时事可为痛哭者一，可为流涕者二，可为太息者六"，因此"数上书陈政事，多所欲匡建"，但文帝并未采纳他的建议。后来他呕血而亡，年仅三十三岁。李商隐此时二十七岁，此处他以贾生自比。

④ 王粲：东汉末年人，建安七子之一。《三国志·魏书·王粲传》载，王粲年轻时曾流寓荆州，依附刘表，但并不得志。诗人以寄人篱下的王粲自比。

⑤ 鹓雏：传说中一种像凤凰的鸟。李商隐以鹓雏自比，表明自己有高远的心志，并非汲汲于官位利禄之辈，但谗佞之徒却以小人之心度之。

On the Tower of the City Wall

From hundred-foot-high city wall I look afar;

Beyond green willow trees the sandy islets are.

I remember a scholar while young shed vain tears,

And a famed scholar roamed in the spring of his years.

I can't forget white-haired General on the lake floating,

After changing the face of the world he went boating.

An owl might feed on dead rats with good appetite,

But a phoenix would perch on trees of lofty height.

天涯 ①

春日在天涯②，天涯日又斜。

莺啼③如有泪，为湿最高花④。

---

① 天涯：此处泛指家乡以外的极远之地。

② 天涯：此处特指具体的天边。

③ 啼：语意双关，即啼叫和啼哭。

④ 最高花：树梢顶上的花，也是盛开在最后的花。

The End of the Sky

Spring is far, far away

Where the sun slants its ray.

If orioles have tear,

Wet highest flowers here!

日日^①

日日春光斗日光^②，山城斜路杏花香。

几时心绪浑无事^③，得及游丝^④百尺长。

---

① 日日：一天天。

② "日日"句：春光，泛指春天明媚妍丽、富于生命力的景象。日光：既指艳阳春日，又兼有时光之意。

③ 浑无事：全无事。浑，全。

④ 游丝：指春天时，虫类吐在空中四处飞扬的细丝。

From Day to Day

From day to day in splendor spring with sunlight vies,

The sloping hillside way sweet with apricot bloom.

When could my heart-string be as free from worldly ties

As the hundred-foot-long gossamer in the gloom?

龙池

龙池^①赐酒敞云屏，羯鼓^②声高众乐停。

夜半宴归宫漏永^③，薛王^④沉醉寿王^⑤醒。

---

① 龙池：既是地名，也是舞曲名，此处指隆庆宫。
② 羯鼓：一种外夷的乐器，据说来源于羯族，因其用公羊皮做鼓皮，故叫羯鼓。羯鼓两面蒙皮，腰部细，它发出的音主要是古音十二律中阳律第二律一度。
③ 漏永：漫漫长夜。漏，滴漏，是古代的计时器。
④ 薛王：唐玄宗的弟弟李业之子。
⑤ 寿王：唐玄宗之子李瑁。杨玉环先为寿王妃，后被唐玄宗看中，将其立为贵妃。

Dragon Pool Feast

At Dragon Pool feast spread screens embroidered with
cloud,

All music drowned in the emperor's drumbeats loud.

Come back at midnight to hear the waterclock's song,

The prince not drunken lay awake all the night long.

流莺

流莺^①漂荡复参差^②，度陌临流不自持。

巧啭岂能无本意？良辰未必有佳期。

风朝露夜阴晴里，万户千门开闭时^③。

曾苦伤春不忍^④听，凤城何处有花枝^⑤。

---

① 流莺：指漂荡流转、无所栖居的黄莺。
② 参差：本是形容鸟儿飞翔时翅膀张敛振落的样子，此处用作动词，指张翅飞翔。
③ "风朝"二句：意指京华莺声，无论风露阴晴、门户开闭，皆漂荡啼啭不已。
④ 不忍：一作"不思"。
⑤ "凤城"句：此句言凤城虽有花枝，而流莺难以借寓，故有伤春之苦吟，而令人不忍卒听。凤城，借指京城长安。花枝，指流莺栖息之所。

To the Roving Oriole

Oriole roving high and low,

Are you happy over fields and streams?

What does your warbling want to show?

Can the fine days fulfil your dreams?

You are careless of shine or rain,

Dawn or dusk, open or closed door.

I'm grieved to hear your sad refrain,

When spring is gone and blooms no more.

嫦娥

云母①屏风烛影深，长河②渐落晓星③沉。

嫦娥应悔偷灵药，碧海青天④夜夜心⑤。

---

① 云母：一种矿石，晶体透明有光泽，古代常用来装饰屏风等家具。
② 长河：指天上的银河。
③ 晓星：启明星，清晨时出现在东方。
④ 碧海青天：本形容天空碧蓝如海，此处借喻嫦娥枯燥的生活。
⑤ 夜夜心：指嫦娥每晚都感到孤寂。

To the Moon Goddess

Upon the marble screen the candlelight is winking;

The Silver River slants and morning stars are sinking.

You'd regret to have stolen the miraculous potion;

Each night you brood over the lonely celestial ocean.

贾生

宣室^①求贤访逐臣，贾生才调^②更无伦。

可怜夜半虚^③前席^④，不问苍生问鬼神。

---

① 宣室：汉代长安城中未央宫前殿的正室，此处指帝王。
② 才调：才华，指贾生的政治才能。
③ 虚：徒然。
④ 前席：在座席上移膝靠近对方。

A Bright Scholar

The emperor recalled the banished scholar bright,

Peerless in eloquence and in ability.

Alas! His Majesty drew near him at midnight

To consult not on man but on divinity.

陈陶

CHEN TAO

作者简介

陈陶（812—885），字嵩伯，自号三教布衣，唐代诗人。

早年游学长安，善天文历象，尤工诗。举进士不第，遂恣游名山。唐宣宗大中时，隐居洪州西山，后不知所终。

有诗十卷，已散佚，后人辑有《陈嵩伯诗集》一卷。

陇西行①四首（其二）

誓扫匈奴不顾身，五千貂锦②丧胡尘。

可怜无定河③边骨，犹是深闺④梦里人。

---

① 陇西行：古代曲名。
② 貂锦：此处指战士。
③ 无定河：位于今陕西北部。
④ 深闺：指战死者的妻子。

The River Side Battleground

They would lay down their lives to wipe away the Huns;

They've bit the dust, five thousand sable-clad brave sons.

Alas! Their bones lie on riverside battleground,

But in dreams of their wives they still seem safe and

sound.

李群玉

LI QUNYU

作者简介

李群玉（808—862），字文山，澧州（今湖南澧县）人，唐代诗人。

曾授弘文馆校书郎，三年后辞官回乡，死后追赐进士及第。

极有诗才，《湖南通志·李群玉传》称其诗"诗笔妍丽，才力遒健"。

赠人

曾留宋玉^①旧衣裳，惹得巫山^②梦里香。
云雨无情^③难管领，任他别嫁楚襄王^④。

---

① 宋玉：战国后期楚国辞赋作家，相传他长相秀美，风流倜傥。
② 巫山：代指巫山神女。
③ 云雨无情：指男女间的私情。
④ 楚襄王：战国时楚国国君，楚怀王之子。

To A Deserted Lover

Your literary fame was once loved best;

Your muse then came in dreams to lovebirds' nest.

We cannot rule over fickle cloud or shower.

So let it water any thirsting flower!

曹邺

CAO YE

作者简介

曹邺（816—875），字业之，一作邺之，桂州（今广西阳朔）人。诗人。

曾任吏部郎中、扬州刺史等官职，其诗多是抒发政治上不得志的感慨，少数是讽刺时政，也有一些山水佳篇。有不少千古名诗，如《官仓鼠》，对官吏盘剥百姓的讽刺入骨三分。

官仓鼠

官仓老鼠大如斗①，见人开仓亦不走。

健儿②无粮百姓饥，谁遣朝朝入君口③？

348

---

① 斗：古代容量单位，十升为一斗。一作"牛"。
② 健儿：前线守卫边疆的将士。
③ "谁遣"句：谁遣，谁让。朝朝，即天天。君，指老鼠。

The Rats in the Public Granary

The rats in the public granary so fatted grow;

When they see man come in, they do not run away.

The soldiers not provided, and people hungry go.

Who allows the rats to eat so much from day to day?

赵嘏

ZHAO GU

作者简介

赵嘏（约806—约853），字承祐，山阳（今江苏淮安）人，唐代诗人。

会昌四年（844年）进士及第。大中年间任渭南尉，人称"赵渭南"。

工诗，风格清迥豪迈，语言疏朗流畅，音律圆熟。《长安秋望》有"残星几点雁横塞，长笛一声人倚楼"之句，为杜牧激赏。《全唐诗》编诗二卷。

江楼感旧①

独上江楼思渺然②，月光如水水如天。

同来望月人何处？风景依稀③似去年。

---

① 江楼感旧：江楼，江边的小楼。感旧，感念旧友旧事。
② 思渺然：思绪怅惘。渺然，悠远的样子。一作"悄然"。
③ 依稀：仿佛，好像。

On the Riverside Tower

Alone I mount the Riverside Tower and sigh

To see the moonbeams blend with waves and waves with

the sky.

Last year I came to view the moon with my compeers.

But where are they now that the scene is like last year's?

崔珏

CUI JUE

作者简介

崔珏，生卒年不详，字梦之。

唐宣宗大中间登进士第，由幕府拜秘书郎，为淇县令，有惠政，官至侍御史。

其诗工丽旖旎、委婉含蓄，构思丰富，比喻为多。《全唐诗》录其诗十五首，《哭李商隐》历来广受好评。

哭李商隐二首（其二）

虚负凌云万丈才，一生襟抱①未曾开。

鸟啼花落人何在，竹死桐枯②凤不来。

良马足因无主踠③，旧交心为绝弦④哀。

九泉莫叹三光⑤隔，又送文星⑥入夜台。

---

① 襟抱：怀抱，此处指远大的理想。
② 竹死桐枯：传说中的凤凰非甘泉不饮，非竹不食，非梧桐不栖，此处指社会残酷地剥夺了李商隐生存下去的条件。
③ 踠：屈曲、弯曲。
④ 绝弦：断绝琴弦，比喻失去知音。
⑤ 三光：古人以日月星为三光。
⑥ 文星：即文曲星，传说中天上掌管人间文事的星宿，通常指富有文才的人，此处指李商隐。

Elegy on Li Shangyin

In vain you could have soared to the azure sky;

Before your long, long wings are fully spread, you die.

The birds bewail with fallen flowers: "Where are you?"

The phoenix won't alight when dead is the bamboo.

A steed may be crippled if ridden by a cur;

The lutist broke his lute without a connoisseur.

In nether world not sun or moon or stars in sight,

You are the brightest star in the eternal night.

罗隐

LUO YIN

隐

作者简介

罗隐（833—910），原名罗横，字昭谏，新城（今浙江富阳）人。唐代诗人，与温庭筠、李商隐合称"三才子"。

一生怀才不遇，屡次失意于科场，后改名罗隐，隐居于九华山。光启三年（887年），归依吴越王钱镠，历任钱塘令、司勋郎中、给事中等职。

善属文，诗笔尤佳。其诗多讽刺现实生活的黑暗。有著作《谗书》《两同书》，诗作《自遣》中的"今朝有酒今朝醉"至今广为传诵。

赠妓云英

钟陵^①醉别十余春，重见云英掌上身^②。

我未成名卿^③未嫁，可能俱是不如人。

---

① 钟陵：地名，今江西省南昌市进贤县。
② 掌上身：形容云英体态窈窕美妙，此处用赵飞燕之典。
③ 卿：第二人称词，表尊敬或爱意，此处指云英。

To a Fair Dancer

Drunken, we parted here more than ten years ago;

Again I meet you as light a dancer as then.

You are not married and my fame remains still low;

Maybe we are not equal to all other men.

自遣

得^①即高歌失^②即休，多愁多恨亦悠悠^③。

今朝有酒今朝醉，明日愁来明日愁。

---

① 得：指得到高歌的机会。
② 失：指失去高歌的机会。
③ 悠悠：悠闲自在的样子。

For Myself

Sing when you're happy and from worries keep away!

How can we bear so much regret and so much sorrow?

When you have wine to drink, O drink your fill today!

Should sorrow come, alas! Tell it to come tomorrow!

鹦鹉

莫恨雕笼^①翠羽残，江南地暖陇西^②寒。

劝君^③不用分明语，语得分明出转难。

---

① 雕笼：指雕刻精美的鸟笼。
② 陇西：指陇山以西，即六盘山南段，传说是鹦鹉的产地，所以鹦鹉又被称
　　为"陇客"。
③ 君：此处指鹦鹉。

To the Parrot

Do not complain of golden cage and wings cut short;

The southern land is far warmer than the northwest.

Don't clearly speak if you listen to my exhort!

You will offend if clearly your complaint's expressed.

雪

尽道丰年瑞^①，丰年事若何^②。

长安有贫者，为瑞不宜^③多。

① "尽道"句：尽，全。道，讲、说。丰年瑞，即瑞雪兆丰年。
② 若何：如何，怎么样。
③ 宜：适合。

Snow

All say that snow forebodes a bumper year.

What if it should arouse less joy than fear?

There are poor people in the capital,

Who are afraid much bumper snow will fall.

韦庄

WEI ZHUANG

作者简介

　　韦庄（836—910），字端己，长安杜陵（今陕西西安）人，韦应物四世孙，晚唐诗人、词人。

　　早年屡试不第，乾宁元年（894年），再试时进士及第，出任校书郎。乾宁四年（897年），以判官职随谏议大夫李询入蜀宣谕，归朝后升任左补阙。天复元年（901年），入蜀为王建掌书记，自此终身仕蜀。

　　以近体诗见长，其律诗圆稳整赡、音调响亮，绝句情致深婉、包蕴丰厚。《全唐诗》录其诗三百一十六首，其长诗《秦妇吟》《孔雀东南飞》《木兰诗》并称"乐府三绝"。

忆昔

昔年曾向五陵①游，子夜②歌清月满楼。

银烛树前长似昼，露桃③花里不知秋。

西园公子名无忌④，南国佳人号莫愁。

今日乱离俱是梦，夕阳唯见水东流！

---

① 五陵：汉代五座皇帝的陵墓，因当时每立一陵都把四方富豪和外戚迁至陵
　　墓附近居住，故又指代豪贵所居之处。

② 子夜：半夜。南朝乐府民歌有《子夜歌》数十首，皆为吟咏男女爱情的，
　　歌极清丽。此处双关。

③ 露桃：比喻艳若桃花的美女。

④ "西园"句：西园公子，指曹丕。西园，为曹操所筑，位于今河北省。无
　　忌，本为信陵君之名，此处代指曹丕。

Bygone Days

I'd visited the capital in bygone days:

The bowers filled with midnight songs and clear

moon rays.

Candlelight shed on trees lengthened evening hours;

No autumn ever came among dewy peach flowers.

The noble son of west garden had a free hand;

The beauty knew no sorrow in the southern land.

Now the state torn by war, all's turned into a dream;

The setting sun sees only the east-flowing stream.

台城^①

江雨霏霏江草齐，六朝^②如梦鸟空啼^③。

无情最是台城柳，依旧烟笼十里堤。

---

① 台城：位于今南京玄武湖旁，六朝时是帝王荒淫享乐的场所。南朝陈后主在台城营造结绮、临春、望仙三座高楼，以供游玩，并自谱《玉树后庭花》，中有"玉树后庭花，花开不复久"之句。

② "六朝"：指东吴、东晋、宋、齐、梁、陈六个朝代。

③ 鸟空啼：既衬托出梦一般的景色，又隐含了诗人对历史兴衰的感慨。空，白白地、徒劳地。

The Lakeside Land

Over the riverside grass falls a drizzling rain;

Six Dynasties have passed like dreams, birds cry in vain.

Three miles along the dike unfeeling willows stand,

Adorning like a veil of mist the lakeside land.

聂夷中

NIE
YIZHONG

作者简介

聂夷中，生卒年不详，字坦之，一说河东（今山西永济）人，一说河南（今河南洛阳）人。

咸通十二年（871年）登第，官华阴尉。

其诗语言朴实，辞浅意哀。《全唐诗》编诗一卷，有《聂夷中诗》二卷。

田家

父耕原上田，子劚^①山下荒。

六月禾^②未秀^③，官家已修仓。

---

① 劚：大锄，此处作动词，有掘的意思。
② 禾：禾苗，特指稻苗。
③ 秀：指谷物吐穗扬花。

Poor Peasants

Up in old fields the fathers toil;

Down in new fields the sons break soil.

The corn in sixth moon still in blade,

Government granaries are made.

章碣

ZHANG JIE

作者简介

章碣（836—905），字丽山，桐庐（今浙江）人。

乾符三年（876年）登进士。乾符中，侍郎高湘自长沙携邵安石来京，高湘主持考试，邵安石及第。章碣赋《东都望幸》诗讽刺之："懒修珠翠上高台，眉目连娟恨不开，纵使东巡也无益，君王自领美人来。"表达了对科场制度的不平，广为人们传诵。

著有《章碣集》等，《焚书坑》为其最著名的诗作。

焚书坑 ①

竹帛 ② 烟销帝业虚，关河 ③ 空锁祖龙 ④ 居。

坑灰未冷山东 ⑤ 乱，刘项 ⑥ 原来不读书。

---

① 焚书坑：位于今陕西省西安市临潼区，据传是秦始皇时焚书的一个洞穴。秦始皇采纳丞相李斯的奏议，下令在全国范围内搜集焚毁儒家《诗》《书》和百家之书，诏令下发之后三十日不烧者，罚做筑城的苦役。这是一场文化的浩劫，使得汉代承担了传统文化复兴的艰巨任务。

② 竹帛：指书籍。西汉蔡伦发明纸以前，中国的书籍大多刻写在竹简上，以及一些帛上。因为帛质料好价高，故所载书籍较少。

③ 关河：指函谷关和黄河，此处指秦国险固的地理优势。

④ 祖龙：秦始皇自称。祖，"始"之意。龙，皇帝的象征。

⑤ 山东：此处是指秦末山东农民起义。一说指太行山之东，即秦始皇所灭的六国旧有之地。

⑥ 刘项：指刘邦、项羽，他们是秦末农民起义最大的两支力量，楚汉之争后，刘邦得胜，建立汉朝。

The Pit Where Emperor Qin Burned the Classics

Smoke of burnt classics gone up with the empire's fall;

Fortresses and rivers could not guard the capital.

Before the pit turned cold, eastern rebellions spread,

The leaders of revolts were not scholars Well-read.

曹松

CAO SONG

作者简介

曹松（828—903），字梦徵，舒州（今安徽潜山）人。
光化四年（901年）中进士，特授校书郎（秘书省正字）。
其诗风格似贾岛，工于铸字炼句，意境深幽。有《曹梦
征诗集》三卷。

己亥岁二首（其一）

泽国^①江山入战图，生民何计乐樵苏^②。

凭君莫话封侯事，一将功成万骨枯。

---

① 泽国：泛指江南各地，因湖泽星罗棋布，故称。
② 樵苏：指日常生计。一作"樵渔"。

A Year of War

The lakeside country has become a battleground.

How can the peasants and woodmen live all around?

I pray you not to talk about the glories vain;

A victor's fame is built on thousands of men slain.

韩偓

HAN WO

作者简介

韩偓（844—923），字致尧，一云字致光，自号玉山樵人，京兆万年（今陕西西安）人，"南安四贤"之一。

龙纪元年（889年）进士及第，佐河中幕。光化中，自司勋郎中兼侍御史知杂入翰林充学士，迁左谏议大夫、中书舍人、兵户二部侍郎、学士承旨。天复三年（903年），以不附朱全忠，贬濮州司马，再贬荣懿尉，徙邓州司马。天祐二年（905年），复召为学士，偓不敢归朝，入闽依王审知，卒。

善写宫词，辞藻华丽，人称"香奁体"。有《香奁集》，后人辑有《韩翰林诗集》。

效崔国辅体四首（其一）①

淡月照中庭，海棠花自落。

独立俯闲阶，风动秋千索。

---

① 本诗为诗人的仿作，以唐诗中的"闺怨"为主题，写春夜庭院中，海棠花
悄然凋落，春又要过去，女主人孤独地等待有人归来的幽静寂寥之景。

A Lonely Woman

On the mid-court the moon sheds a pale light

And petals float down from crabapple trees.

On vacant steps she fixes her lonely sight

Only to see the swing sway in the breeze.

杜荀鹤

DU XUNHE

作者简介

杜荀鹤（846—904），字彦之，自号九华山人，池州石埭（今安徽石台）人。

出身寒微，中年始中进士，仍未授官，乃返乡闲居。曾以诗颂朱温，后朱温表荐他，授翰林学士，知制诰，故入《旧五代史·梁书》。

工近体诗，于晚唐自成一体。今存《杜荀鹤文集》三卷。

山中寡妇

夫因兵死守蓬茅，麻苎衣衫鬓发焦^①。

桑柘^②废来犹纳税，田园荒后尚征苗。

时挑野菜和^③根煮，旋斫^④生柴带叶烧。

任是深山更深处，也应无计避征徭^⑤。

---

① 鬓发焦：因吃不饱，身体缺乏营养而头发变成枯黄色。

② 柘：树木名，叶子可以喂蚕。

③ 和：带着，连着。

④ 旋斫：现砍。旋，现（做）。斫，砍。

⑤ 征徭：赋税、徭役。

A Widow Living in the Mountains

Her husband killed in war, she lives in a thatched hut,

Wearing coarse hempen clothes and a flaxen hair.

She should pay taxes though down mulberries were cut,

And before harvest though fields and gardens lie bare.

She has to eat wild herbs together with their root,

And burn as fuel leafy branches from the trees.

However deep she hides in mountains as a brute,

From oppressive taxes she can never be free.

黄巢

HUANG CHAO

作者简介

黄巢（生年不详，卒于884年），曹州冤句（今山东菏泽西南）人。唐朝末年农民起义领袖。

出身盐商家庭，善于骑射，喜任侠，粗通笔墨，少有诗才。

乾符二年（875年）六月，响应王仙芝起义。王仙芝战死后，成为起义军领袖，号称"冲天大将军"，年号"王霸"。广明元年（880年），进入长安，即位于含元殿，国号"大齐"，年号"金统"。中和三年（883年）退出长安。

题菊花

飒飒西风^①满院栽，蕊寒香冷蝶难来。

他年我若为青帝^②，报^③与桃花一处开。

---

① 西风：此处指秋风。古人用四个方向来代指四个季节：东为春，南为夏，西为秋，北为冬。

② 青帝：指司春之神。古代传说中的五天帝之一，住在东方，主行春天时令。

③ 报：告诉，告知，此处有命令的意思。

To the Chrysanthemum

In soughing western wind you blossom far and nigh;

Your fragrance is too cold to invite butterfly.

Some day if I as Lord of Spring come into power,

I'd order you to bloom together with peach flower.

菊花①

待到秋来九月八②，我花③开后百花杀。

冲天香阵④透长安，满城尽带黄金甲⑤。

---

① 又作《不第后赋菊》。
② 九月八：指九月九日是重阳节，说"九月八"是为了押韵。古代重阳节有赏菊、喝菊花酒的风俗。
③ 我花：这里指菊花。
④ 香阵：这里指菊花的芬芳。
⑤ 黄金甲：此处指菊花的形状与颜色像黄金制成的盔甲。

The Chrysanthemum

When autumn comes, the Mountain-climbing Day
is nigh;
My flower blows when other blooms come to an end.
In battle array its fragrance rises sky-high,
The capital with its golden armour will blend.

王 驾

WANG JIA

作者简介

王驾（生于851年，卒年不详），字大用，自号守素先生，河中（今山西永济）人。

大顺元年（890年）登进士第，仕至礼部员外郎。后弃官归隐。

与郑谷、司空图友善，诗风亦相近。其绝句构思巧妙，自然流畅。有《王驾诗集》六卷，已佚。《全唐诗》存诗六首。

社日^①

鹅湖^②山下稻粱^③肥，豚栅鸡栖半掩扉。

桑柘影斜春社散，家家扶得醉人^④归。

---

① 社日：古代祭祀土神、谷神的日子，分春秋两祭，即春社和秋社。
② 鹅湖：位于今江西省铅山县，此地一年两稻，本诗为此地春社日。
③ 粱：古代对粟的优良品种的通称。
④ 醉人：祭祀后喝醉酒的人。

A Spring Feast

The paddy crops wax rich at the foot of Goose-lake Hill,

Door half closed, pigs in sty and fowls in cage are still.

The shade of mulberries lengthens, the feast is over,

All drunken villagers are helped back to their door.

雨晴

雨前初见花间蕊，雨后全无叶底①花。

蜂蝶②纷纷过墙去，却疑③春色在邻家。

---

① 叶底：绿叶中间。底，底部。

② 蜂蝶：蜜蜂和蝴蝶。

③ 疑：怀疑。

After the Rain

Before the rain I still see blooming flowers;

Only green leaves are left after the showers.

Over the wall pass butterflies and bees;

I wonder if spring dwells in my neighbor's trees.

秦韬玉

QIN TAOYU

作者简介

秦韬玉，生卒年不详，字中明，京兆（今陕西西安）人，或云邠阳（今陕西合阳）人，唐代诗人。

出身尚武世家，父为左军军将，累举不第，后附宦官田令孜，充当幕僚，官丞郎，判盐铁。中和二年（882年）特赐进士及第，编入春榜。

工歌吟，有《投知小录》三卷，已佚。

贫女

蓬门①未识绮罗②香，拟托良媒益自伤。

谁爱风流高格调③，共怜时世俭梳妆④。

敢将十指夸针巧，不把双眉斗⑤画长。

苦恨年年压金线⑥，为他人作嫁衣裳。

---

① 蓬门：用蓬茅编扎的门，代指穷人家。
② 绮罗：华贵的丝织品，此处指富贵妇女的华丽衣裳。
③ "谁爱"句：风流高格调，指格调高雅的妆扮。风流，指意态娴雅。高格调，高品格、高情调。
④ "共怜"句：怜，喜欢、欣赏。时事俭梳妆，当时妇女的一种妆扮。时世，当世，当今。
⑤ 斗：比较，竞赛。
⑥ "苦恨"句：苦恨，非常懊恼。压金线，用金线绣花。压，刺绣的一种手法，此处作动词用，是刺绣的意思。

A Poor Maid

In thatched hut I know not fragrant silks and brocade;

To be married I can't find a good go-between.

Who would love an uncommon fashion though

self-made?

All pity my simple toilet and humble mien.

I dare boast my fingers' needlework without peer,

But I won't vie with maidens painting eyebrows long.

I regret to stitch golden thread from year to year,

But to make wedding gowns which to others belong.

于武陵

YU WULING

作者简介

于武陵，生卒年、字与号均不详，唐代诗人。

工五言诗，题材上以写景送别为主，寄寓浓浓的乡思友情，悠扬沉郁。佳作很多，流传颇广。

赠卖松人

入市虽求利，怜君意独真。

劚将寒涧树^①，卖与翠楼^②人。

瘦叶几经雪，淡花应少春^③。

长安重桃李，徒染六街^④尘。

---

① 寒涧树：松树。
② 翠楼：华丽的楼阁，又指旗亭酒楼等场所。
③ 应少春：意为大概也见不到几许春意。
④ 六街：本意为长安城的六条大街，此处指闹市街区。

To a Pine-Ellep

Men come to market to seek gain.

Why are you so sincere in vain?

You sell creekside tree without flower

To those who live in emerald bower.

Its leaves are meager under snow,

Its pale blooms even in spring won't blow.

The rich love but peach and plum sweet;

Dusted pines can't be sold in the street.

皮日休

PI
RIXIU

作者简介

皮日休（约838—883），字袭美，自号鹿门子，晚唐诗人、文学家。与陆龟蒙齐名，世称"皮陆"。

咸通八年（867）进士及第，历任苏州从事、著作佐郎、太常博士、毗陵副使。黄巢称帝后，被迫任翰林学士，最后不知所终。

其诗文兼有奇、朴二态，且多同情民间疾苦之作，对于社会民生有深刻的洞察和思考。著有《皮日休集》《皮子》《皮氏鹿门家钞》等。

Lament of an Acorn-eater

Acorns ripen in autumn cold;

Falling into scrubs, they seem lost.

A hunched gray-haired woman old

Gathers them, treading morning frost.

To get a handful will take long;

To fill her basket needs a day.

She suns and steams them,

In winter her hunger to stay.

By hillside there's ripening rice,

From purple spikes fragrance pervades.

She reaps and hulls the grain so nice,

Each kernel like an earring of jade.

She takes the grain the tax to pay;

Not much is left for her to store.

How can the tax-collecter say

She has paid but half and no more!

Officials would commit a crime;

Taking bribes, greedy ones are worse.

Peasants owe them debt in busy time,

But debt paid goes to private purse.

From winter even into spring

She has only acorns to eat.

I've heard the premier helped the king

To give more and take less to cheat.

Seeing this woman old,

Can I keep back tears streaming from the eye?

To My Love

When you were gone, in dreams I lingered you know
where:
Our courtyard seemed the same with zigzag balustrade.
Only the sympathetic moon was shining there
Over fallen petals melting like you into the shade.

代后记

中国学派的文学翻译理论

中国学派的文学翻译理论源自中国的传统文化，主要包括儒家思想和道家思想，儒家思想的代表著作是《论语》，道家思想的代表著作是《道德经》。

《道德经》第一章开始就说："道可道，非常道；名可名，非常名。"联系到翻译理论上来，就是说：翻译理论是可以知道的，是可以说得出来的，但不是只说得出来而经不起实践检验的空头理论，这就是中国学派翻译理论中的实践论。其次，文学翻译理论不能算科学理论（自然科学），与其说是社会科学理论，不如说是人文学科或艺术理论，这就是文学翻译的艺术论，也可以说是相对论。后六个字"名可名，非常名"应用到文学翻译理论上来，可以有两层意思：第一层是原文的文字是描写现实的，但并不等于现实，文字和现实之间还有距离，还有矛盾；第二层意思是译文和原文之间也有距离，也有矛盾，译文和原文所描写的现实之间，自然还有距离，还有矛盾。译文应该发挥译语优势，运用最好的译语表达方式，来和原文展开竞赛，使译文和现实的距离或矛盾小于原文和现实之间的矛盾，那就是超越原文了。这就是文学翻译理论中的优势论或优化论，超越论或竞赛论。文学翻译理论应该解决的不只是译文和原文在文字方面的矛盾，还要解决译文和原文所反映的现实之间的矛盾，这是文学翻译的本体论。

　　一般翻译只要解决"真"或"信"或"似"的问题，文学翻译却要解决"真"或"信"和"美"之间的矛盾。原文反映的现实不只是言内之意，还有言外之意。中国的文学语言往往有言外之意，甚至还有言外之情。文学翻译理论也要解决译文和原文的言外之意、言外之情的矛盾。

　　《论语》说："知之者不如好之者，好之者不如乐之者。"知之，好之，乐之，这"三之论"是对艺术论的进一步说明。艺术论第一条原则要求译文忠实于原文所反映的现实，求的是真，可以使人知之；第二条原则要求用"三化"法来优化译文，求的是美，可以使人好之；第三条原则要求用"三美"来优化译文，尤其是译诗词，求的是意美、音美和形美，可以使人乐之。如果"不逾矩"的等化译文能使人知之（理解），那就达到了文学翻译的低标准；如果从心所欲而不逾矩的浅化或深化的译文既能使人知之，又能使人好之（喜欢），那就达到了中标准；如果从心所欲的译文不但能使人知之、好之，还能使人乐之（愉快），那才达到了文学翻译的高标准。这也是中国译者对世界译论做出的贡献。

翻译艺术的规律是从心所欲而不逾矩。"矩"就是规矩，规律。但艺术规律却可以依人的主观意志而转移，是因为得到承认才算正确的。所以贝多芬说："为了更美，没有什么清规戒律不可打破。"他所说的戒律不是科学规律，而是艺术规律。不能用科学规律来评论文学翻译。

孔子不大谈"什么是"（What？）而多谈"怎么做"（How？）。这是中国传统的方法论，比西方流传更久，影响更广，作用更大，并且经过了两三千年实践的考验。《论语》第一章中说："学而时习之，不亦说（悦，乐）乎！""学"是取得知识，"习"是实践。孔子只说学习实践可以得到乐趣，却不说什么是"乐"。这就是孔子的方法论，是中国文学翻译理论的依据。

总而言之，中国学派的文学翻译理论是研究老子提出的"信"（似）"美"（优）矛盾的艺术（本体论），但"信"不限原文，还指原文所反映的现实，这是认识论，"信"由严复提出的"信达雅"发展到鲁迅提出"信顺"的直译，再发展到陈源的"三似"（形似，意似，神似），直到傅雷的"重神似不重形似"，这已经接近"美"了。"美"发展到鲁迅的"三美"（意美，音美，形美），再发展到林语堂提出的"忠实，通顺，美"，转化为朱生豪"传达原作意趣"的意译，直到茅盾提出的"美的享受"。孔子提出的"从心所欲"发展到郭沫若提出的创译论（好的翻译等于创作），以及钱钟书说的译文可以胜过原作的"化境"说，再发展到优化论、超越论、"三化"（等化，浅化，深化）方法论。孔子提出的"不逾矩"和老子说的"信""言不美，美言不信"有同有异。老子"信""美"并重，孔子"从心所欲"重于"不逾矩"，发展为朱光潜的"艺术论"，包括郭沫若说的"在信达之外，愈雅愈好。所谓'雅'不是高深或讲修饰，而是文学价值或艺术价值比较高。"直到茅盾说的："必须把文学翻译工作提高到艺术创造的水平。"孔子的"乐之"发展为胡适之的"愉快"说（翻译要使读者读得愉快），再发展到"三之"（知之，好之，乐之）目的论。这就是中国学派的文学翻译理论发展为"美化之艺术"（"三美""三化""三之"的艺术）的概况。

许渊冲

2011年10月